COMMUNITY-BUILT

Throughout history and around the world, community members have come together to build places, be it settlers constructing log cabins in nineteenth-century Canada, an artist group creating a waterfront gathering place along the Danube in Budapest, or residents helping revive small-town main streets in the United States. What all these projects have in common is that they involve local volunteers in the construction of public and community places; they are community-built.

Although much attention has been given to specific community-built movements such as public murals and community gardens, little has been given to defining community-built as a whole. This volume provides a preliminary description of community-built practices, with examples from the disciplines of urban design, historic preservation, and community art.

Taken as a whole, these community-built projects illustrate how the process of local involvement in adapting, building, and preserving a built environment can strengthen communities and create places that are intimately tied to local needs, culture, and community. The lessons learned from this volume can provide community planners, grassroots facilitators, and participants with an understanding of what can lead to successful community-built art, construction, preservation, and placemaking.

Katherine Melcher is an Associate Professor of Landscape Architecture at the University of Georgia's College of Environment and Design, U.S. Her research focuses on the interaction between design and community development—in particular, participatory processes in the design of community spaces. Her design work has been featured in *Landscape Architecture, Designer/Builder, 1000x Landscape Architecture*, and *Architecture for Change*.

Barry L. Stiefel is an Associate Professor in the Historic Preservation and Community Planning program at the College of Charleston, U.S. He is interested in how the sum of local preservation efforts affects regional, national, and multi-national policies within the field of cultural resource management and heritage conservation. Dr. Stiefel has published numerous books and articles.

Kristin Faurest worked as an Associate Professor in the Faculty of Landscape Architecture, Corvinus University of Budapest, Hungary, where she taught and researched in the areas of community-based planning, social justice in spatial planning, and the connections between culture and landscape. Last year she returned to her native U.S. to direct the Portland Japanese Garden's new International Institute for Japanese Garden Arts and Culture in Portland, Oregon.

The Community Development Research and Practice Series

Volume 7

Series Editor:

Rhonda G. Phillips
Purdue University, USA

As the series continues to grow with the seventh volume, it is our intent to continue to serve scholars, community developers, planners, public administrators, and others involved in research, practice, and policymaking in the realm of community development. The series strives to provide both timely and applied information for researchers, students, and practitioners. Building on a long history since 1970 of publishing the Community Development Society's journal, *Community Development* (http://www.comm-dev.org), the book series contributes to a growing and rapidly changing knowledge base as a resource for practitioners and researchers alike. For additional information, please see the series page at http://www.routledge.com/books/series/CDRP/.

The evolution of the field of community development continues. As reflected in both theory and practice, community development is at the forefront of change, which comes to no surprise to our communities and regions that constantly face challenges and opportunities. As a practice focused discipline, change often seems to be the only constant in the community development realm. The need to integrate theory, practice, research, teaching, and training is even more pressing now than ever, given rapidly transforming economic, social, environmental, political, and cultural climates locally and globally. Current and applicable information and insights about effective research and practice are needed.

The Community Development Society, a non-profit association of those interested in pushing the discipline forward, is delighted to offer this book series in partnership with Routledge. The series is designed to integrate innovative thinking on tools, strategies, and experiences as a resource especially well-suited for bridging the gaps between theory, research, and practice. The Community Development Society actively promotes continued advancement of the discipline and practice. Fundamental to this mission is adherence to the following core principles of good practice. This book series is a reflection of many of these principles:

> Promote active and representative participation toward enabling all community members to meaningfully influence the decisions that affect their lives.
>
> Engage community members in learning about and understanding community issues, and the economic, social, environmental, political, psychological, and other impacts associated with alternative courses of action.
>
> Incorporate the diverse interest and cultures of the community in the community development process, and disengage from support of any effort that is likely to adversely affect the disadvantaged members of a community.
>
> Work actively to enhance the leadership capacity of community members, leaders, and groups within the community.
>
> Be open to using the full range of action strategies to work toward the long-term sustainability and well-being of the community.

We invite you to explore the series and continue to do so as new volumes are added. We hope you will find it a valuable resource for supporting community development research and practice.

Other books in the series:

Theory, Practice, and Community Development
Mark Brennan, Jeffrey Bridger, and Theodore Alter

Schools and Urban Revitalization
Rethinking Institutions and Community Development
Kelly L. Patterson and Robert Mark Silverman

Knowledge Partnering for Community Development
Robyn Eversole

Social Capital at the Community Level
An Applied Interdisciplinary Perspective
John M. Halstead and Steven C. Deller

"From DIY urbanism to rural barn-raising, *Community-Built* describes both a growing movement and a social and cultural practice that has long existed in human civilization. With a diverse collection of cases in contexts and project types, this book is a timely addition to a growing literature on the power of communities in transforming and creating places. Focusing on the building of both physical places and social relationships, it offers a refreshing look at the scope and significance of community-driven process while examining the persistent tensions and challenges."

Jeff Hou, Professor and Chair of Landscape Architecture,
University of Washington, Seattle, U.S.

"The community-built movement is alive, well, and thriving internationally. This book stands as a testament to this movement's vitality as evidenced by its coverage of theory development and the wide range of examples of community-built projects in all types of places. This book is a must read for anyone wishing to be a part of this important movement."

Melvin Delgado, Ph.D., Professor of Social Work, Boston
University School of Social Work, U.S.

"This comprehensive inquiry into community built design offers a transdisciplinary and multicultural perspective, exemplified in the fascinating case studies from Eastern Europe, Canada and the United States. These intimate stories celebrate the local, address historic community injustices, and document how environments are transformed into celebrations of symbolic meaning and cultural heritage. This welcome and essential text offers both practical information and inspirational narratives. *Community-Built* offers alternatives to rethink the meaning and importance of art and identity, vernacular expression and building, and preservation and narrative."

Professor Daniel Winterbottom, RLA, FASLA, Department of Landscape
Architecture, University of Washington, Seattle, U.S.

COMMUNITY-BUILT

Art, Construction, Preservation, and Place

Edited by Katherine Melcher,
Barry L. Stiefel, and Kristin Faurest

NEW YORK AND LONDON

First published 2017
by Routledge
711 Third Avenue, New York, NY 10017

and by Routledge
2 Park Square, Milton Park, Abingdon, Oxon, OX14 4RN

Routledge is an imprint of the Taylor & Francis Group, an informa business

© 2017 Taylor & Francis

The right of Katherine Melcher, Barry Stiefel, and Kristin Faurest to be
identified as the authors of the editorial material, and of the authors for
their individual chapters, has been asserted in accordance with sections 77
and 78 of the Copyright, Designs and Patents Act 1988.

Library of Congress Cataloging-in-Publication Data
Names: Melcher, Katherine, editor. | Stiefel, Barry, editor. | Faurest, Kristin,
   editor.
Title: Community-built : art, construction, preservation, and place /
   edited by Katherine Melcher, Barry L. Stiefel, and Kristin Faurest.
Description: New York : Routledge, 2016. | Series: The community
   development research and practice series ; Volume 7
Identifiers: LCCN 2016022821 | ISBN 9781138682566 (hardback) |
   ISBN 9781138682580 (pbk.)
Subjects: LCSH: Architecture and society. | Community development. |
   Building—Social aspects. | Social participation.
Classification: LCC NA2543.S6 C637 2016 | DDC 720.1/03—dc23
LC record available at https://lccn.loc.gov/2016022821

ISBN: 978-1-138-68256-6 (hbk)
ISBN: 978-1-138-68258-0 (pbk)
ISBN: 978-1-315-54506-6 (ebk)

Typeset in Bembo
by Apex CoVantage, LLC

*In memory of Rev. Clementa Pinckney, Cynthia Hurd,
Rev. Sharonda Coleman-Singleton, Tywanza Sanders, Ethel
Lance, Susie Jackson, Depayne Middleton Doctor, Rev. Daniel
Simmons, and Myra Thompson, who were killed at
AME Emanuel Church, Charleston, South Carolina,
on June 17, 2015*

*And to the people of Charleston who came together to build
solidarity and unity in their mourning, as well as art and
placemaking as a positive response to the tragedy.*[1] *That is*
Charleston Strong.

Note

1 See Kate Abbey-Lambertz, "The Incredible Ways Art Is Helping Charleston Unite after Church Massacre," *Huffington Post*, 27 June 2015, accessed 29 June 2015, http://www. huffingtonpost.com/2015/06/27/art-charleston-church_n_7654802.html?cps= gravity_2691_-354746021980783934.

CONTENTS

FIGURES AND TABLE

Figures

Table

ACKNOWLEDGMENTS

This volume could not have come about without the Community Built Association and its members. They are a rock of support and networking in respect to furthering the theory and best practices of community-built art, construction, preservation, and placemaking.

1

INTRODUCTION

Defining Community-Built

Barry L. Stiefel, Kristin Faurest, and Katherine Melcher

Throughout history and around the world, community members have come together to build places, be it rural farmers raising a barn in North America, Malian villagers holding a festival to re-plaster their adobe mosque, or neighbors in New York City's Lower East Side turning vacant lots into a community garden. What all these places have in common is that they are community-built; they "meet a set of criteria that stress participation and result in an environmental change" (Delgado 2000, 76); they bring community members together to construct projects in public and semi-public spaces.

The concept of community-built is deeply embedded within the world's heritage. Historically, community-built works can be found in the civilizations of both nomadic and sedentary peoples. One of the earliest recorded instances of a community-built project is found within the Hebrew Bible, concerning the creation of the Tabernacle, the transportable house of worship that the ancient Israelites used during their wanderings in the wilderness: "Every man whose heart inspired him came; and everyone whose spirit motivated him brought the portion of God for the work of the Tent of Meeting [Tabernacle], for all its labor and for the sacred vestments" (Exodus 35:21).

The contemporary American practice of community-built emerged in the 1960s, with activists such as Karl Linn and Paul Hogan building common spaces and playgrounds in inner-city Philadelphia; Lilli Ann Rosenberg creating murals with children in Harlem housing projects; and Bob Leathers working with parents to construct playgrounds in upstate New York. These individuals, along with other artists and designers, formed the Community Built Association (CBA) in 1989. The CBA defines community-built as a "collaboration between professionals and community volunteers to design, organize and create community projects that reshape public spaces. Projects accomplished through community initiative and professional

FIGURE 1.1 Barn raising, farm of Joseph Bales, Lansing, North York, Canada, circa 1900–1919

Source: Photograph by Alexander W. Galbraith, City of Toronto Archives, Fonds 1568, Item 177

FIGURE 1.2 Community members refinishing a mud plaster floor, Togo, 1996

Source: Katherine Melcher

guidance include murals, playgrounds, parks, public gardens, sculptures and historic restorations" (Community Built Association 2014).

Today, community-built spaces, artworks, and other elements can be found in almost every community around the globe. For example, school murals across the

FIGURE 1.3 Community garden in Berkeley, California, 2008

Source: Katherine Melcher

United States connect youth with their heritage and local history. Community gardens in places as diverse as Budapest, Hungary, and Roanoke, Virginia, engage both neighborhood residents and university design students. In Pennsylvania, volunteer-driven sidewalk and facade improvements are intended to revive small-town main streets.

FIGURE 1.4 A community-built park in New Orleans, Louisiana, 2010

Source: Katherine Melcher

Despite its widespread existence, most community-built work is rarely classified as such, perhaps because of its grassroots and multi-disciplinary nature. Beyond
Melvin Delgado's (2000) book, *Community Social Work Practice in an Urban Context*,
little research about community-built practices as a whole exists. Multiple case
studies focus on one realized work or practitioner (see, for example, Rofe 1998;
Semenza 2003; Hutzel 2007; Semenza and March 2009), and other research investigates one type of project—for example, playgrounds (Daniels and Johnson 2009;
Wilson, Marshall, and Iserhott 2011), murals and community art (Delgado 2003;
Rossetto 2012), or community open spaces and gardens (Francis, Cashdan, and
Paxson 1984; Hou, Johnson, and Lawson 2009; Draper and Freedman 2010). Most
of this research and writing remains within their specific disciplinary boundaries,
failing to draw connections across the spectrum of community-built projects. As far
as the editors of this volume are aware, this is the first interdisciplinary volume to
analyze the concept of community-built across the fields of urban design, historic
preservation, and community art. This volume brings together research into a variety of community-built practices in order to explore their commonalities, while at
the same time describing community-built in the broadest sense.

The quest to expand the concept of community-built beyond the work of
Community Built Association members resulted in the call for contributions that
formed this book. In the responses, we found a diversity of projects that include
local people in the construction and preservation of community places. This book

FIGURE 1.5   A community-built mural under construction at Maxwell Park, Oakland, California, 2008

Source: Katherine Melcher

contains examples of community-built projects from the United States, Canada, and Europe; these include art projects, gardens, streetscapes, and buildings. The projects included celebrate the small and the specific, the often immeasurable yet meaningful. However, taken as a whole, they illustrate a cross-disciplinary approach to community development and placemaking. They provide a powerful illustration of how local engagement with built projects can strengthen communities.

FIGURE 1.6 A community-built playground under construction in a village in Thailand, 2006

Source: Katherine Melcher

The Trans-Disciplinary Nature of Community-Built

The contributors to this book come from three primary disciplines: urban design, historic preservation, and the visual arts. Despite this, all of their community-built examples can also be classified as a form of asset-based community development: "a planned effort to build assets that increase the capacity of residents to improve their quality of life" (Green and Haines 2008, 7). Like other community development initiatives, community-built projects emphasize the use of local resources and community-controlled, collaborative decision-making. Each of the three primary disciplines has a subdiscipline that utilizes an asset-based approach: community design and placemaking within urban design, community-based historic preservation within historic preservation, and community arts within the visual arts. The following is a brief overview of these subdisciplines and how community-built projects can be categorized within them.

Community Design and Placemaking

Community design is "based on the principle that the environment works better if the people affected by its changes are actively involved in its creation and management instead of being treated as passive consumers" (Sanoff 2000, x). In the 1960s, in reaction against the U.S. government urban renewal program's displacement of minorities, community design proponents advocated for involving local residents in the design decision-making that impacted their neighborhoods (Hester Jr. 1989; Toker 2007). Today, at least within the United States, local involvement in public design projects is often mandated; and terms such as public interest design and social impact design are used more frequently to describe design processes that focus on social concerns. Additionally, terms such as DIY urbanism and tactical urbanism describe small-scale community design projects that can be easily implemented with or without government support (Iveson 2013; Pagano 2013; Lydon and Garcia 2015).

Placemaking, a term that describes a specific approach to spatial design, incorporates much of community design's philosophy and applies it specifically to the public realm. In placemaking, a public space's design is driven not by designers or decision makers, but by the local community's assets, identity, character, and needs (Massachusetts Institute of Technology, Department of Urban Studies and Planning 2013). Placemaking takes a trans-disciplinary approach to public space design: the benefits of a community space are not just limited to the provision of recreation and the contribution to urban ecology but instead viewed as a complex web that encompasses other factors such as public health, social capital, climate change amelioration, and economic well-being.

Within urban design and placemaking, more attention is being focused on small-scale community projects and their ability to impact larger issues such as neighborhood cohesion, crime, public health, and socioeconomic mobility. This isn't a completely new paradigm: back in the 1960s, Jane Jacobs (1992) pointed out the importance of vibrant, lively sidewalks and the contributions of small stores and other community institutions to make our cities safe, happy, equitable places. During that same period, urban planner Oscar Newman's (1976) defensible spaces approach in subsidized housing developments demonstrated that when we give people the power and the responsibility to change their communities on a manageable scale, they respond by taking charge. Collective efficacy—people's willingness to help each other out, to connect, to make an effort—increases, and the sense of helplessness and apathy that can so often be the product of life in government-owned housing decreases. When people are given the opportunity to shape their environment in a way that makes their surroundings more comfortable, more colorful, or more personalized, they feel a greater power to make other changes as well. They also have an enhanced sense of stewardship and a closer relationship with the friends and neighbors who helped them realize the project.

From the general concept of placemaking, more specific categories have emerged: tactical placemaking, using small-scale, incremental improvements to help stimulate larger-scale positive change; strategic placemaking, a targeted process that uses activities and projects to attract talented workers to a place; and creative placemaking, which is based upon using visual arts and cultural activities to shape a place (Wycoff 2014).

In placemaking, the opinions and preferences of the future users inform the design of the place, which strengthens stewardship. The mutual stewardship of place and community sets up a symbiotic relationship in which communities transform places and the places continue to transform communities. Community designers observed this symbiosis as well; they found that places designed with community participation experience more use and less vandalism (Francis 1983). These designers believe that by being involved in the design process, participants can develop a sense of pride and an attachment to the place (Hester Jr. 1989; Sanoff 2008).

Community-built projects—because they often take place in small-scale, semi-public places—fit well within the placemaking paradigm. They often come to fruition in what might be considered a third category of public space: neither private nor public, but semi-public (for example, community gardens or other shared spaces). At the same time, community-built projects remain distinct within the field of placemaking because of their emphasis on community involvement in the construction phase of the project.

Within this volume, we have five chapters that highlight community involvement in the building of public and semi-public places. Kristin Faurest, in Chapter 3, "*Kalaka*: Four Stories about Community Building in a New Democracy," discusses a variety of neighborhood projects within Hungary, including a school fruit orchard, community courtyard gardens, and a re-imagined public space. In Chapter 4, "Reflections on Community Engagement: Making Meaning of Experience," Terry L. Clements and C. L. Bohannon share their experience with similar projects—a community park, bus stop, and community garden—in a very different context, the Hurt Park neighborhood of Roanoke, Virginia. Barry L. Stiefel's "Community Eruvin: Architecture for *Semi*-public/private Neighborhood Space" (Chapter 6) describes a unique form of shared community space: eruvin, physio-psychological enclosures used by halachic-observing[1] Jews that enable them to "carry" in the public domain on their Sabbath. Daniela Patti and Levente Polyak, in Chapter 10, "Building Informal Infrastructure: Architects in Support of Bottom-Up Community Services and Social Solidarity in Budapest," explore adaptive reuse of a public park and waterfront in Budapest. In Chapter 12, "Building Streets and Building Community," Katherine Melcher shares three examples of community-built streetscapes in the United States.

Community-Based Historic Preservation

In most countries, historic preservation (often called heritage conservation outside of the United States) is a top-down initiative from the national or regional government. However, within the United States, the historic preservation movement began as a grassroots, community-based endeavor. For instance, in 1816, due to public outcry by the citizens of Philadelphia, the city purchased Independence Hall (then called the State House) from the State of Pennsylvania, which had plans to demolish it. Again, in 1853–58, under the leadership of Ann Pamela Cunningham, women across the United States came together to save Mount Vernon, George Washington's plantation estate in Virginia, from neglect and proposed redevelopment.

While separated by more than a century from these earliest preservation-related achievements, the contemporary American practices of historic preservation also emerged in the 1960s, most significantly related to the National Historic Preservation Act of 1966. Specifically, within the act, Congress specified in Section 101(4) that "the Secretary [of the Interior] may accept a nomination directly from any person . . . for inclusion of a property on the National Register," (National Historic Preservation Act 1966) whereas before for National Historic Monuments or National Historic Sites, only the president and the secretary of the interior had the specific authority to nominate a place nationally historic. So, besides the physical maintenance or repair of historic places, the designation and heritage interpretation of them is frequently a community undertaking, and often initiated at the grassroots level in some way. The typical history of historic preservation practice is, more often than not, one of success stories where a group of citizens came together to save an old place from demolition or neglect that they held to be important for them and their community (see the analysis and various essays within Page and Mason [2004]). A testament to the results of enabling any person or group to nominate a historic place to the National Register is that there have been more than 90,000 successfully listed (National Park Service 2014).

Community-based historic preservation aims to preserve and express local identity and heritage. Within historic preservation, any person or group has the ability to nominate a place as historic; therefore the inventory of the National Register of Historic Places represents well what the American public considers to be historically and culturally significant. By comparison, the National Historic Monument and National Historic Sites programs are designated by the president and the secretary of the interior, respectively, in a top-down authoritative manner.

While typical places on the National Register tend to include architectural monuments or places attributed to famous people or events, they can also include what is called a Traditional Cultural Property. In short, a Traditional Cultural Property is a place that has an "association with cultural practices or beliefs of a living community that (a) are rooted in that community's history, and (b) are important in maintaining the continuing cultural identity of the community" (Parker and King 1998, 1). So, while community-based historic preservation does often entail a community of people coming together to save a formal-built place, such as in the examples of Independence Hall or Mount Vernon, it can even come full circle and focus on the preservation of community-built projects and art. Examples include the entire historical spectrum, from the Anasazi ruins of Salmon Pueblo in New Mexico (built c. 1100) to the murals of Chicano Park in San Diego, California (painted 1970–89). Preserving places (or the lack thereof) is a reflection of what society believes to be important, or not. This, of course, changes over time as our society reacts to the ever-evolving issue of cultural sensitivity and appropriateness. Local community-level preservation is often at the forefront of the preservation movement in respect to best practices as well as theory.

Three chapters within this volume share examples of community historic preservation where the inhabitants of a particular area came together to save, restore, or rehabilitate already-built environments. In Chapter 7, "Community-Built and Preserved Material Culture: Square-Log Cabins in the Village of Mont-Tremblant, Quebec," Mariana Esponda Cascajares investigates grassroots preservation efforts of log cabins, often requiring great creativity and a planned budget, among other logistical issues. Taking a different perspective to community historic preservation, Ildikó Réka Báthory-Nagy looks at the issues of memory conservation in Chapter 9, "Yellow-Star Houses: A Community-Generated Living History Project in Budapest," which discusses the community-driven effort to commemorate the "yellow-star" houses where Jews were relocated during the Holocaust. In Chapter 11, "The Main Street Approach to Community Design," Jeremy Wells looks at how volunteer-driven community preservation efforts are applied in the United States' Main Street Program.

Community Arts

During the 1930s, the U.S. government experimented with public art as a means to put unemployed artists back to work during the Great Depression—creating over 5,000 jobs and 225,000 works of art across the country—first with the Public Works of Art Project (1934–35) and then followed by the Works Progress Administration (1935–43) (see Figure 1.7). With the end of the Great Depression during World War II, this centralized, government-funded approach to community arts

FIGURE 1.7   The poster, *Murals for the Community,* announcing a Federal Art Project, Works Progress Administration exhibit of murals at the Federal Art Gallery, 225 West 57th St., New York City, 1936

Source: Library of Congress Prints and Photographs Division

faded away and re-emerged in a more decentralized form in the 1960s (Chilvers, Osborne, and Farr 1988).

In the late 1960s—at the same time when community design was developing in reaction to urban renewal and community-initiated historic preservation efforts were becoming more frequent—grassroots community arts emerged as an alternative art form. Community arts emphasized the participation of non-professionals in the creation of artwork. Community art challenged how art was defined and valued. While traditional art was valued by the aesthetics of the artwork produced, community artwork was valued for its inclusive process and its impact on the community (Lowe 2000).

Community art projects have since spread across the globe. Some are government-sponsored as public art or art-in-the-schools projects, while individual artists initiate others. Common community art projects include murals and public sculptures, but they can also be performance pieces and works of literature. Community art as a "process of community members coming together to pursue shared goals" can create "a feeling of connectedness and belonging, develops trust, and creates organizational skills and a habit of civic involvement" (McCarthy et al. 2004, 15). Similar to historic preservation, community arts can also help groups (often marginalized groups) explore and express individual and shared identities.

When a community art project is installed in a public or semi-public place, it can be classified as community-built. Such a project "may be more likely to serve as a reminder of solidarity and identity. Permanently installed art may also be more likely to encourage future social interaction" (Lowe 2000, 383). By bringing the art into public spaces, community-built art overlaps with urban design and can be classified as creative placemaking. Creative placemaking, as defined by Ann Markusen and Anne Gadwa, "animates public and private spaces, rejuvenates structures and streetscapes, improves local business viability, and public safety, and brings diverse people together to celebrate, inspire, and be inspired" (2010, 4).

This volume contains three chapters that focus on community arts projects. Tiva Lasiter, in Chapter 5, "Impacts of Participatory Mural Making on Youth Empowerment," explores how designing and painting a high school mural impacted the empowerment of the youths involved. Anastasia L. Pratt, in Chapter 8, "Constructing and Preserving History through Community Art Projects," demonstrates how a community arts project—in this case, a mosaic tile mural in upstate New York—can be a vehicle for learning and expressing a community's history. Additionally, Katherine Melcher's Chapter 12, "Building Streets and Building Community," includes the muralist Dave Loewenstein's work on the Mid-America Mural Project.

Themes within Community-Built Work

As a hybrid of design, preservation, and art, community-built can provide a unique approach to community development. In order to emphasize the cross-disciplinary nature of community-built, we have grouped the contributing chapters by three themes that cross the disciplinary boundaries of urban design, historic preservation, and art. The examples within this book illustrate how community-built projects strengthen communities through three primary means: community-built processes build trust, empowerment, and community capacity through carefully orchestrated participatory processes; community-built projects help define and express local identity and culture through symbolic meaning; and community-built places often involve community members taking control of their local environment. These three themes—participation and empowerment, culture and identity, and local control of place—form the organizing structure of the book.

Part 1: Participation and Empowerment

Contemporary community-built practices aim to provide more than basic, functional services; they aim to bring people together and build relationships. Ever since industrialization, social theorists have observed an increasing isolation within contemporary life. As people move to cities, the traditional bonds of family and community can break down. More recently, increasing demands on our leisure time mean that we spend less time connecting with others outside our immediate family—we end up "bowling alone" (Putnam 2000).

The physical design of where we live can reinforce this isolation. City design that prioritizes automobile traffic and separates commerce, culture, and residential areas results in isolated neighborhoods and streets void of pedestrian presence. With such empty places, it is no wonder that people find it easier to connect with others through computer screens than on the streets. By bringing people together in order to revitalize local places and develop stronger interpersonal relationships, community-built has the potential to counteract the isolation of modern times.

The methods undertaken in community-built projects not only counter the isolation created by our physical environment but also can overcome social isolation. Through meaningful community engagement, community-built processes aim to foster social change by developing a groups' capacity to manage and realize projects (Delgado 2000). The power of community-based projects to bring in marginalized groups and build their sense of empowerment is starting to gain recognition across disciplines, not just in the design fields. Leading social scientists such as Robert J. Sampson (2011) and Eric Klinenberg (2013) are doing research that shows important connections between the presence of community-based or community-built initiatives and a neighborhood's ability to recover from extreme weather events or fight crime.

This book starts with the chapter "Community-Built as a Professional Practice" by Katherine Melcher. Her study of professional artists and designers within the Community Built Association developed the preliminary definition of community-built that was then used to select the other cases included within this volume. She identifies three core elements within CBA members' work: community involvement, the construction of something in a public or semi-public space, and the ultimate goal of building stronger communities. She describes some commonalities CBA members share and how both community involvement and the act of building something can contribute to building stronger communities.

The following chapters describe community-built projects within communities who are wary of participatory initiatives: groups in post-Communist Hungary, a low-income African American neighborhood in the United States, and teenage youth in a California high school. In these projects, the development of mutual trust becomes a central focus, and the methods of participation become as important as the fact that participation is allowed.

In Chapter 3, through four stories about community-built projects in Hungary, Kristin Faurest explores how to revive public engagement in a newly democratic state after many decades of authoritarian and Communist rule. In this challenging environment, building a culture of participation is best attempted first through small scale projects, such as the collaborative re-envisioning of the small urban space of Teleki Square, or working with a specific, closed special-needs group such as the severely autistic residents of the Miskolc Autism Foundation.

In a very different context (the neighborhood of Hurt Park in Roanoke, Virginia), Terry L. Clements and C. L. Bohannon grapple with a similar question in Chapter 4: How does a university community (faculty and students) build trust within a community that has been characterized as "a poor, crime-ridden" place where residents are frustrated with past projects because the community residents were not a part of the process? Their answer was a process that places an emphasis on trust, reciprocity, and mutually supportive networks. Through a series of projects—oral histories, a place inventory, the design of a gateway park, and the creation of a community garden—they emphasize developing relationships within the community over creating a built project.

In Chapter 5, the final piece in Part 1, Tiva Lasiter documents how a high school mural project helped students develop different types of empowerment. Using surveys, photographs, and participant observation, Lasiter concludes that the students experienced seven different forms of empowerment. She concludes that social capital can be developed through many different methods within one community-built project.

Part 2: Culture and Identity

Our built environment provides not only the practical functions of shelter and transportation; it also has a symbolic function. Traditionally, local materials and construction methods expressed not only the character of the local environment but also cultural and religious meaning for its inhabitants. Community-created and maintained material objects can be symbolic representations of intangible cultural heritage practices. Conversely, contemporary construction with its "one size fits all" approach and global access to materials has been criticized for creating generic places that lack connections to the specific place and to the past. Many community-built projects, such as the ones presented in this section, counteract this force by creating ways to express or preserve local culture within their built environment.

Barry L. Stiefel's Chapter 6 explores how the eruvin—physio-psychological enclosures used by halachic-observing Jews that enable them to "carry" in the public domain on their Sabbath—have shaped some neighborhoods in Charleston, South Carolina, and brought people together in unexpected ways. This process demonstrates how an ancient, community-built tool that allows a group to maintain a separate spiritual space can evolve over time to become a symbolic cultural device that allows the group to maintain religious tradition while still being an integrated part of the urban fabric.

Mariana Esponda Cascajares's study on the square-log cabins in the village of Mont-Tremblant, Quebec, in Chapter 7 describes how the preservation and adaption of historic log cabins reveal the collective memory of a Quebecois community and its powerful connections with the local environment. Several preserved log cabin examples serve as illustrations of how they were historically used to colonize the area. Preservation of these log cabins becomes significant not only because of their technological aspects but also because of the material culture that becomes inseparable from its landscape. These log cabins reflect a local connection to the surrounding environment—historically out of necessity and currently as a tourism draw.

In Chapter 8, Anastasia L. Pratt uses an example of a school mural project in Clinton County, New York, to illustrate how community art can help define the historical identity of a community. Over the course of 2008 and 2009, seventh graders from every school district in the county worked with their social studies and art teachers, the Clinton County Historian, and three artists to create a mosaic to showcase the county's history. From researching the history of their school and their region to proposing images for the tiles and then making the tiles, the students were actively involved in a project that created a huge ceramic tile mosaic, which graces the side of the county's government center.

In the final chapter of Part 2, Chapter 9, Ildikó Réka Báthory-Nagy looks at the issues of memory conservation. On June 16, 1944, the mayor of Budapest issued a decree where 220,000 persons were forced to wear a yellow Star of David on their clothing. They had to leave their homes by midnight on June 21 and move into one of 1,944 designated apartment buildings in the city, also marked with a yellow star. They were the so-called yellow-star houses. The houses served the same purpose as the ghettos, a preparatory stage for deportation. For half a year, everyone passing by could see precisely who the persecuted Jews were, and where they lived. Today, 1,600 former yellow-star houses still stand, but barely a trace of their past role remains in public memory.

In 2014, the Memorial Year of the Hungarian Holocaust, several centralized events were launched, organized by national institutions. As a counterpoint of a centralized governmental program in January 2014, the Open Society Archive (OSA) of Central European University invited current residents of the existing former yellow-star houses to organize a collective memorial event for June 21, 2014. More than 7,000 volunteers participated and worked out their own memorial project in over 130 locations across the city in order to preserve the memory of place and people together.

Part 3: Local Control of Place

Necessity is the mother of many community-built initiatives. As with the Amish barn-raising example, larger-scale projects need a community in order for them to be realized. By coming together to build projects, people can combine their resources to improve their environment and living conditions. Community-built projects often arise out of a specific need experienced within a community—whether it is caused by a natural disaster, economic downturn, or lack of government support. Many community-built projects make better use of decaying, demolished, or over-looked spaces such as vacant lots, neglected public spaces, or abandoned buildings.

When citizens gather and organize themselves to serve their shared needs, it places them in an interesting relationship with governing organizations. It becomes a political act. Whether officially sanctioned or not, community-built projects can be seen as acts of claiming space. These acts require negotiating a balance between official control and local use. In this way, community-built projects provide a con-crete illustration of what theorists call the "right to the city." The expression first came into prominence with Henri Lefebvre's book of the same name, *Le Droit a la Ville* (1968), which called for a transformed and renewed access to urban life. The idea has since been taken up by the members of the Los Angeles school of urban sociology, particularly Mike Davis and Edward Soja, who argue that the power of the privileged few has, for a number of reasons, made it impossible for the vast majority of the urban population to have truly open access to the city and its resources.

The concept of community-built is inherently linked to the idea of the right to the city, particularly as it has been expressed in recent times by David Harvey (2008). Harvey describes the inherent human need to be able to freely modify one's urban environment and the importance of understanding the ability to change the city as a fundamental right:

> The right to the city is, therefore, far more than a right of individual access to the resources that the city embodies: it is a right to change our-selves by changing the city more after our heart's desire. It is, moreover, a collective rather than an individual right since changing the city inevi-tably depends upon the exercise of a collective power over the processes of urbanization.
>
> *(Harvey 2008, 1)*

The expression "right to the city" has since been interpreted and appropriated by many groups, including squatters in Germany, the New York–based social jus-tice organization the Right to the City Alliance, and a South African antieviction movement. The need for people, especially marginalized communities, to assert their right to equal access to common urban resources is a critical issue worldwide. A city that offers its residents possibilities for individual expression will by nature be more welcoming. For example, in his recent book on Berlin, Peter Schneider

(2014) describes how the city's somewhat unfinished, less-than-perfect appearance is far more attractive to young creative people than more polished metropolitan centers like Paris or Singapore. A combination of a difficult history and an enlightened urban management has resulted in a place where people feel that they can leave their individual mark:

> Young visitors to a beautiful, expensive, and perfectly restored city feel excluded. Looking around, it is clear to them: every space here is already occupied. Cinderella Berlin offers an inestimable advantage over these princess cities: it gives all newcomers the feeling that there is still room for them, that they can still make something of themselves here. It is this peculiarity that makes Berlin the capital of creative people from around the world today.
> *(Schneider 2014, 8)*

In encouraging local control of the environment, what is the relationship between the local residents, the authorities, and private corporations? It does not always have to be antagonistic. Local authorities can provide the space and the possibility for people to use their city in creative and collaborative ways. For instance, in Vienna, the local government allows graffiti artists and other bottom-up urbanism initiatives to take control of portions of the Danube Canal, which has, in turn, revitalized the area. But still, in many cases, community-built projects are spurred on by belief that the authorities aren't providing the services they should, and it is often in times of economic downturn, with the increase of empty lots or storefronts, that community-built projects thrive.

Part 3 contains three chapters that demonstrate three very different ways that citizens claim their rights to adapt their living environments to better suit their needs.

Daniela Patti and Levente Polyak outline in Chapter 10 a diversity of do-it-yourself urbanism movements in Budapest. They observe an increasing number of designers facilitating community projects to meet community needs long neglected by the authorities. This process unfolded in a particular way in Budapest, where budget cuts and reformulated policy priorities undermined a variety of important social services. Bottom-up community infrastructure emerged, relying on either private commercial support or volunteer community capacities. Focusing on two cases—VALYO, an informal and itinerant public space along the Danube riverbank, and Művelődési Szint, a cultural center established as an adaptive reuse of an underused department store—they reflect on the impact these projects have had as well as the downside of their potential to be instrumentalized by large-scale urban development programs.

Patti and Polyak's insights proved accurate in an entirely different context in Budapest during the refugee crisis of late summer and fall 2015, when, in face of government inaction to provide even a minimum humanitarian standard for the refugees, small community groups and until-then unheard-of charities maintained temporary transit camps in public spaces in train stations. The transit camps took on a specific spatial character of their own in particular at the Keleti Train Station, where the black walls of the underpass took on a secondary role as an improvised creative forum and communications channel for locals to express their sympathies and welcome to the refugees.

The following chapter shares a community-built approach that collaborates with local government initiatives rather than providing an alternative, parallel infra-structure. In Chapter 11, Jeremy C. Wells describes how the United States' National Trust for Historic Preservation Main Street approach can catalyze efforts led by passionate community volunteers and revitalize downtowns. In Main Street pro-grams across the United States, local volunteers help revitalize the local economy, promote the downtown, and design and preserve places. However, these approaches are not without conflict. In Quakertown, Pennsylvania, for instance, Main Street volunteers found their efforts to improve the design of the downtown were often resisted by local government officials and the Borough Council. The Main Street program in Quakertown persevered and garnered the trust of the borough and downtown stakeholders, although the gains—a couple of community parks—took more than a decade to achieve. While these limited results are fairly typical of most Main Street programs, nonetheless, Wells observes that the community buy-in of grassroots preservation initiatives often has the most sustaining long-term results.

In Chapter 12, a second contribution from Katherine Melcher, we learn about community-built streetscape projects across the United States facilitated by archi-tect Mark Lakeman of City Repair, muralist Dave Loewenstein, and landscape designer Steve Rasmussen Cancian. Each of these streetscape projects can be clas-sified as a hybrid of top-down and bottom-up approaches. Within each, the prac-titioners and community members negotiated the tensions between grassroots efforts and city regulations in order to slow traffic, deter gentrification, and turn streets into community gathering places.

These chapters represent only a small sampling of community-built work. The goal of this book is to achieve something that might seem counterintui-tive: to develop an overarching framework for understanding a phenomenon that is inherently informal. While highlighting the themes found within these pro-jects, we hope to also respect the informal, local, and context-specific nature that defines them.

Almost all of the cases included in this book include more than one of these organizing themes: participation and empowerment, culture and identity, and local control. In the conclusion, we will reflect on how these examples of community-built projects further illuminate these themes. Finally, we will conclude with a summary of how community-built, defined as involving local residents in the construction of a built project, helped realize those themes—and ultimately build community.

Note

1 *Halacha* is the Hebrew term for Jewish law.

References

Chilvers, Ian, Harold Osborne, and Dennis Farr. 1988. *The Oxford Dictionary of Art*. Oxford, UK: Oxford University Press.

Community Built Association. 2014. "What Is Community Built?" *Community Built Association*. http://communitybuilt.org/about/. Accessed 7 June 2014.

Daniels, D. M., and E. L. Johnson. 2009. "The Impact of Community-Built Playgrounds on the Community." *Journal of Trauma*, 67: S16–19. doi:10.1097/TA.0b013e3181ac1400.

Delgado, Melvin. 2000. *Community Social Work Practice in an Urban Context: The Potential of a Capacity-Enhancement Perspective*. New York: Oxford University Press.

———. 2003. *Death at an Early Age and the Urban Scene: The Case for Memorial Murals and Community Healing*. Westport, CT: Praeger.

Draper, Carrie, and Darcy Freedman. 2010. "Review and Analysis of the Benefits, Purposes, and Motivations Associated with Community Gardening in the United States." *Journal of Community Practice*, 18(4): 458–92. doi:10.1080/10705422.2010.519682.

Francis, Mark. 1983. "Community Design." *Journal of Architectural Education*, 37: 14–19.

Francis, Mark, Lisa Cashdan, and Lynn Paxson. 1984. *Community Open Spaces: Greening Neighborhoods through Community Action and Land Conservation*. Washington, DC: Island Press.

Green, Gary P., and Anna Haines. 2008. *Asset Building & Community Development*. 2nd ed. Los Angeles: Sage Publications.

Harvey, David. 2008. "The Right to the City." *New Left Review*, II(53)(October): 23–40.

Hester Jr., Randolph T. 1989. "Community Design Today: From the Inside Out." *Landscape Journal*, 8: 128–37.

Hou, Jeffrey, Julie M. Johnson, and Laura J. Lawson. 2009. Greening Cities, Growing Communities : Learning from Seattle's Urban Community Gardens. *Land and Community Design Case Studies*. Seattle, WA: Landscape Architecture Foundation in association with University of Washington Press.

Hutzel, Karen. 2007. "Reconstructing a Community, Reclaiming a Playground: A Participatory Action Research Study." *Studies in Art Education: A Journal of Issues and Research in Art Education*, 48: 299–315.

Iveson, Kurt. 2013. "Cities Within the City: Do-It-Yourself Urbanism and the Right to the City." *International Journal of Urban and Regional Research*, 37(3): 941–56. doi:10.1111/1468–2427.12053.

Jacobs, Jane. 1992. *The Death and Life of Great American Cities*. Reprint ed. New York: Vintage Books.

Klinenberg, Eric. 2013. "Dept. of Urban Planning: Adaptation." *The New Yorker*, 88(42): 32–7.

Lefebvre, Henri. 1968. *Le Droit a La Ville*. 2nd ed. Paris: Anthropos.

Lowe, Seana S. 2000. "Creating Community." *Journal of Contemporary Ethnography*, 29: 357.

Lydon, Mike, and Anthony Garcia. 2015. *Tactical Urbanism: Short-Term Action for Long-Term Change*. Washington, DC: Island Press.

Markusen, Ann, and Anne Gadwa. 2010. *Creative Placemaking*. Washington, DC: National Endowment for the Arts.

Massachusetts Institute of Technology, Department of Urban Studies and Planning. 2013. *Places in the Making: How Placemaking Builds Places and Communities*. http://dusp.mit.edu/cdd/project/placemaking. Accessed 26 August 2016.

McCarthy, Kevin F., Elizabeth H. Ondaatje, Laura Zakaras, and Arthur Brooks. 2004. *Gifts of the Muse: Reframing the Debate About the Benefits of the Arts*. Santa Monica, CA: RAND Corporation.

National Historic Preservation Act. 1966. Public Law 89–665; 16 U.S.C. 470 et seq., Section 101(4).

National Park Service. 2014."National Register of Historic Places Program: Research." *National Register of Historic Places.* http://www.nps.gov/nr/research/. Accessed 5 February 2015.

Newman, Oscar. 1976. *Design Guidelines for Creating Defensible Space.* Washington, DC: U.S. Dept. of Justice, Law Enforcement Assistance Administration, National Institute of Law Enforcement and Criminal Justice: for sale by the Supt. of Docs., U.S. Govt. Print. Off.

Pagano, Celeste. 2013. "DIY Urbanism: Property and Process in Grassroots City Building." *Marquette Law Review*, 97(2): 335–89.

Page, Max, and Randall Mason, eds. 2004. *Giving Preservation a History: Histories of Historic Preservation in the United States.* New York: Routledge.

Parker, Patricia L., and Thomas King. 1998. "Guidelines for Evaluating and Documenting Traditional Cultural Properties." National Register Bulletin. National Park Service.

Putnam, Robert D. 2000. *Bowling Alone: The Collapse and Revival of American Community.* New York: Simon and Schuster.

Rofe, Yodan Y. 1998. "A Community Built Playground in Tel-Aviv." *Built Environment*, 25: 61–5.

Rossetto, Erica. 2012. "A Hermeneutic Phenomenological Study of Community Mural Making and Social Action Art Therapy." *Art Therapy: Journal of the American Art Therapy Association*, 29(1): 19–26.

Sampson, Robert J. 2011. *Great American City: Chicago and the Enduring Neighborhood Effect.* Chicago: The University of Chicago Press.

Sanoff, Henry. 2000. *Community Participation Methods in Design and Planning.* New York: John Wiley and Sons, Inc.

———. 2008. "Multiple Views of Participatory Design." *Archnet-IJAR: International Journal of Architectural Research*, 2: 57–69.

Schneider, Peter. 2014. *Berlin Now: The City After the Wall.* Translated by Sophie Schlondorff. New York: Farrar, Straus and Giroux.

Semenza, Jan C. 2003. "The Intersection of Urban Planning, Art, and Public Health: The Sunnyside Piazza." *American Journal of Public Health*, 93(9): 1439–41.

Semenza, Jan C., and Tanya L. March. 2009. "An Urban Community-Based Intervention to Advance Social Interactions." *Environment and Behavior*, 41(1): 22–42. doi:10.1177/0013916507311136.

Toker, Zeynep. 2007. "Recent Trends in Community Design: The Eminence of Participation." *Design Studies*, 28: 309–23. doi:10.1016/j.destud.2007.02.008.

Wilson, David Sloan, Danielle Marshall, and Hindi Iserhott. 2011. "Empowering Groups That Enable Play." *American Journal of Play*, 3: 523–38.

Wycoff, Mark A. January, 2014. "Definition of Placemaking: Four Different Types." *Planning and Zoning News.* http://www.canr.msu.edu/uploads/375/65824/4typesplacemaking_pzn_wyckoff_january2014.pdf. Accessed 26 August 2016.

PART I

Participation and Empowerment

2

COMMUNITY-BUILT AS A PROFESSIONAL PRACTICE

Katherine Melcher

In 1965, artist Lilli Ann Rosenberg brought youth and seniors together in Harlem to create a street mural. In 1973, architect Bob Leathers organized a group of parents in Ithaca, New York, to construct a playground at his children's elementary school. At the same time, landscape architect Karl Linn was bringing together residents in inner-city Philadelphia to build neighborhood commons on vacant lots. Today the tradition of professionals working with communities to design and build shared places continues. Artist Laurel True works with communities in Haiti, Ghana, and New Orleans to create mosaic murals that not only express their local cultures but also generate new sources of income. Rusty Keeler of Earthplay works with early childcare centers to construct natural play-scapes across the United States. The Pomegranate Center works closely with communities in the Pacific Northwest to create gathering spaces within their neighborhoods.

What all these professionals have in common is that they engage in community-built practices, defined by the Community Built Association (CBA) as a "collaboration between professionals and community volunteers to design, organize and create community projects that reshape public spaces" (2014).

Within the United States, community-built as a professional practice has existed since the 1960s, and the CBA, a national organization of community-built practitioners, is nearing thirty years of existence. Still, beyond Melvin Delgado's *Community Social Work Practice in an Urban Context* (2000), community-built has not been defined or described as a distinct field of practice, despite practitioners' acknowledgement that "even though they were from Habitat or they were painters or they were architects or they were designers, all these different fields, we felt that we had more in common than we do with other people in our field" (Donch 2012).

Although academic research into community-built practices is scarce, popular press coverage of community-built projects is extensive. This preliminary description of contemporary, professional community-built practices is based on texts by and about CBA members[1] and CBA member responses to a 2012 survey.[2] This description of community-built as a professional practice is neither comprehensive nor definitive. Each person's community-built experience is different, creating unlimited variety and possibility within the practice. Still, through a collection of individual interactions and interpretations, one can catch a glimpse of that collective understanding that is the social world of community-built. The analyzed texts were primarily written by community-built enthusiasts, and therefore they provide an optimistic description of the practice. Regardless of these limitations, this description, as a preliminary step into community-built research, can broaden the public's understanding of the practice, inform discussions about the practice's value and purpose, and provide a basis for future research.

Defining Elements

Two elements appeared repeatedly in CBA members' definitions of community-built: creating a built project and the involvement of the local community. According to one respondent, community-built "is differentiated from participatory design in that the community is also empowered to organize and participate in every stage of a project's development. Not just design input." This implies that community involvement in the construction phase is what distinguishes community-built from other design practices. "By preference and necessity it involves community organizing and involvement of the community at each stage from design to creation of the project."

Definitions found within the analyzed texts suggest a third defining element: the ultimate goal of community-built is to build connections between participants—in other words, to build community. For example (emphases added by author),

- Community-built "celebrates not only the physical accomplishment of building *but also the experience of interdependence and community*" (Linn 2007, 99).
- "The reason community built was done originally in many, many areas was not only the building and the resources coming together, *but it was really about the building of community*" (Donch 2012).
- It is not only about "stretching your play dollar while increasing quality and celebrating what makes your community special; *there is the added benefit of building community*" (Learning Structures, n.d.).

Community-built is therefore defined by three elements: a built project, community involvement, and the ultimate goal of building community. In the following sections, these three elements of community-built are described in more detail.

Community-Built Projects

Community-built projects exist in public and semi-public places. They can be of any size; one practitioner described his projects as "small but potent" (Matanovic 2007, 8). They can be temporary or lasting. They can be something newly made or the preservation of something already existing. Despite this diversity, community-built projects typically fit into three main types: play spaces, public art, and gathering spaces.[3]

The beginnings of contemporary community-built practice can be traced to the 1960s and 1970s when playground designers such as Bob Leathers, Jimmy Jolley, and Paul Hogan began involving community members, especially children, in the design and construction of playgrounds. Their choices of materials differed—Leathers is known for his complex wood structures (figure 2.1), Jolley for his creative use of tires, and Hogan for innovative use of discarded industrial and construction materials—but the collaborative nature of their approaches were similar.

Today most community-built playground professionals, such as Leathers and Associates, Learning Structures, and Meyer Design, work in private companies of two or more employees, and they work with community groups nationwide and sometimes internationally. Recently, the practice has evolved to include the nature-play movement, with companies such as Earth Play and Bay Tree Design who design natural play areas rather than free-standing play structures.

Public art projects can also be community-built. "Using a range of common materials and collaborative approaches, community public artists work in such forms as art parks, 'garden galleries,' landscape design projects, playspaces, hand-sculpted and cast seating areas, relief sculptures, columns, archways, and pavements"

FIGURE 2.1   World of Wonder playground designed by Leathers and Associates, Athens, Georgia

Source: Katherine Melcher

(Huebner 2013). Murals and sculptures tend to be the most common forms of community-built art, with mosaics being the most popular medium (figure 2.2).

Most community-built artists work on their own as independent contractors (for example, Sherri Warner Hunter, Laurel True, Elizabeth Raybee, and Tom Arie Donch), but some public art practices have evolved into non-profit organizations serving specific cities and hiring multiple artists at a time (for example, the Chicago Public Art Group and the Philadelphia Mural Project).

The third project type, gathering spaces, is the smallest and most eclectic of the three. Gathering space designers create spaces where community members can come together (figure 2.3). Gathering spaces can be created out of overlooked places such as road intersections, in-between spaces, and vacant lots. Designers incorporate elements intended to draw people together and to encourage inter-action, such as gardens, benches, mailboxes, amphitheaters, tea stands, and book trade stations. Gathering spaces have fewer practitioners than other types. Exam-ples include City Repair in Portland, Oregon; Pomegranate Center in the Pacific Northwest; Karl Linn in Philadelphia and Berkeley; and the Village of Arts and Humanities in Philadelphia. Although often known for their dynamic leaders, many of these gathering space practices have grown into independent, non-profit organizations.

FIGURE 2.2 Mosaic being created at a Community Built Association conference, New Orleans, Louisiana, 2010

Source: Katherine Melcher

FIGURE 2.3   Peralta Community Garden gathering space; design facilitated by Karl Linn, Berkeley, California

Source: Katherine Melcher

Community-built projects can contain more than one of these project types and involve more than one practitioner. In the 1970s, Karl Linn worked with Paul Hogan in creating spaces for play and gathering in Philadelphia. Currently, playground companies such as Leathers and Associates collaborate with artists, such as Sherri Warner Hunter and Laurel True to incorporate artwork into their playgrounds.

Although project types vary, and materials range from lumber to mosaics to plant materials, commonalities in qualities of materials, construction methods, and overall character exist. Community-built projects tend to use locally available and often salvaged materials. Typically, the methods of bringing these materials together involves craft, building by hand, and use of low-tech construction methods such as carpentry and masonry.

Additionally, projects often express local culture and history through the content of the artwork and form of design. Playground designers often incorporate place-based themes, drawing from local history and architecture. Muralists are more inclined to use social and cultural themes, allowing individuals to make statements about their own life experiences. Murals often contain political statements, but, in other cases, they are simply a celebration of the place.

These characteristics have practical functions. Relying on local resources (materials, skills, and funding) can make a project more affordable. Low-tech construction encourages people to join in, no matter their level of experience: "'The use of familiar materials engages the energy of many participants,' Weber explains. 'Adults who are too inhibited to join a painting team will help lay pavement, mix cement, etc.'" (Gude and Pounds 2013). Relying on local resources and skills also can increase the sense of ownership a community has over a project: "Even if the project is publicly funded, community contributions of money, time, or skills are important for creating a sense of community ownership" (Gude and Pounds 2013).

The local materials, low-tech methods, and local content all contribute to a character of place that is commonly described in the analyzed texts as unique, beautiful, and meaningful. These characteristics can result in a project that celebrates "local choices, resources, and sensibilities" (Matanovic 2007, x).

Community Involvement

Most community-built practitioners would agree that, "Citizen involvement, participation and collaboration are the heart of the project, and often even more important than what may be physically built as a result" (City Repair 2006, 44). The involvement of the local community can be characterized as the core defining element of community-built, with almost all survey respondents including it in their definitions. But, as one respondent said, you can define community-built "as broadly as you define the word 'community,' intentional and otherwise." People who are involved in community-built projects tend to be "local volunteers." But community can be further defined as the "people who use the place" and the "people who enjoy the place" or "a group of people with some common connection," such as "a town, neighborhood, school church, civic organization, etc." Community can also be a "multi-generational" group that includes "people of all ages and abilities."

Despite small variations in defining who the community is, practitioners often commented that community includes everyone, and therefore the community process should, too. Practitioners value inclusivity because they believe that everyone has something of value to share: "latent talent exists in abundance among many people" (Cockcroft, Weber, and Cockcroft 1977, 115), "every community has surprise resources and talents" (Keeler 2012, 41), and "each community contains a wealth of latent human and physical resources" (Linn 2007, 201). Practitioners stressed the importance of asking who is not already a part of the process and then finding methods to bring them in: "that is the nature of community organizing and community build . . . that drawing in constantly, inclusion, bringing people together" (Donch 2012).

"Usually and preferably," the community is involved from the beginning to the end of the project: "from the beginning with the design process, [continuing] with fund raising, community involvement, volunteer recruitment, and the bulk of installation labor" (CBA member survey response).

In an ideal community-built process, the community not only participates but also leads the project. This community-control is often achieved through the use of a core group, "a 'dream team' of interested and excited volunteers" (Keeler 2011, 27) who organize the process, fundraise, recruit volunteers, and manage the construction. Despite this emphasis on local leadership, volunteers do not have to be involved in every aspect of the project. For example, major infrastructure and more complex construction can be undertaken by professional contractors (Danks 2010). Between the project types, there are significant differences in how the community-built process runs. For example, playground practitioners often work in communities across the United States, which limits how much time they can spend in each community. Therefore, they provide a structured process for the community to follow between their visits. Muralists and gathering space designers tend to work hand-in-hand with the community throughout the process. Nevertheless, the process can be broken down into three main phases: planning and designing, building, and nurturing.

In the planning and design phase, participants work collaboratively with the practitioner to develop ideas for the project. Once a general vision is settled upon, a designer "takes their desires and suggestions and transforms them into a stylized reality" (Schmidt 1986, 32)—in other words, into a design plan. Play space designers often accomplish this through a design day where the designer visits the community for a series of meetings and workshops. Muralists work with the community to decide on a theme around which individual designs can develop. In both approaches, the community is in charge of the theme and vision. They also provide feedback on the proposed design plan before it moves into implementation.

After the design planning phase, the community (usually the core group) prepares for the build days through additional fundraising, material gathering, workday planning, and volunteer recruiting. Although outreach and fundraising start at the beginning of the process, they become critical at this stage. Fundraising can be considered "the biggest obstacle—the most intimidating one, too!" (Megan Dyer and Peter Gibbs qtd. in Keeler 2008b, 171). Fundraising includes looking for monetary donations, grants, as well as donations of materials, food, labor, and other in-kind services such as loaning tents, tables, and tools. For playgrounds, the preparation phases can take anywhere from three months to a year, with most projects lasting an average of five months.

The construction phase, "a big community construction party" (Matanovic and Orseman 2014, 26), differs significantly between the project types. Playgrounds have intense build days over long weekends (an average of five days to two weeks), with hundreds of volunteers, while murals can rely on less formal participation and fewer numbers of volunteers. In all projects, though, construction typically ends with a community-wide celebration.

The end of construction does not mean the end of community involvement. Extending community involvement beyond the building phase is important for the life of the place. Hogan observed, "When this nurturing (construction) stopped, the body (playground) began to die" (1974, 141). Matanovic observed that after about five years, the "on-going maintenance that grew naturally out of this [the community's] investment" started to fade and vandalism began to occur (2007, 42).

Community events and additional construction projects can help keep the site alive. Keeler suggests that a community-built place "should be built and changed and re-changed on a regular basis" (Keeler 2012). Despite the tendency for community interest in the place to fade, sometimes the community's dedication to the project lasts from one generation to the next. Leathers and Associates reports,

> Over the past few years, something very exciting has been happening more and more frequently. Some of our early playgrounds have reached the end of their life expectancy, and many of these communities are coming back to Leathers to design another community-built playground.
>
> *(Leathers and Associates 2007, 6)*

The phases listed here might create the impression that the community-built process is a simple, step-by-step formula to follow, but it is not: "It is not a science. It's an art" (Donch 2012). "Projects evolve as different pieces and new players are added. By the time a project is sixty-percent completed it may look very different from the originally envisioned end result" (Yeh, Moskin, and Jackson 2004, 20).

Community-built practitioners use similes of jazz and dance to describe how the process unfolds:

- "Up front, people involved need to know that the project is like a jazz band as opposed to an orchestra. This is a different project. Not everything in this type of project can be planned in advance."

  (Matanovic 2007, 72)

- "It's like a dance. It's a score . . . . In a sense we are dancing with the community. And, but there are rules, there are patterns, there are techniques, there are things we can use and kind of flow with. In general some of the things are important to do in a specific order, but sometimes you throw them out."

  (Donch 2012)

Like in jazz, a structure allows for improvisation, bringing many people into one composition. Like in a dance, the practitioner decides when to follow and when to step in and take the lead: "I suppose you do let things happen which you think will be more interesting than other things. You do have to have an overall point of view—or you do have one whether you want to or not" (Lilli Ann Rosenburg qtd. in Hubbird 1993, 91). Other practitioners use the terms "planned indeterminacy" (Linn 2007, 88) and "chaordic (chaotically ordered)" (City Repair 2006, 140) to describe this balance between structure and openness. This method helps "leaders try to ensure that the active creativity of each group member is elicited and valued so that it contributes to the give-and-take from which emerges a shared vision" (Cockcroft, Weber, and Cockcroft 1977, 116).

One example of structure and improvisation is the muralist's use of a theme within which each person can improvise. Participants share their ideas through discussion and settle on a theme. Then the artist works with individuals to develop ways to express their individual interpretations into images and art. In this way, the practitioner can "give over as much as possible but still keep an eye on the overall project composition" (Laurel True qtd. in Chtena 2011). Another example of structure and openness can be found within the master plan, which provides a structure for moving forward, but can still "adapt to the shifting needs of their resident populations" (Danks 2010, 14).

Combining the flexibility of an improvisational process with an emphasis on local resources allows the practitioners to incorporate new talents, new ways of giving, and new resources as they arise out of the community: "Having no pre-set ideas, I had the freedom to work with whatever resources came my way and with whoever was willing to participate" (Yeh, Moskin, and Jackson 2004, 1). The openness to local contributions fosters a kind of serendipity, with people finding the right materials or skills at exactly the right time:

- "Wagner ticks off a list of serendipitous local talent discoveries. The museum artist who crafted the dinosaur print sculptures for the park, the planners and construction workers, the PR and marketing whizzes."

  (Hannan 2011, 55)
- "When they needed last-minute donations, such as sod and backfill early on Sunday morning, Fuller and Henningson just rifled through the phone book. So involved was the community that 'if you needed something, you just got on the phone and before long a truck would drive up.'"

  (Henrich 1990, 31)

Rosenberg reflects that these unexpected occurrences are what make the work beautiful: "There are many exciting things that can happen when people work together on a project; chance occurrences and happenings often bring a spontaneous beauty which a preconceived plan does not predict and cannot produce" (Rosenberg and Wittenberg 1968, 109).

Building Community

A community-built practice can create places with unique character and instill a sense of ownership and pride within participants (Melcher 2014), but ultimately, its primary goal is building a sense of community. Within the community-built context, building community consists of, first of all, strengthening relationships among participants and neighbors. Second, building community results from the community group's realization of their own collective capacity for making change.

"When neighbors participate in envisioning, building, and using a shared communal space, they simultaneously build relationships with one another" (Linn 2007, 8). Community-built projects bring people together, often people who may be neighbors but do not have a reason to interact:

In the past, many of our school parents would only see each other at drop-off and pick-up times. The community build gave the parents a chance to really get to know the faces they casually saw each week at school. The process also introduced the church members to the school families.

(Keeler 2008a, 37)

Through a project where they need to work together to realize their shared goals, people create connections that can develop into friendships:

It brought thousands of people together for the first time. And one time the Junior League these ladies were just at each other and we sat down on one of the benches one of the nights that we were working and we were able to just talk.

(Donch 2012)

In some cases, a sense of interdependence develops between people that lasts beyond the project:

Deep and lasting relationships are found when people work together on a common cause. I frequently see many of the volunteers around town from that project with Rusty and I know that we will help each other out whenever we can. I like being connected that way.

(Jill Elizabeth qtd. in Keeler 2008b, 196)

Through these strengthened connections, a sense of community emerges: "I am forever connected to my fellow-community members because of this. This project put me in touch with my community in a way that has never happened before. It forced me to truly examine my community and appreciate what we have" (community participant qtd. in Matanovic 2007, vi).

When people work together to accomplish a shared goal, relationships are not the only thing developed; by working together to complete a large community project, participants realize their collective ability to make positive change in their everyday environment and their world. In community-built projects, participants create visible change by working together, often in a way that is larger and greater than they thought possible: "There is something magical about this project. Who could believe that 2,800 volunteers of all different skill levels and abilities could come together to make this happen in six days?" (Schanen IV 2008, 2).

Often this realization strengthens bonds between community members and empowers them to continue working together on new projects: "Possibility playground will be a great resource, but an even more valuable one is the band of motivated citizens who created it. There is much to be done in this community, and they've shown they know how to do it. We have no doubt they will answer another call" (Schanen IV 2008, 3). This act of realizing one's collective abilities can lead to a sense of empowerment in children as well: "By producing real objects that beautified their common environment, the children at Henry Street learned valuable lessons, not only about ceramic art, but about their own power to change their world" (Hubbird 1993, 78).

Community-built practitioners have observed that this sense of empowerment can transfer to other aspects of their lives: "Community control of these small-scale neighborhood commons gives residents a place where they can take a stand . . . As people realize their shared vision by successfully constructing a commons through cooperative efforts, they are empowered to take on larger issues" (Linn 2007, 204).

This sense of empowerment can, in turn, lead to the creation of stronger bonds between members—a building of community: "At 5 p.m. Sunday, work stopped. The project, with the exception of concrete work, was finished. Volunteers, many with tears in their eyes, stood staring at what they had done, shaking hands and hugging one another. 'People say small towns and close-knit communities are disappearing,' Mayer said. 'Not here. Just look as what this community came together to accomplish. The only word for it is amazing'" (Schanen IV 2008, 2).

Community-built as a professional practice is defined by the involvement of local volunteers in the creation of a built project. Usually the community leads the process and builds the project using donated materials and hand construction. By valuing all contributions (money, skills, and materials), the built project becomes unique and valued by the community. Local involvement and built projects are not just defining elements of community-built practices. They also appear to be fundamental components for the building of a community. It is the combination of these two elements that people see as having the potential to achieve the ultimate goal of community-built—the building of a sense of community by strengthening relationships between participants, helping groups realize their capacity for completing a large project.

A process that involves local community in a careful, deliberate manner is important for strengthening relationships within a diverse community: "Over the years, we found ways to encourage more people to participate in creating commons and developed methods for resolving conflicts and maintaining open communication, allowing both ideas and emotions to be expressed. These are the paths to deeper mutual understanding and stronger bonds among diverse members of a community" (Linn 2007, 12). Valuing everyone's contributions can also lead to a sense of individual empowerment that ties a person to their community: "It also raised the realization that I was capable of bringing change and improvements to my community—just by participating and caring—that I had a responsibility to my community" (community participant qtd. in Matanovic 2007, vi).

Somewhat more surprisingly, the physical construction of a project can also help strengthen relationships and empower groups. As one participant observed, "There is something about working hard, sweating, pushing yourself beyond what you thought you could do, and having others doing the same, right beside you, that forges bonds of community and caring" (community volunteer qtd. in Keeler 2008b). For example, "Being a teacher and having a parent work alongside you builds that relationship. Later in the year, when you need to tell them their child isn't doing so well or need, to work on certain things, they are more able to listen and accept what you have to say. . . . They've worked and sweated alongside you building something special for their kids. They've seen your passion" (community volunteer qtd. in Keeler 2008b).

Additionally, the public and permanent nature of the projects inspires pride within the community group; it serves as tangible evidence of the community group's abilities. "What's been the best? Seeing children and adults point to something they helped create and say with pride: 'I did this.'" (*Grist Magazine: Environmental News and Commentary* 2005).

The special synergy of creating places together appears to be central to the "empowering process" that is community-built. As one survey respondent said, "I love the magic that happens when you connect with others in a creative context." When asked why they engage in community-built practices, survey respondents cited the rewards found in the act of creating (thirteen total) and in working with other people (sixteen total). Several respondents included both in their statements (seven total), rather than just one or the other. This suggests that the two in combination create a synergy that is special to community-built practice, which can result in experiences that they describe as "fun," transcendent," and "a celebration."

Conclusion

Community-built as a contemporary professional practice can be defined through three key elements—local community involvement, a built project in a shared place, and an ultimate goal of building community. Each defining element contained within it some common (but not necessarily universal) characteristics. Projects are made with locally available materials, knowledge, and skills. The process follows some basic steps (planning and designing, building, and nurturing), but an openness characterized by improvisation is also emphasized. However, many challenges exist in the process, including negotiating collective decision making, managing volunteer construction, and retaining and motivating volunteers.

In analyzing the texts on community-built practices, several hypotheses were formed on how defining elements, common characteristics, and desired outcomes are interrelated, more specifically:

1 An emphasis on local resources plus an improvisational process is open to local contributions fosters "spontaneous beauty" and a form of serendipity, finding just the right resource at the right time.
2 In community-built projects, building community is accomplished by strengthening relationships between participants and realizing the capabilities of the group as a whole.
3 The practice of building together creates a special magic; local volunteer involvement in construction helps both strengthen relationships between participants and empower groups to take on additional projects.

These observations suggest that the defining elements of community-built (community involvement in the process and a built project in a public place) not only make the practice unique but also contribute to its ability to build community.

Still, throughout the texts, community participation in the process remains the most important defining element. Leathers and Associates explain, "The process IS the most important product" (Leathers and Associates 2012), and Lilli Ann Rosenberg concludes, "The final mural will be effective if the process of creation has been exciting and satisfying" (Rosenberg and Wittenberg 1968, 53). Although community-built can be defined through its outcomes of a built project and a stronger sense of community, it appears that the inclusive, adaptive process remains the most critical defining element. Participation in the process not only defines community-built; it also is critical to its outcomes. As Lily Yeh remarks, "the right process becomes the right product" (Yeh, Moskin, and Jackson 2004, 19).

Acknowledgments

The research in this chapter was funded by a grant from the National Endowment for the Arts, Research: Art Works. The author is also indebted to the Community Built Association members for their participation in the survey.

Notes

1 Ninety-five texts matched the selection criteria: twenty-four magazine articles, fifteen books, fourteen newspaper articles, ten journal articles, eight online reports, eight newsletters, seven websites, three blog entries, two theses, two recorded conference presentations, and one video. Forty-two of the texts were written by community-built practitioners, and fifty-three were written by non-practitioners (participants and observers). The selected texts cover the work of eighteen community-built practitioners, whose projects range from play spaces (seven practitioners, forty-nine texts), gathering spaces (five practitioners, twenty-six texts), and murals and sculpture (six practitioners, nineteen texts), reflecting the breadth of community-built projects. The selected texts also span all decades from the 1960s to the present day, with the majority of the texts being published in the 2000s (thirty-three) and the 2010s (thirty-two).
2 In 2012, the survey was distributed to members of the Community Built Association (CBA). Twenty-three respondents completed the questionnaire. Nineteen completed the online questionnaire, while four were completed at a CBA conference. The respondents' experience with community-built projects ranged from one year to forty years, with an average of seventeen years. Over half (twelve) of the respondents had seventeen or more years of experience, and two had more than thirty-five years each, suggesting that, on the whole, the respondents had significant experience with community-built projects.
3 Of these three types, the majority of the survey respondents identified more closely with public art (sixteen), while six worked primarily on place space, and one selected both. None of the respondents selected "Gathering places, community commons, amphitheaters, community gardens" as their main type of work, even though it was listed as an option.

References

Chtena, Natascha. 2011. "True Mosaics: Interview with Mosaic Artist Laurel True." *Think Africa Press*. http://thinkafricapress.com. Accessed 1 August 2015.

City Repair. 2006. *Placemaking Guidebook: Creative Community Building in the Public Right of Way*. 2nd ed. Portland, OR: City Repair.

Cockcroft, Eva Sperling, John Pitman Weber, and James D. Cockcroft. 1977. *Toward a People's Art: The Contemporary Mural Movement.* New York: Dutton.

Community Built Association. 2014. "What Is Community Built?" *Community Built Association.* http://communitybuilt.org/about/. Accessed 7 June 2015.

Danks, Sharon Gamson. 2010. *Asphalt to Ecosystems: Design Ideas for Schoolyard Transformation.* Oakland, CA: New Village Press.

Delgado, Melvin. 2000. *Community Social Work Practice in an Urban Context: The Potential of a Capacity-Enhancement Perspective.* New York: Oxford University Press.

Donch, Tom Arie. 2012. "Community-Building," presented at the Community Built Association conference, Portland, Oregon, June.

Grist Magazine: Environmental News and Commentary. 2005. "Miracle Milenko." Accessed 1 August 2015.

Gude, Olivia, and Jon Pounds. 2013. *Chicago Public Art Group's Community Public Art Guide: Making Murals, Mosaics, Sculptures, and Spaces.* Chicago: Chicago Public Art Group. http://www.cpag.net/guide/. Accessed 15 November 2015.

Hannan, Maureen. 2011. "We'll Build It Ourselves The Community-Built Playground Movement Now Addresses Safety, Accessibility, and Long-Term Maintenance Concerns." *Parks and Recreation*, 46: 52–5.

Henrich, George. 1990. "Designs in Good Citizenship: Monticello Builds a Sense of Community by Building a Playground." *Architecture Minnesota*, 16: 30–1.

Hogan, Paul. 1974. *Playgrounds for Free: The Utilization of Used and Surplus Materials in Playground Construction.* Cambridge, MA: MIT Press.

Hubbird, Ann R. 1993. *Lilli Ann and Marvin Rosenberg, Community Artists: A Case Study in Calling Forth Creativity.* Eugene, OR: University of Oregon.

Huebner, Jeff. 2013. "Community Artist as Space Designer." *Community Public Art Guide.* Chicago: Chicago Public Art Group. http://www.cpag.net/guide/4/4_pages/4_1.htm. Accessed 16 November 2015.

Keeler, Rusty. 2008a. "Community-Built Playscapes." *Exchange: The Early Childhood Leaders' Magazine Since 1978*, May/June: 36–8.

———. 2008b. *Natural Playscapes: Creating Outdoor Play Environments for the Soul.* Redmond, WA: Exchange Press.

———. 2011. Earth Play Possibilities. *Rattler (Sydney)*, no. 97 *(March):* 15–17.

———. 2012. "Play Environments for the Soul." *Landscape Online.* http://www.landscape online.com/research/article.php/732. Accessed July 11, 2016.

Learning Structures. n.d. "Community Built Value." *Learning Structures.* http://www.learn ingstructures.com/value.asp. Accessed 16 November 2015.

Leathers and Associates. 2007. "Summer Newsletter."

———. 2012. "Frequently Asked Questions." http://www.leathersassociates.com. Accessed 15 September 2013.

Linn, Karl. 2007. *Building Commons and Community.* Oakland, CA: New Village Press.

Matanovic, Milenko. 2007. *Multiple Victories: Pomegranate Center's Art of Creating Community-Crafted Gathering Places.* Issaquah, WA: Pomegranate Center.

Matanovic, Milenko, and Alison Orseman. 2014. *Building Better Communities.* Issaquah, WA: Pomegranate Center. http://www.pomegranatecenter.org/wp-content/uploads/2011/04/Pomagrante_Center_How_To.pdf. Accessed 20 January 2016.

Melcher, Katherine. 2014. "Community-Built Projects, Processes, and Practices." *National Endowment for the Arts.* http://arts.gov/artistic-fields/research-analysis/research-art-works-grants-final-papers. Accessed 20 January 2016.

Rosenberg, Lilli Ann Killen, and Ken Wittenberg. 1968. *Children Make Murals and Sculpture; Experiences in Community Art Projects.* New York: Reinhold Book Corp.

Schanen IV, Bill. 2008. "The Playground Volunteers Built." *Ozaukee Press*. http://possibility
playground.org/2011/01/the-playground-volunteers-built/. Accessed 24 September 2015.
Schmidt, Mark J. August 1986. "Greenwood School Playground." *Iowa Architect*.
Yeh, Lily, Bill Moskin, and Jill Jackson. 2004. "Warrior Angel: The Work of Lily Yeh." Bainbridge Island, WA. Available at: *http://www.virtuevision.org/lily_yeh.pdf*.

3

KALAKA

Four Stories about Community Building in a New Democracy

Kristin Faurest

Environmental pollution and degradation are among the grimmest legacies of Communist Eastern Europe. But what often is not so obvious to those not deeply acquainted with post-Communist societies is the linguistic pollution left in its wake. Words and expressions with original meanings that are positive and bright were corrupted and twisted to become Orwellian perversions of their original selves: *volunteering* meant being coerced into weekend labor brigades; *communal* or *shared* were construed to refer to the centralized economy and a lack of individual choice. One of the paving stones on the route to an open society is finding the words to express these concepts without unwillingly referencing the unhappy past.

In Hungary, the term *kalaka* has an ancient rural meaning. It is similar to the Amish concept of a barn-raising, for example—a communal effort to build something good and useful, either for a group or an individual, but with the understanding that working together is a common value that benefits everyone. The idea of recovering something ancient and rural in order to express a new, international, and modern identity is not new in Hungary. In many European countries at the turn of the twentieth century, architects, industrial designers, and artists sought to connect to the international secessionist movement by creating a specifically national identity, drawn from folk art and medieval peasant architecture. In this way, something local, rural, and ancient became part of something international, urban, and modern. This was the case in Finland, the Czech lands, and Hungary, to name a few countries. It is this same phenomenon that now informs the idea of community design and building; no words of the recent past will do, so we return to the more distant past, one free of the jargon of a centrally controlled economy and totalitarian rule. The word for "community" has always existed, but until recently denoted a physical settlement, not a social group. Only in recent years has it taken on the same broad connotation and usage that it has in English—a physical or virtual group with a common purpose and shared values. The word *kalaka*, which until a decade ago had more of an ethnographic connotation besides being the name of a favorite children's music group, has undergone a revival of sorts to describe the process of working together with the common purpose of improving a community space.[1] *Kalaka* is used both in the rural and urban context, but generally to describe projects in which friends and neighbors work together to create a community garden, clean up a park, build playground equipment, or carry out other similar projects. One of the leading landscape architects in Hungary founded the Ars Topia Foundation, which describes its activity as carrying out kalaka projects in former Hungarian provinces in Romania, mostly restoring old community thermal bath facilities.

Along with finding the words to describe community building, Hungarian greening activists are looking to find the right approaches to community building. Community gardens and collaborative urban greening projects have only become commonplace in the region in the last five years or so. Part of this can be attributed to the fact that there was not a perceived need for producing food in the city until recently; much of the population own weekend homes with plots of land, and farmers' markets are still quite abundant in the city. Still, some of the obstacles can also be attributed to the legacy of communist rule. The emphasis is less on food and more on creating new informal, volunteer-controlled green spaces, beautifying dense urban neighborhoods, and improving the quality of life of disadvantaged groups including but not limited to Roma, people with mental or physical disabilities, and the elderly poor. The influence of community gardens and allotments in nearby cities such as Berlin and the emergence of non-governmental organizations (NGOs) and informal activist groups advocating DIY urbanism and community gardening have all contributed to an increase in know-how and interest in community building.

A quarter of a century after Hungary became a democracy, community-based building processes are starting to work. This chapter details four different community-generated projects: one in an autistic institute, designed to help support the therapeutic goals and economic sustainability of the institute; another in a school garden in a working-class neighborhood of Budapest that emphasizes fruit production and seeks to build stronger connections among generations and neighbors; is the third via a series of courtyard gardens in a densely built-up, disadvantaged area of Budapest; and lastly through a community-based reinvention of an extremely deteriorated but storied public square. Each is an individual example of how community building can thrive and be nurtured in a new democracy, while at the same time serving as a building block for it.

Seedling Garden, Miskolc Autism Foundation, Miskolc, Hungary

The Miskolc Autism Foundation serves as a permanent home for about sixty profoundly autistic young people and adults. Miskolc is situated in one of the poorest areas of eastern Hungary, an area with high poverty and unemployment where it is far more difficult to mobilize volunteer help than in Budapest. In 2013, the foundation received a grant from the Swiss-Hungarian fund to develop a sustainable agriculture project that involved chickens, geese, sheep, two large greenhouses, and a therapeutic herb and vegetable garden. My firm, Artemisia Landscape Design, was entrusted with the design work. We approached it in a collaborative way; working closely with the staff of the institution, we developed a spatial plan and a conceptual document listing plants, potential furnishings and decorative elements, and a budget calculation for the materials needed. We cooperated with another group that was constructing hothouses for the site so that in the future no plants would need to be purchased; all would be grown on-site.

We designed the garden as a series of concentric circles planted with herbs, vegetables, and ornamentals, arranged by their dominant sensory effect, with a living willow sculpture in the middle. This had multiple meanings: the willow sculpture serves as a place that provides shelter or solitude, but it is also symbolizes a living basket. This is of particular local significance because the institute supports its operations in part through basket weaving workshops, since it is a craft that permits the kind of repetitive, easily readable activity for which many people with autism have an affinity. The raised beds are constructed from reclaimed brick and roof tiles, with other ornaments and features from upcycled materials. This makes the garden economically and ecologically efficient, since most of the materials were found

FIGURE 3.1 Raised beds in concentric circles, with plants arranged according to sensory interest, in the Seedling Sensory Garden in Miskolc, Hungary

Source: Kristin Faurest

abandoned on the institute's grounds, but it is also meant to express the idea that all materials and all people have some sort of inherent value and affinity; nothing should be discarded as useless.

Involving the residents of the institute in the traditional sense in the design was not plausible; most cannot speak and they understand their daily routines by the pictograms posted in the dormitories and common areas. There was a gap between the vision of the funders and the institute itself. The funders saw it as an important opportunity for community connection and outreach, envisioning such things as the residents selling the surplus at the local market or having visitors to the institute come to purchase produce or secondary products. The institute's directors did not see this as possible, pointing to the tendency of many of the residents to be disturbed by encounters with crowds or individual strangers. In spite of this gap in understanding, the project will mean that the institute can grow fresh produce for its residents and sell the surplus and secondary products in the future.

Instead of taking the approach that we would have taken at a school or urban neighborhood, which would have meant directly involving the site's future users in the design and construction, we observed the daily routines and used what we saw to inform the design, and involved the local office of a multi-national corporation, Accenture, in the site preparation. Some other local volunteers and a couple of landscape architecture students from Budapest's Corvinus University contributed, too. The garden is now rich with texture, color, fragrance, and flavor, crowned with the beautiful living willow sculpture in the center. It is still a work in progress and probably always will be—like any other garden, it is a continuously growing process, not a product—but it is a significant work of cooperation in a part of the country that has become synonymous with poverty and unemployment since 1989.

The Jam Garden, Eötvös Elementary School, Budapest

This project came about after the local district mayor expressed a desire to create a public fruit orchard. Again, Artemisia Landscape Design was hired by the city to manage the design process. We chose the school's courtyard and the adjoining public area for planting fruit trees and vines. The question remained: How can we involve the school's community, primarily residents of the surrounding prefabricated housing estate? These Communist-era planned communities from the 1950s and 1960s are often problematic in terms of social cohesion because of the tendency of the block towers to isolate people from each other and the surrounding environment, and also because, in some cases, people were moved into them in large numbers at once so that the organic fabric of a neighborhood never got a chance to develop. Schools are an excellent vehicle for community organization—to get the parents interested, the best tactic was to get the kids to have an active stake in the process.

We met over eight weeks with eight classes, grades second through fifth. We focused on building an interactive educational program for the students to get them to make a large mental and emotional investment in the garden. We started by asking them to think about where on the planet different kinds of fruit come

FIGURE 3.2 Posters made by students at Eotvos Elementary School making presentations about their fruit research in preparation for planning the Jam Garden

Source: Kristin Faurest

from, how fruits reach, and how we could grow our own. We also sought to get the students to reach out to the older generation in inquiring about how fruit used to be cultivated, what was available in stores many years ago, and what recipes they used for homemade fruit desserts or drinks. The students built models of how the garden should look out of Lego building blocks, clay, and other materials, and we also carried out "living models" in the courtyard, with each of the students or groups of students taking on the role of tree, fountain, arbor, and so on. The students made funny drawings of fruit with the caption "What can we do for the Jam Garden?" and were then asked to take them home to their parents and bring them back with responses. In this way, we directly but discreetly reached out to the parents through the students for individual donations. There were very few parents who did not respond; offers for building materials, plants, seeds, soil, compost, and various in-kind donations came back.

After two months of these workshops and take-home assignments, we looked at what the kids drew and built and listened to what they were saying during the workshop sessions. Based on that, we established four loose concepts for how the garden could be designed, and they voted on the one they liked best. Ultimately what was chosen included a labyrinthine series of allotment beds (one per class), an outdoor classroom with a long arbor and gazebo, and a number of mostly native fruit trees and vines.

FIGURE 3.3   Each class in the school has its own raised bed, which contributes to class pride and gives opportunities for outdoor learning

Source: Kristin Faurest

That was the design process. In terms of the construction, the municipality provided much of the funding and carpentry work to ensure that the larger elements, particularly the gazebo and arbor, were constructed according to safety standards. The parents also contributed a considerable amount of materials and labor. We organized several Saturday workdays and scheduled workdays around the schooldays as well. The staking out of the raised beds—complex given its labyrinthine shape and precise geometry—was given to sixth graders as a math assignment, with several of the school community's fathers doing the construction with the timber delivered by the municipality.

The garden is now in its third season. It is still a work in progress. Some elements have not yet been built, and the arbor is not yet the vine-covered structure we had originally envisioned, but the garden is an integral part of the school's curriculum. If a recent observation is typical, students are constantly jockeying to get to be the one who waters the allotment beds, which are filled with lavender, strawberry plants, red currant bushes, a multitude of colorful annuals, and other plantings, depending on each class's preference.

GANG Group, Budapest

District 8, also known as Józsefváros (Joseph City), is located in central Budapest. It is similar in character to neighborhoods like San Francisco's Mission District or

Berlin's Kreuzberg in that it is divided into strikingly, abruptly different quarters—for example, the Palace Quarter with its renovated buildings and young intellectuals and the Magdolna Quarter with some of the highest unemployment and lowest education and income levels in the city (Rev-8 2008). After World War II, the Jewish population was largely replaced by the Roma minority, which now constitutes 30 percent of the district. Budapest, like Vienna, is defined by a large ring road that encircles the inner city. Part of the district lies within the ring road and the other outside of it. Areas outside of the ring road have always constituted, in the mental map of Budapest citizens, a periphery of sorts, historically plagued with prostitution, petty gang crime, and homelessness. The Magdolna Quarter, a subsection of District 8 located just outside the ring road, is one of the poorest and most neglected parts of the city. It has some of the highest unemployment and lowest school-finishing rates. Since 2004, it has been undergoing a massive municipally driven social rehabilitation, designed to improve the local quality of life for the original residents, while also adding higher-end housing and retail; in other words, revitalization without gentrification.

This kind of urban regeneration program, already in practice in other European cities, was new for Budapest: a renewal approach that simultaneously deals with social, economic, environmental, and architectural renewal, with particular attention to improving the quality of life of the most disadvantaged. Crime prevention, family support, community development, occupational training, and architectural and public space renewal are all essential components.

The revitalization program is mostly large scale, focusing on renovation of public squares, construction of major new retail and housing developments, and renovation of existing old buildings. The GANG[2] group—four women, all in environment-related fields, working as volunteers—saw the critical importance of small-scale interventions in the form of greening the district's courtyards. The four members of the group, all longtime friends in their twenties and thirties, were a landscape architect, an herbalist, an environmental engineer, and an educator. They first came up with the idea in 2007 to carry out three pilot projects in the Magdolna Quarter. Initially the members thought that they were reviving an old tradition—after all, these courtyards are in century-old buildings, so surely they had originally been intended as gardens. In fact, the spaces originally had very functional purposes—providing space for tinkers to repair broken crockery or maids to beat carpets, for instance. The group's strategy was not to create a huge number of gardens—their total number to date is five—but rather to create a few very well done projects that could be extensively promoted to the public as success stories. This was because they recognized their limited capacity as a small team of volunteers and thought it was more effective to do pilot projects and then campaign in the hopes that others would feel inspired to do the same. The group launched a blog and also made a documentary film about the project; they also organized neighborhood festivals and street fairs. The basic philosophy was that rather than spending limited time and resources on making many gardens that may or may not be sustained, it was better to try to change the public's attitude and open their minds to the possibilities.

The basic idea of making these spaces into gardens could seem obvious to any-one looking at the Google Earth image of downtown Budapest. Most of Buda-pest's buildings constructed before World War I have inner courtyards. Building regulations of the time required that the courtyard be at least 15 percent of the building's footprint. Most developers stuck to this minimum in order to have the maximum amount of sellable built space, so most of the courtyards are shady, some of them long and narrow. Yet because of their number (there are some neighbor-hoods in Budapest where they constitute well over 80 percent of the housing stock), these humble, shady courtyards represent a huge potential for increas-ing urban green space. This is especially true in some inner-city neighborhoods, where green space is less than a square yard per capita. Further, the courtyards function as a type of shared outdoor space that is neither entirely private nor entirely public, just like the green squares of London and other UK cities, and provide social and environmental benefits that neither private gardens nor public parks do. Most buildings keep their gates locked, and visitors who don't live in the building can only enter by ringing or punching in a code, so the garden's security level is high and people feel free to put out more expensive plants or decorative items or furniture. The small scale of the courtyards and the limited user group make it relatively easy to convince people that it's worth the effort and money to make a garden there.

The GANG team's approach was to begin with informal gatherings to talk about what the courtyard could be, then progressing to get residents involved in the planning and design and, finally, the construction. Funding came from various private grants as well as some support from the crime prevention department of the Ministry of Justice, which showed a certain level of awareness on the part of the authorities that these kinds of initiatives promote stronger social ties, get peo-ple paying more attention to their environment, and as a result can lower crimes like break-ins and vandalism. Raised beds were made of found or salvaged mate-rials; the plants were chosen based on quick growth and low maintenance. This was all done as a collaborative effort by volunteers, and without professional assis-tance. Given that the buildings in question were dilapidated structures with small, council-owned apartments, it was a remarkable feat to get people interested in improving their environment in such a dramatic way. Three pilot projects were real-ized in 2007, all three of them thriving today and cared for by the same people who use them—the residents. As the activist team noted on their blog,

> Walking through the streets of Budapest, entering the courtyards, one can discover wonderful gardens full of plants and charm. The majority of court-yards, though, are empty and dreary, containing nothing but concrete. In April 2007 three gardens of Buda and Pest were born. Plans were elaborated according to the wishes of locals. People living in the house and our vol-unteer team realized the gardens with their own hands. Help from outside was limited—just enough to let it happen. We believe that the rebirth of gardens is not a question of money, as in a building of 20–50 flats much more

depends on self-organisation. As a result, empty spaces gain their stories, and the courtyard becomes the integral part of people's life.

(GANG group blog)

Remaking the Agora: The Community-Based Design of Teleki Square

Teleki Square is one of Budapest's most storied squares, in one of the city's most disadvantaged neighborhoods. New Directions Landscape Architects, commissioned by Budapest's District 8 with European Union funds, set out in 2013 to work with a team of residents to turn a barren, crime-ridden, functionless space into a vital neighborhood center. The project—part of the same social rehabilitation project as the GANG gardens—was funded by the European Union through the local municipality, which strongly endorsed the idea of a citizen-driven design process.

Teleki Square's identity was less as a green space than as a hive of commerce. It was a literal and metaphorical meeting of urban and rural worlds. Its namesake was László Teleki, a mid-nineteenth-century statesman noted for his advocacy for the rights of minority nationalities in Hungary. This legacy of inclusiveness as part of the history of the square became a determining factor in the space's reinvention. Teleki Square has a distinctive place, too, in local Jewish life, since the market had a significant number of Jewish merchants and the square's synagogue is the city's only Sephardic one. Many of Teleki market's poor Jewish peddlers originated from the more insular Hasidic communities of the Eastern Carpathian Mountains. In 1910, this area had some of the highest density in the city, with 70,000 people per square kilometer. Conditions in Teleki were harsh, as a 1917 newspaper account described: "Teleki tér even in peacetime is one of Budapest's most sorrowful squares, but now, since the war has placed its own sad stamp on it, Teleki tér itself with its boisterous, loud marketplace is truly a bleak place" (*Népszava* newspaper, June 24, 1917).

In between the two wars, the unemployed and unskilled waited for day labor here, while others stood in line for scarce foodstuffs. World War II brought tragic days to Teleki as everywhere else in the city, including a pogrom in October 1944 and some of the city's first yellow-star houses, indicating where Jews lived (described in Chapter 9, "Yellow-Star Houses: A Community-Generated Living History Project in Budapest," by Ildikó Réka Báthory-Nagy). Losing the used-goods market to another location in the 1950s led to a decline in the square's life, as it lost its raison d'être. It only half-heartedly filled the role of urban park—the trees and grass were there, but there was no playground, gathering place, furniture, or seasonal colorful plantings to draw people. Clearly there was no one who felt a sense of community or ownership, because littering, vandalism, and other destructive behavior were the norm.

Teleki Square serves as an experiment with how interventions that promote cooperation, interaction, and participation can build community identity and have an active role in creating lively and livable cities with an open society. To achieve the goal of making Teleki a real neighborhood gathering place that would be welcoming and approachable to the many ethnic, socioeconomic, and age groups in the area, it was necessary to use a wide range of communication and outreach tools. The aim was to examine how urban design, public art, and creative strategies contribute to communication platforms that foster and strengthen social bonds.

The community planning process spanned a dozen meetings over two months and engaged a diverse neighborhood team, including elderly people who have lived there for fifty years and still recall the horse-drawn carriages that brought goods to the old square's market, the young tattooed rabbi from the neighborhood's synagogue, young intellectuals, and Roma families. Meetings took place at the site and at the Glove Factory community house nearby. Communication outside meetings was run primarily through Facebook, which the elderly residents used with equal enthusiasm. A core design team of landscape architects plus about fifteen residents consistently took part in the design work. The first task was to create mental maps of the site's history and potential. With its awkward triangular geometry and ragged reputation, Teleki Square was never known as a green space or for its attractive architectural features; it was a commercial exchange for rags, used goods, and foodstuffs, characterized by ramshackle bodegas and non-descript storage facilities. This liberated the design team from having to conform to historic preservation guidelines, and priority was placed upon the simple, sturdy, and functional. History was treated in the abstract: the design team took Teleki's nineteenth century notions of inclusiveness and openness as a defining idea for the park's mood.

The visioning began with the square's potential and desired functions. Next came a physical rendering. A planting scheme and hardscape materials were selected by what would be most appropriate and sustainable. A variety of tools helped actively engage community workers in the research, mapping, and planning work. This was done in order to provide a way for anyone who wanted to contribute. Some residents only felt comfortable engaging in the discussion. Others were happy to make slideshow presentations about the area's history. Still others were comfortable picking up markers and indicating their wishes on the printed-out maps. Informal installations, including "wish lists" for the park tied with twine onto trees, served as a fun way to get people to move through the park to envision its new forms. Most of the exercises were done in the community center, which served as the headquarters of the planning process, but there were also exhibits in the park featuring the documentation of the process, so that people who had not come to the meetings could also view them. After each meeting, photos and a summary film were posted on Facebook, and the sheets of butcher paper covered with hieroglyphic sketches and scribbles were rapidly translated into a legible, attractive digital form to be displayed at the next meeting. In the process, the group formed a Friends of Teleki Square Association, to ensure that the square is filling its role as a community catalyst.

The design was realized in spring of 2014. Its functions are a direct reflection of the residents' input. Entering the space, a visitor first encounters the forum area, for festivals or other events, where historic signage sets a strong sense of identity. There is a stage, a playground for small children, a leisure area, asymmetrical beds for ornamental gardens to be planted by the residents, a dog run, and a corner for teenagers. The place that was once clutter and chaos is now a diverse hub for neighborhood social events, play, and quiet reflection. It is once again a meeting of town and country, as a visitor can sense by passing through the park's paved, very urban entrance and transiting through its green areas in the direction out of the city.

Conclusion

Part of the legacy of Communism in the former Eastern Bloc countries is a negative perception of terms such as *volunteer* and *community*. In the half-century of communist rule, the public became accustomed to the state controlling and deciding all matters of design and planning, and there has remained a residual skepticism and cynicism toward volunteer-driven, community-based green space projects. Fortunately, this has begun to rapidly change in the last half-decade, as a critical mass of activists and designers has found culturally and socially accepted ways to advocate for and carry out community design projects. Some of the factors driving this positive development include foundations offering grants for such developments as well as the emergence of many new NGOs that advocate and try to build capacity for do-it-yourself urbanism, community gardening, and other practices. This is how community building can thrive in a new democracy, while at the same time serving as a building block for it.

What are the challenges to community building projects in new democracies, particularly those of the former Eastern Bloc, and how can we as designers devise ways to overcome them? Institutional barriers still exist. For older people, there is still the mentality that they don't have the right, the power, or the responsibility to change their environment; these decisions are to be made from above, and to challenge that is only inviting trouble. For younger people, the educational system and child-rearing tendencies lean toward the Prussian tradition—questioning conventional truths or coming up with new ideas are not generally rewarded. High taxes are one reason there is a general tendency to think that the state or the municipality are responsible for our surroundings, and to contribute time or materials to such projects is doing a job that should be done by the authorities. And there is a general cynicism about the willingness of others to take care of a commonly developed space, a lack of social sustainability generated by years of communist rule.

Ironically, in the last few years, the decidedly undemocratic practices of the right-of-center government of Viktor Orbán have stimulated public interest in community activism. Social media has also helped promote ideas and projects that previously stayed in more limited circles. This has even extended across previously existing generational boundaries: in the case of Teleki Square, it was not unusual to see the elderly residents posting photos and comments on Facebook. The four projects described previously had many commonalities that contributed to their success—for example, all involved small-scale projects that directly impacted a well-defined community. In the case of the Seedling Sensory garden, it was important to design the planning process in a way that would be sensitive to the particular needs of people with autism. That was the priority, along with engaging the larger community. In fact, the project's funder encouraged us to try to set up systems for using the produce from the garden as a way of building connections with the surrounding community and have the institute's residents sell produce at local markets or even host markets on site. This might have strengthened the project, but the institute's administration strongly felt that this would be more of a trauma than a positive experience to many of the autistic residents, who cannot tolerate large crowds of strangers or diversion from daily routine.

In all four projects, it was easy to convince the user group that working together to build a better place would be directly beneficial for them. That was the simplest part. Using hands-on educational approaches was also a helpful tool—the kids who helped design the Jam Garden were thrilled to be given open-ended, creative assignments that allowed them to learn more about fruit cultivation and its history in Hungary. The Teleki Square residents were very motivated and inspired by the slide shows of public space design ideas that we showed them. With the residents involved in the GANG projects, part of the challenge was getting them to perceive the courtyards as potential gardens, since they have traditionally been empty, utilitarian spaces and their shady conditions and concrete flooring seemed contradictory to the idea of a garden to many people who were not aware of how many low-maintenance shade plants could thrive there in raised beds built of reclaimed materials.

In all cases, it was important to not rush the planning process; spending time beforehand to build knowledge and awareness created the necessary social bonds. The GANG group would begin each of their garden projects with social events, usually involving plenty of food and drink and casual conversation. With the Jam Garden, we spent many weeks giving the kids fun lectures and art assignments about fruit before we asked them to help with the garden's layout. We spent a lot of time observing everyday routines at the autism institute before planning the garden, even if we could not directly involve the residents much in the planning. At the Jam Garden, the teachers initially just thought we were going to plant a couple of fruit trees and be done with it, and they were quite apprehensive about the ambitious scope of the project and skeptical of the promised municipal funding. We repeatedly had to debate with various teachers and administrators about the garden's layout— we had to negotiate with the gym teacher about where the long jump course and the running track would go and convince him that the garden would not interfere with the courtyard's sports functions. Putting the students in a position to make bold decisions about the garden made it a much more convincing argument to win the hearts and minds of parents and teachers alike.

With the Teleki Square plan, people were highly skeptical about whether the realized project would continue to be successful, given the high rate of petty crime in the neighborhood. So a lot of the planning process included helping them develop the Friends of Teleki Square group, and we tried to persuade them that the best way to keep a park in good shape is not by having strict rules and a police presence, but rather by ensuring that people associate it with a variety of enjoyable events. Although we might not have liked the idea ourselves, we agreed with the residents' desire to have the park fenced in and locked at night, because it made them feel enabled to protect the square and also made them willing to do such things as plant flowers in the community ornamental garden. In the case of Teleki Square, it proved of key importance to give people hands-on assignments, such as researching the park's history or finding cost estimates for a clock or furnishings or other elements. It caused them to make an emotional and mental investment resulting in their wanting the process to succeed. Having individual assignments made people accountable and enabled us to avoid the situation of a task being everyone's and no one's.

Finally, one of the lasting lessons for us from all of these projects was that sometimes people are not receptive to the idea of participatory design because of the entrenched belief that it is the professional designer's competence and a layperson could not possibly contribute. The notion of the layperson as expert is still foreign to some. What they have to be aware of is that the designer's role changes to that of educator and communicator. So often people do not see how a place can be made better—it is just too familiar, and they are not aware of the possibilities. We have to take advantage of the opportunity to show people what could be better.

Notes

1 The word, by the way, is unrelated to the *kalaka* referenced as the ancient Babylonian word for "carpool" in a comic American public service announcement from the 1970s.
2 Gang is the word used in Budapest for the internal walkways that characterize these courtyard buildings. They're common areas that can become, if everyone works together, beautiful little communal spaces.

References

"Bleakness at Teleki Square." *Népszava newspaper*, June 24, 1917. Courtesy of Ervin Szabó Metropolitan Library, Budapest Collection, Budapest, Hungary
GANG group blog. http://www.gang-gong.blogspot.com. Accessed 26 January 2016.
Rev-8. 2008. "Magdolna Quarter Rehabilitation Program." Revitalize District VIII, Inc. http://rev8.hu/aktualis-projektek/magdolna-negyed-program-iii/. Accessed 26 January 2016.

4

REFLECTIONS ON COMMUNITY ENGAGEMENT

Making Meaning of Experience

Terry L. Clements and C. L. Bohannon

Communities are not built *through* the making of a thing within a community. They are built *around* the making of a thing. Meaningful community engagement has the potential to reshape the way a community builds relationships with their members and partners. Community engagement processes directly influence the success of community building and building in a community. This chapter reflects on the challenges and opportunities community members and partners faced as they developed mutual trust, and a sense of shared values and goals, while engaged in a sequence of three community-engaged projects with landscape architecture, architecture, and planning students over a two-year period.

All three projects took place in the Hurt Park neighborhood of Roanoke, Virginia. Each project was the focus of a semester's work. The first project inventoried neighborhood physical assets using on-site investigations, oral histories, and local neighborhood data. The second project developed conceptual site plans for a community gateway park and bus stop. The final project resulted in the design and construction of a centrally located community garden.

Within these projects, community residents had the opportunity to increase self-identification—their sense of self and community—and meet goals that might improve the physical and social qualities of their neighborhood. Students learned and applied knowledge essential to their studies and development of their civic lives. Faculty developed their research in the scholarships of engagement, teaching, and learning. Through the sequence of the three projects, community engagement among the neighborhood, university students, and faculty addressed a wider range of goals and results than possible through a single course offering. The mixed success of these sequential projects demonstrate the importance of community social capital: developing and sustaining trust between community members and their partners, understanding the quality and nature of relationships among the residents and each of the partner groups throughout the projects' development, and building reciprocal partnerships around shared goals and values (Field 2003; Halpern 2005).

Neighborhood Context and Project Initiation

The Hurt Park neighborhood in Roanoke, Virginia, was once a vibrant, traditional neighborhood. Originally laid out in the 1880s, it was developed throughout the early twentieth century to house Norfolk and Western Railroad's executives and other middle income residents. By the 1940s, the neighborhood had transitioned into one of the city's premier African American neighborhoods as white residents moved out to the suburbs (Division of Historic Landmarks 1985). Large American foursquare houses with well-kept front lawns lined tree-shaded streets. Neighbors visited across close-set front porches and backyards separated by narrow service alleys.

After desegregation in the 1960s and as long-term residents aged or passed on, the hilltop neighborhood went into a steady decline. More recently, the neighborhood has the uneasy distinctions of containing a high percentage of substandard housing, poorly maintained properties, vacant lots, and abandoned buildings, as well as high rates of drugs and prostitution, personal and property crime, and limited neighborhood businesses. Many of the large two-story houses have been converted into multi-family rental properties; only 32 percent of the houses remain single family (Hurt Park/Mountain View/West End Neighborhood Plan 2003). Light industrial uses have replaced small neighborhood-based commercial businesses.

Today, the neighborhood is on an upswing. In 2008, long-time residents, neighborhood church leaders, and younger transplants helped form the Hurt Park Neighborhood Alliance, Inc. (HPNA). As part of the Roanoke City Neighborhood Partnership, the HPNA and its members are working with a number of government and nonprofit organizations to stop and reverse the neighborhood's decline. The United Way, Habitat for Humanity, Total Action for Progress (formerly Total Action Against Poverty), Community Housing, the city police department, and others are working together to support families and improve the social and physical environment in the neighborhood by Rebuilding a Community That Cares, a campaign to bring city resources to the neighborhood in a collaborative and coordinated partnership (Hurt Park 2014). All are active participants in the neighborhood's efforts to build a stronger community based on trust, reciprocity, and mutually supportive networks.

Faculty from Virginia Tech's College of Architecture and Urban Studies (VT CAUS) approached the Roanoke City Neighborhood Partnership seeking opportunities to partner with a neighborhood group in a university-community engagement project. The Hurt Park Neighborhood Alliance responded. A faculty member in the Urban Affairs and Planning Program needed a community and neighborhood setting to teach graduate students community participation skills. In return, students offered the neighborhood their developing expertise in community identification and asset mapping. Early in exploratory discussions, HPNA members expressed interest in a longer-term relationship to explore opportunities for continued development of the physical neighborhood. The HPNA thought this might strengthen the neighborhood's social capital by continuing to bring community members together to learn more about each other and their needs and desires as they discussed possible future projects. As a result, Landscape Architecture Program faculty were invited to join the developing partnership. The discussions led to a series of projects engaging community members across multiple courses and extra-curricular offerings. The student-community projects were developed to assist the community in identifying the neighborhood's physical and social assets and to envision other possibilities within the community.

Project Goals: Community Building through Community Engagement

Community Engagement describes the collaboration between higher education institutions and their larger communities (local, regional/state, national, global) for the mutually beneficial exchange of knowledge and resources in a context of partnership and reciprocity.

(Carnegie 2014)

[Community engagement is a] direct two-way interaction between communities and external groups through the development exchange, and application of knowledge, information, and expertise for mutual benefit.

(Carnegie 2014)

The challenge in any university-community engagement is to negotiate a partnership that fits project needs as defined by the community, other community partners and stakeholders, and the faculty's responsibility to create a teaching and learning environment that addresses a course's particular learning objectives. Importantly, this includes recognizing and developing a sense that the community is at least an equal part of the project ownership and would hold primary ownership of each community product as they were completed.

As faculty, we were interested in exploring project opportunities for our students focused on community building through community engagement that could also contribute to our research in the scholarship of engagement (see Figure 4.1). During early discussions, community leaders told of other groups and government programs that had done things "for" the neighborhood without working "with" or "alongside" community members, without building a sense of partnership or trust with residents. The HPNA was frustrated with past "service" projects undertaken in the neighborhood where the community residents "received" but were not a part of the process of making in their community. The HPNA was also sensitive to the neighborhood's characterization as "a poor, crime-ridden" place in need of "being helped" or of "being provided for."

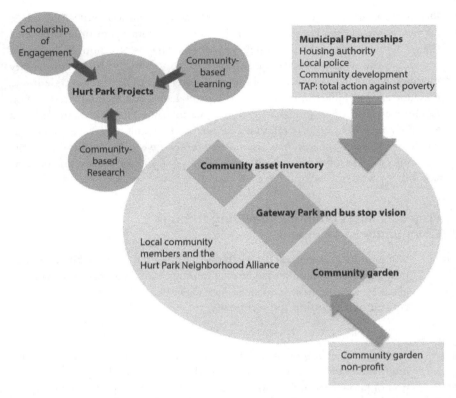

FIGURE 4.1 Faculty helped frame the projects to contribute to the teaching, research, and service missions of the university. Neighborhood leaders ensured that project objectives aligned with community goals.

Source: Terry L. Clements and C. L. Bohannon

Desiring to be effective university partners, we were particularly interested in creating constructive and meaningful relationships among community members, students, and faculty. Together we quickly determined that all would be better served and engaged if the HPNA and faculty worked cooperatively to develop a sequence of projects that could span across university courses and academic semesters. This also would provide flexible openings to adjust or develop additional project partnerships where and when need and desire arose. This approach characterized our partnership and pattern of care as we developed project collaborations that met course learning objectives and neighborhood needs.

In each project, the faculty and HPNA leadership strove to meet the Kellogg Commission's seven-part test for engagement: responsiveness, respect for partners, academic neutrality, accessibility, integration, coordination, and resource partnerships (Kellogg Commission 1999). Virginia Tech faculty and students offered mutually beneficial partnership opportunities where students could offer their developing expertise in community participation and community design to assist residents in learning about themselves and identifying building projects to enhance their physical neighborhood. Students would enhance their educational experiences through mentored real-world training with community residents and other partners. Faculty facilitated processes that voluntarily brought community members together to discover, articulate, and share their goals to improve their neighborhood. Faculty also helped frame the projects so that they contributed to the teaching, research, and service missions of the university. Community leaders helped ensure that project objectives aligned with community goals.

Community Engagement Methods

Before any physical project could be developed, the community needed additional support building social capital among community residents and partners. A currency of trust, reciprocity, and networking is necessary to develop community social identity, resiliency, knowledge, and empowerment. Through the Hurt Park Neighborhood Alliance (HPNA) and other internal bonding relationships, community residents were already building and reinforcing informal networks based on shared values and mutual cooperation. They were also building formal networks with external partners—the city police, housing authority, code enforcement officials, and area nonprofit associations. These intercommunity partnerships bridged between internal community members and external people and organizations holding such shared values and/or goals as reduced crime, better housing, and supporting families.

The HPNA and VT CAUS worked to employ engagement methods that encouraged community building, recognizing that small gains and actions over time can develop or reinforce a community's sense of self as well as build the sense of trust and respect between community members and partners. In order to foster community trust, a sense of reciprocal purpose, and goals, we used a number of engagement methods that regularly brought people together during each project (see Table 4.1). Students were coached in the basics of building trust: to talk straight, demonstrate respect (not patronize), create transparency, right wrongs, show loyalty, get better, confront reality, clarify expectations, practice accountability, listen first, keep commitments, and extend trust (Covey 2006).

The methods reflect a desire to build community social capital such that each activity might create a stronger sense of community empowerment through recognition and celebration of the community and its members—past, present, and future—as well as develop an ethos of engagement in the students and faculty. These methods aimed to build a bridge of trust between community residents and external partners.

Each of the three projects built upon the previous one and incorporated work that other community partners were doing or had done to improve the neighborhood. The first project introduced the university partners to residents through oral histories and mapping exercises. The mapping and oral history projects allowed

TABLE 4.1 Engagement tools employed by Virginia Tech's College of Architecture and Urban Studies and the Hurt Park Neighborhood Alliance during the three neighborhood projects

Engagement Tool	Description	Outcome
Oral histories (Project one)	Students conducted one-on-one recorded interviews with community members as they recalled their history with the neighborhood, its people, and its places. HPNA invited participants rather than the faculty "outsiders."	Compiled audio archive and transcript of the neighborhood members and their stories for use in next steps toward community building. The process of collecting and sharing stories reinforced bonds between community residents. The histories are now part of the city library's permanent archive.
Community mapping (Project one)	Students first walked the neighborhood with community members and later by themselves to collect specific physical and social spatial data. They consulted with local government and non-profits for land use and ownership issues and other information.	The maps spatially located an inventory of the community's physical assets as well as socially valued places discovered in the oral histories. These were re-presented to the community and community partners for verification, and for discussion on potential project development.
Member checking (Projects one, two, and three)	Frequent communication between local and university leaders developed and maintained a sense of trust and common direction. This also helped make sure "we were doing it right" during the process.	Developed a common sense of various goals and purposes, and the direction of each project as well as a sense of where the university supported projects and other community projects might overlap or coincide.
Community forum (Projects one, two, and three)	Work and/or reporting sessions to listen, share, and review the process and products. Developed to generate feedback as well as discussion of new information and thinking around the process and the projects. These were designed so members shared with each other rather than having "outside experts" reporting results.	Transparent and direct critique and discussion of the projects as they were developing at larger community gatherings allowed students and members to develop and refine throughout the ongoing work process. Small table discussions encouraged active participation and voice from all members rather than privileging the community's more vocal participants.

Engagement Tool	Description	Outcome
Story circle (Projects one, two, and three)	These were held throughout the process in each project. Small groups shared individuals' stories about the neighborhood, what was there, and what was/ is valued. Facilitators direct traffic but encourage all members (across age, gender, etc.) to tell tales and share thoughts.	Informal sharing of stories and values contributed new information and verified community values and aspirations.
Design charrette (Project three)	Two short intense work sessions of multi-representational teams—charrettes—were held at key points during the site design projects: one with neighborhood residents and local garden advocates to garner ideas about what the community garden might include, the other to refine these ideas into a tangible, buildable form.	Landscape architecture students prepared conceptual site design and supporting objectives for the community's garden. These were given to the HPNA and the community garden non-profit association for further development.

students and community members to better know the neighborhood and celebrate local knowledge and experience. They also provided necessary information for the next projects. In the second project, landscape architecture students conducted a series of community workshops to develop conceptual sites plans envisioning a gateway park and bus stop as a new neighborhood gathering space. The third project resulted in construction of a community vegetable garden. The gateway park bus stop envisioning project and the community garden project intended to draw out many community voices to discover possibilities for the future of the neighborhood as they built neighborhood relationships and, finally, places.

Each of the community building projects was the focus of a semester's work, each with a unique combination of instructors and students. The projects all directly involved the HPNA and its members and included a range of official and unofficial community partners. In each project, participants shared their stories, their sense of community and place, and developed ideas for rebuilding their community.

Although the projects included varying degrees of engagement among community members, students and faculty, and other partners (see Figure 4.1), in all of them, the HPNA was responsible for bringing local neighborhood knowledge as well as active participation in community initiated meetings and workshops. University partners were responsible for co-facilitating numerous partners, listening and interpreting, and developing materials that community residents could use as they continued to build and strengthen a community that cares.

Project 1: Community Inventory: Oral Histories and Community Asset Mapping

It is extraordinarily difficult for outsiders to make a social or cultural inventory of a community, as they rarely have deep connections to the community members' lived experiences and knowledge of place. It was critical that the community leaders, as gatekeepers, introduced the university participants and the project to the neighborhood. Without these gatekeepers' explicit endorsement, trust or respect would not have been extended to university faculty and students, the "outsiders."

After meeting with the university faculty and students, a core group from the HPNA introduced the team and the project to the larger community at a monthly HPNA meeting held at the elementary school. Students from two planning courses, Multi-cultural Cities and Community Participation, presented an overview of the semester-long project. Together they would develop an inventory of the community's cultural history by collecting oral histories and mapping the neighborhood's physical and social assets.

The oral history project collected local stories that were then spatially located on community maps. Oral histories from the neighborhood residents allowed each to learn of each other, much like the early phases of dating. The oral history project revealed numerous desires for a community garden, neighborhood park, and bus stop. Maps of the neighborhood's physical and cultural history were created and re-presented to the community by an interdisciplinary team of graduate students who worked with community members, community stakeholders, and local officials to collect information on historic and current land uses, community places, opportunities, and problem areas.

The oral histories were developed to be included in the city library's permanent archive. While these methods collected essential information for future work within the community, the histories and maps were valuable artifacts in and of themselves. The histories could celebrate the neighborhood's past and people through collecting, compiling, and sharing individual experiences and artifacts. Residents knew that their histories would also become part of the city library's archive, providing a tangible record to be passed down to their children and future generations. Privileging local knowledge over outsider knowledge also built trust between the "outsiders" and individual neighborhood members.

Inventorying the neighborhood's physical resources using site observation and additional data collection, as well as spatial analysis of the oral histories, produced inventory and analysis maps that tied the place to people and their stories. The resulting maps revealed that, other than limited use of the neighborhood elementary school and schoolyard and local churches, the neighborhood lacked intentional and functional community places. The maps and stories also located problem areas, such as high crime corners and problem houses, that could be prioritized for revitalization. The maps also helped identify potential areas to reclaim lost or diminished social opportunities. This final analysis revealed a prime location for a new community gateway park and potential sites for a neighborhood community garden.

Project 2: Envisioning a Community Gateway Park and Bus Stop

In project 2, landscape architecture students who were learning design development from conceptual design through construction drawings worked with community members to design a range of alternatives for a new neighborhood park. The corner lot selected for the project could become a primary entrance into the neighborhood. Located at a key automobile entrance to the neighborhood, it had been cleared of a dilapidated garage and junkyard that had been a popular spot for drug dealing and prostitution. Once city partners gained ownership of the physical property and removed the buildings, community members were having difficulty envisioning a different future for the corner. Students worked with the HPNA to create alternate visions for what could become a community gateway park (see Figures 4.2, 4.3, and 4.4).

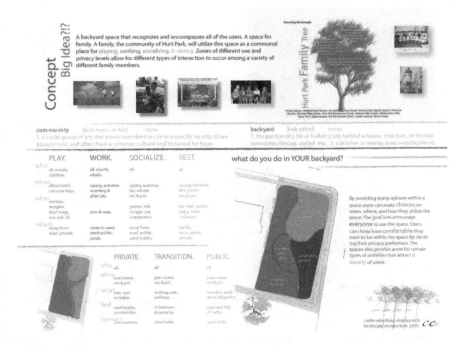

FIGURE 4.2   Site design plans for the park included descriptions of design opportunities for community involvement in the park.

Source: Caitlin Edenfield

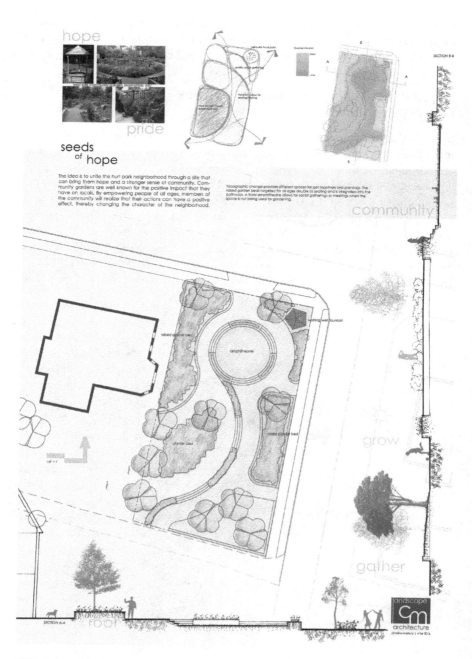

FIGURE 4.3 After numerous community forums, students produced illustrative posters that highlighted a park alternative as well as how it might help build a sense of community and place within the neighborhood.

Source: Christine Ly

While this project has not yet resulted in the making of an actual park, it has resulted in building positive social capital in the neighborhood. The lot is now regularly maintained by the neighborhood and includes a long-awaited bus shelter. The shelter, supplied by the city, provides a place where people can informally meet in a neighborhood place that is not "owned" or otherwise controlled by an undesirable person or group. The students' work emphasized the importance of the bus stop for this low-income neighborhood and its potential role in developing a visible central and neutral location for everyone—elderly, young, employed or not—to meet informally in the neighborhood. The community members used the students' work to support their petition to the city to provide the shelter.

The community forums and informal sharing of illustrative posters after the forums gave more neighborhood residents a voice on what could be possible within the neighborhood (see Figure 4.4). When the project was proposed as a site for the landscape architecture students to practice small park design, it was understood that the highest priority was a physical community bus shelter. Even though a developed park was and is not a high priority item for this site, the process of developing and discussing future possibilities for a park reinforced many neighborhood residents' sense of a need to create a welcoming point that marks the entrance to the neighborhood, as well as other places within the neighborhood that could draw a diversity of residents together. The oral histories and community asset maps were used by the students and during the community forums to reveal and support the community's values and history to a new set of students, and as a resource for envisioning the park alternatives. While development of the park plan alternatives met the students' course learning objectives, the social building resulting from the engagement processes was more important for neighborhood residents.

FIGURE 4.4 Community engagement in action: students, community members, and partners discuss the pros and cons of individual site designs for the gateway park

Source: Terry L. Clements and C. L. Bohannon

Project 3: Developing a Community Garden or Building a Community

As the first two projects were underway, a new non-profit advocating community gardens was established in the city. The director was actively looking for sites to build a second garden and saw the city's focus on the Hurt Park neighborhood as a viable entrée into the area. In the third project—the construction of a community vegetable garden—a team of undergraduate and graduate students worked with community residents to envision a place for food production and communal gathering.

The oral histories from Project 1 revealed community members' fond memories of their parents or grandparents tending vegetable gardens and the neighborhood camaraderie it fostered. Community asset maps identified a few viable vacant lots that could be used for a community garden. The HPNA began to envision a place for a diverse group (age, race, gender) to come together to grow household vegetables, share gardening knowledge, be social, and meet neighbors in a less-charged environment. At least, that is what the neighborhood intended.

The HPNA worked with VT CAUS students and faculty at a series of community forums and story circles to develop ideas about what a community garden should include and what activities it could encourage. The VT CAUS teams used these as the basis for a design charrette, quickly producing a set of design alternatives to share and discuss at a HPNA monthly meeting. Attendees, including representatives from the garden non-profit, discussed the merits of each and identified key components they thought necessary for the success of the garden; community members then voted on their favorites. Students refined the results into a single concept that was then shared with the HPNA and the director of the garden non-profit.

However, the community garden non-profit was focused on making a garden, not on building the neighborhood's social capital through making a garden. In an effort to move forward quickly, the director chose not to include neighborhood residents or the design proposal residents had developed in making the final garden plan. Rather, the director worked with someone from outside the neighborhood to create a simpler plan and submitted it for municipal approval. The Hurt Park community's plan, developed through a series of engagement practices, was not acknowledged. Ultimately, neighborhood alliance members did not build the garden; nor did the construction team include many neighborhood residents. The community garden non-profit recruited its own members as well as a volunteer service group from outside the neighborhood to provide labor. Only after municipal approval did the director alert the HPNA of the final construction plans and invite Hurt Park neighborhood residents to help on construction day. In its first year, gardeners living outside the neighborhood maintained most of the plots. The non-profit's process was messy, and it challenged many people's concepts of trust, reciprocity, and engagement. The "do unto the neighborhood" approach led to hard feelings among many of the partners and neighborhood residents who were or had been championing the idea of a community garden. The non-profit built a garden that was instantly regarded as a place apart, something that was done to the community instead of through the community. It represents a significant disconnect between building a community and building in a community.

Only, now that the garden has been managed for two growing seasons and that Hurt Park's community center run children's activities there, do neighborhood adults see the garden as a part of their community. A few of the HPNA members are still enraged about the process. But they are beginning to see improvements in the social networks in the neighborhood. The garden is providing a site for social, community interaction. Perhaps they are even seeing the community building goals they envisioned during the community asset mapping and gateway park planning exercises become tangible.

Lessons Learned

The community engagement partnership between Virginia Tech faculty and students and the HPNA offered valuable opportunities to both partners. HPNA was able to enhance the neighborhood's community social capital through strengthening a sense of trust, respect, and shared values as they participated in the creation of meaningful tangible products to their neighborhood. The faculty, working across departments and courses, were able to provide a wide range of students with learning experiences as they met multiple course objectives. The students realized the value of the knowledge and skills they developed through undertaking the projects in partnership with community members. It was not easy. It did take more time than non-community-based courses. But community and student evaluations conducted after the projects were complete revealed that the processes and final products were meaningful to each group. The HPNA and neighborhood residents have taken ownership of the histories, maps, and site design proposals. They continue to refer to the community asset maps and gateway park objectives as they work with their city partners to prioritize and implement neighborhood improvements. As seen in the students' final course evaluations, the neighborhood's validation of the students' work evoked a sense of satisfaction and achievement in the students. Students have used the communication skills and community empathy developed during the projects to frame subsequent coursework as well as employment choices upon graduation.

As for the faculty, we offer the following lessons:

1   *Communities are not built through the making of a thing within a community, but around the making of a thing.*

   This process began with individual involvement, creating initial conceptions of what is desired, what is possible, and what can be gained. Building Hurt Park's social capital can be seen as setting the stage for the physical building of a place or places within Hurt Park. One of these includes the actual building of a project. Building partnership with the HPNA included working with municipal authorities and non-profit organizations. Each partner began with their own agenda and goals; some converged, some were incidental to one another, others conflicted. Where partners' goals aligned, it was easier to develop excitement and a sense of purpose, direction, and accomplishment. This proved neither as easy nor delightful where goals differed or the prioritization of a particular outcome varied. Contention was particularly apparent during the final making of the community vegetable garden.

2   *It takes time for outsiders to develop effective relationships with neighborhood groups and residents.*

Developing strong relationships with a new community for each course takes a lot of effort for both partners. Establishing longer-term relationships with one neighborhood and multiple faculty who span related courses saves all partners the time and effort necessary to build strong relationships. After being invited into the neighborhood for discussions to form a mutually beneficial partnership, faculty and neighborhood leaders must devise an engagement plan that addresses and bridges the needs of each. Interactions during the initial project established ground rules and expectations based upon respect, trust, shared goals, and a reciprocity of needs. Subsequent projects built upon the gains and lessons of the proceeding ones.

3   *Bridges between partners can be damaged or broken if the ground rules or expectations of any of the partners are not respected.*

Strong bridges between community members and outside partners can be tenuous. Community members and partners must maintain transparent and respectful communication about their own goals and expectations throughout the project. If either side perceives a "wrong," it can be difficult to recover and repair the direct relationship, and this may affect other partners.

4   *Extending partnerships over a longer, sustained period of time allows relationships room to grow.*

The community's perceived value of each project's tangible products led to proposals for new projects in subsequent courses. The faculty could frame projects to meet teaching and learning objectives in subsequent courses, as they knew the neighborhood and its resources. At the same time, students developed and tested their professional and relationship skills in settings that had lasting significance outside of their class. In the first project, neighborhood residents valued having their sense of community formally verified by the students who delved into the social and physical history of the neighborhood, and again when the Oral History Project was archived in the city library. The histories and the Community Asset Maps were used in subsequent courses and with municipal partners to develop ideas for a gateway park, and later to promote construction of a neighborhood bus stop and a community garden.

5   *Community engagement projects in a course can have meaning outside of course learning objectives. The projects are a tangible demonstration of how neighborhood social capital can be influenced through university and community partnerships.*

Engaged students and faculty were very aware of their contributions and obligations to the neighborhood and committed to meeting project and relationship expectations. The faculty were also respectful of their role relative to the neighborhood's other partners.

At the end of these projects, the neighborhood-university experiment in long-term community engagement did address a wider range of goals and results than possible through a single course offering. The Hurt Park neighborhood's social capital is growing stronger, and the neighborhood's physical landscape is continuing to develop to meet their needs. The faculty continues to challenge their community engagement practices, and many of the students have gone on to pursue their own community engagement projects.

References

Carnegie Foundation for the Advancement of Teaching. 2014. *Community Engagement Classification.* http://classifications.carnegiefoundation.org/descriptions/community_engagement.php?key=1213. Accessed 30 May 2014.

Covey, Stephen M.R. 2006. *The SPEED of Trust: The One Thing that Changes Everything.* New York: Free Press, Imprint of Simon and Schuster.

Division of Historic Landmarks Staff. 1985. "National Register of Historic Places Inventory/Nomination: Southwest Historic District." *Virginia Department of Historic Resources.* http://www.dhr.virginia.gov/registers/Cities/Roanoke/128–0049_Southwest_Historic_District_1985_Final_%20Nomination.pdf. Accessed 30 May 2014.

Field, John. 2003. *Social Capital.* Key Ideas. London and New York: Routledge.

Halpern, David. 2005. *Social Capital.* Cambridge, UK; Malden, MA: Polity.

Hurt Park Neighborhood Alliance. 2014. City of Roanoke, VA. http://www.roanokeva.gov/85256A8D0062AF37/CurrentBaseLink/N26F3LUY795RLAREN. Accessed 29 May 2014.

"Hurt Park/Mountain View/West End Neighborhood Plan." 2003. Neighborhood Plan. Vision 2001–2020. Roanoke, VA: City of Roanoke. http://www.roanokeva.gov/DocumentCenter/View/1238. Accessed 29 May 2014.

Kellogg Commission on the Future of State and Land-Grant Universities. 1999. *Returning to Our Roots: The Engaged Institution.* National Association of State Universities and Land-Grant Colleges, Office of Public Affairs, February 1999. http://www.aplu.org/library/returning-to-our-roots-the-engaged-institution/file. Accessed 15 May 2014.

5

IMPACTS OF PARTICIPATORY MURAL MAKING ON YOUTH EMPOWERMENT

Tiva Lasiter

Community-built art projects can empower young people by helping them gain social capital through acquiring new skills, receiving mentorship from community leaders, making connections with their peers through teamwork, and participating in peer leadership opportunities. Art can be a tool for empowerment, because through art making, people build connections, receive recognition, and foster their own creativity (Grams 2010). Community mural-making as a tool for youth development teaches young people to think outside of the box—outside of the norms of art to be made for an elite class of educated museum goers. Through participatory creative placemaking, students can develop the courage to try, the skill to execute, and the resources to accomplish something new. As a form of youth-led action research, art projects can be a powerful means to inform and catalyze community organizing and revitalization (London 2007).

This chapter presents a case study of a large-scale community mural created with eighty high school art students at Winters High School, located in the small rural town of Winters, California. As a community researcher, educator, and artist, I facilitated the project while also using qualitative research to explore the question, "How are individuals and communities affected by participating in public art making? Are they empowered? By what means?" The project was designed to incorporate opportunities for relationship building, mentorship, teamwork, leadership, and student ownership of ideas, concepts, design, and imagery. A community participation approach emphasized student involvement and leadership in a variety of capacities. The desired outcome of the mural was to create social change in the lives of the youth and other community members involved, while transforming a bare physical space into a beautiful gathering place.

Throughout this chapter, empowerment is defined as "the development of individual leadership skills and knowledge regarding the practice of leadership, and formal recognition by the community of their newly acquired skills (status) in the

FIGURE 5.1 Winters High School art building before transformation

Source: Tiva Lasiter

community" (Pigg 2002, 118). I will refer to youth development as "the process all young people undergo as they build the individual assets or competencies needed to participate in adolescence and adult life" (Listen 2000, 6).

Project Description

The aim of the Winters High School Mural Project was for it to be a student-driven, designed, and produced project. My role as a visiting artist and community development graduate student from the University of California at Davis was to lead and facilitate the creative process from design inception to mural completion. This project was made possible through a partnership with Winters Joint Unified School District, Winters High School art teacher Kate Humphrey, Winters High School art students, and myself. The mural project set out to meet and exceed the Visual and Performing Arts Content Standards for California Public Schools. These standards served as a guideline for designing and building the mural project curriculum, and many of the key learning areas from the mural project exemplify these standards at the "advanced" level for grades nine through twelve (O'Malley 2001).

Tools for student engagement and participation included design charrettes, story sharing, collaborative teamwork, leadership development opportunities, and decision-making processes. The students explored the history of mural making and sought inspiration from viewing current and past mural projects and public art. Through photography, drawings, and words, students had the opportunity to share their stories and ideas to create the themes of the mural. Students had a high level of involvement and, through team assignments, were held accountable for the project outcomes.

At the beginning of the project, each student took an assessment survey of their existing skills and the skills they wished to develop. Within the survey, they also were able to select their team preferences, opt to take leadership roles, or be involved in team training. In order to give everyone the greatest opportunity possible to both develop the skills they wanted to learn and be placed on a team they preferred, I coded the survey answers for what skills the students wanted to develop, cross-referenced the skill sets with the teams they selected as their top choices, and assigned students to teams accordingly. Everyone was expected to help paint the mural and also to participate in one of the following planning teams: project planning and logistics, site repair and assessment, design, design transfer, fundraising, or photography. Dividing students into different planning teams allowed the students to take on responsibility for a part of the project they selected.

Next, students submitted ideas about what most inspires them and then designed mural ideas on a template of the building. We had group discussions and design charrettes to determine themes and to develop a collective voice through imagery. We did activities as a whole class to choose what inspirations to move forward to the mural design team. The process of sharing ideas, visions, hopes, and dreams created a bond seldom incorporated in a high school curriculum. I met with each team to discuss the duties and timeline for that team, and to establish team captains. Each time I came to the school, I met with the teams and got them organized and prepared to conquer their assigned tasks.

The mural design team started working with the selected inspirations by brainstorming ideas in writing and through drawing. It was important for the design teams to think beyond their own needs and desires and try to design something that expressed the collective ideas and experiences of the community of youth. The students had close ties to their local environment, and they wanted a reflection of a sense of place, of Winters, California, to be incorporated in the mural. For the base of the design, students decided to re-create the mountain range they looked at every day—the set of hills that, to them, embodied Winters. Through a participatory design process, we were able to meld complex ideas and graphics into one design. After coming to a finalized design for the mural, all design team students worked collaboratively on the final drawn-to-scale design drawing and selected colors for the mural.

Meanwhile, the site repair team prepared the site wall. They filled cracks, primed and painted, and taped off the windows and detail areas. The fundraising team coordinated two fundraisers at local restaurants to gain funding for the mural. I worked with the design transfer team to grid the wall and transfer the design, section by section. After sorting and setting up materials and learning important safety

FIGURE 5.2 Design charrette

Source: Kate Humphrey

FIGURE 5.3 Site assessment and repair workday

Source: Kate Humphrey

FIGURE 5.4 Student-led painting workday

Source: Kate Humphrey

precautions, students were now ready to start painting. Students started by painting the mountain range, a large area at the bottom of the mural requiring many layers for the realistic effect they wanted.

For most of the painting days, I was able to be there for the entire day; but on the days that I was not available, the students took it upon themselves to take out all the materials and lead the mural painting process. Students were left in charge of certain areas of the mural, and they were instructed on the right colors to use in specific sections. Students then led their teams to paint the mural according to our plan, acting as peer trainers and leaders. It was quite remarkable how well the students did when I was not there, how they took responsibility for painting the mural and made sure to create with a thoughtful and careful process.

We held a commemoration event to honor the completion of the mural. This event was attended by a former Winters mayor, administrators and teachers at the school, students, parents, and the community of Winters. Finally, students took a post-project survey to share their experiences with me.

Contextualization within Current Literature

Research indicates that community art can be a powerful tool for youth engagement and that murals involving youth have the power to teach both skills and history (Conrad 1995). Elizabeth Garber's (2006) article "Why Teach Public Art? A High School Primer" shows that public art projects motivate students and engage them in meaningful learning experiences. Judy Baca (2009, 29) speaks of the power of murals in Los Angeles in her article *Public Memory*, stating, "Sites of public memory were created by hundreds of artists and thousands of community members and youth, and these sites creatively solved myriad problems in blighted neighborhoods."

Public works of art are a form of discourse, helping communities communicate and work toward empowerment and unity (Prigoff 2005; Buffington 2007). Public art has the ability to address key community concerns such as urban sprawl, lack of visual identity, crime, poverty, race relations, and the underestimation of the benefits of public art (Nikitin 2000). Successful creative placemaking crosses boundaries to act as a catalyst that can address social, cultural, and economic issues. It is an approach that invites artists and communities to work together as a cooperative team (Stephens 2006). Public art has a far-reaching ability to engage communities, even with very little funding (Berk 2001). As Judy Baca states in *Public Memory*,

> Growing directly out of the hopes, dreams, and desires of the surrounding population, community-driven public art gives a voice to those who inspire it and provides a breath to all those who pass it as it speaks from the streets.
>
> *(Baca 2009, 29)*

Case studies of community-driven art indicate that young people who are intimately involved in community mural projects experience great joy through the process, and more importantly, gain social capital and become empowered. Student empowerment is directly related to holding important roles in the project. When young people are involved in the decision-making and design processes, they gain skills, build relationships, and create meaningful places that can lead to community change in and of itself. Students are empowered through claiming and creating their own cultural space (Griswold 2007).

One case study, *The Diversity Mural Project: A Partnership between the University and the Community*, provided local teens with the opportunity to work in a diverse group to design and paint a mural that represented diversity (Chin-Newman, Min, and Fleming 2011). Research findings indicated that participants enjoyed meeting people different from themselves and the experience of working together as a team.

Another case study, Janelle Turk's (2012) *Collaboration, Inclusion, and Empowerment: A Life Skills Mural*, uses action research, phenomenological study, participant observation, and interviews to illustrate how youth are empowered through active responsibility for a collaborative community mural at their school. Turk's mural project was based on authentic instructional practices in that it engaged students in higher-level thinking, active inquiry, and real-life problem solving. In this study, student interactions took a completely different approach than what the researcher often saw in the regular classroom. As Turk states,

> When students play an active role in making important decisions, especially in an inclusive environment, they are given the chance to develop self-esteem, empathy, and dependability. These values foster social justice, rendering art education a very powerful part of the K-12 experience in American public education.
>
> *(Turk 2012, 53)*

The product of the artwork is a visual reflection of a collective identity and communal experience, so it needs to be reflective of professionalism and high standards (Rice 1999). It is important that the art created meets certain standards of artistic integrity, because it not only makes it a better learning experience, but the students also have more pride and sense of accomplishment when the finished piece is created with high aesthetic standards. Students need to be invested in the outcome of the mural. Support for this idea is illustrated in Elizabeth Garber's article "Why Teach Public Art? A High School Primer":

> Public art offers insights into many dimensions of art beyond the expression of self; the art becomes something larger than the individual and self-expression. Public art in high schools motivates students, engages them in meaningful learning experiences, gives students hand-on experiences, increases their self-esteem, and provides them with a sense of ownership of the created space.
>
> *(Garber 2006, 29)*

There is a great need for evaluation of community art (Craig 2002). There is little research based on firsthand feedback from participants; rather, most evaluation is done through participant observation and phenomenological study. With this need mind, one aim of my research is to provide evidence of youth empowerment through direct student feedback, solicited through surveys. I aim not only to repeat the success of similar projects but also to add a researched example that illustrates how students become empowered through participating in community-built art.

Research Methods

I used a case study methodology to evaluate the process and outcomes of this participatory community mural project at Winters High School. I used several tools to engage the students in the project so that they gained a variety of skills through participating in both project planning and painting the mural. Included in the case study method were group development, team building, participant observations, process tracking through journaling and project planning documents, photograph analysis, and evaluation of pre- and post-participation surveys taken by all willing participants (Clifford, French, and Valentine 2010; Creswell 2013).

The student participants were selected through the partnership fostered between Winters High School, art teacher Kate Humphrey, and myself. At the time, Kate was teaching six high school art classes, totaling 110 students. I wanted to involve as many students as possible, while still allowing for each student to be meaningfully engaged. Kate and I decided that I would work with the four two-dimensional design classes, which together consisted of 85 students.

All students present in class on the day of the project introduction (82 out of 85) took a project assessment survey, where they selected teams and roles for the project. I hand-coded the surveys and created a database in Microsoft Excel that enabled me to cross-reference students' desired skill building areas, their present strengths, and their top choices for teams. I placed students together who would offer a variety of skills to their teams, and each team was assigned a captain who would keep their team motivated.

Because there was a second project happening simultaneously, an altered book project that Kate was leading, we allowed students to choose not to participate if they did not want to. One or two students in each class did choose to opt out of most mural-related activities. The students who opted out of the mural process did not participate in planning teams or mural painting.

Seventy-nine of the 85 participants took a post-project survey, which was administered via an online survey host. The students all took the survey on school computers during the last day of school, just days after the mural was completed. Each student who was present in the class that day took the survey. We gave students the option to opt out of being surveyed, but no one opted out. Those who took the survey included the full range of students, from those who participated entirely, to those who participated somewhat, to the few students who opted out of most or all of the process. The large majority of students were engaged on planning teams and in painting, while a few students in every class did either planning or painting, but not both.

With the vast majority of participants taking the post-project survey, the percentages and comments are a good reflection of students' actual experiences. I analyzed and coded the student survey comments to see what was most often repeated, which comments were representative of popular opinion, and which were especially poignant. I selected student quotes and survey data points that represented the project with the most clarity to include in this chapter.

Throughout the project, I took notes that reflected upon the project, process, and research. At the end of each day spent at the mural site, I wrote participant observations and project reflections in my field journal. After the project was completed, I studied and analyzed all of my participant observation entries to see what patterns emerged. I created a list of key findings based on reading all student comments from the post-participation survey and analyzed the percentages of students engaged in the process. I combined these findings with my analysis of the project, participant observations, and analysis of project photographs taken by students. Once I had established that the large majority of students were empowered through participating on this project, I formulated the key factors that influenced the empowerment experienced by participants. I then coded my journal entries and participant observations into categories supporting my key findings.

Key Findings: Forms of Empowerment

The ways individuals and communities are affected by participating in public art making are multifaceted and complex. Students' responses to the mural experience indicate that there is positive personal development from participating in a collaborative mural project; in the post-project survey, 74 percent of students either agreed or strongly agreed that creating the mural was a "positive experience" for them. Student comments indicate that they felt involved in the decision-making process, and a significant majority was empowered through participation in the project.

Student empowerment came in many forms. The students' feedback indicates that skill development, confidence building, and leadership experience all empowered them. From an analysis of the survey, I classified the students' empowerment into the following seven key forms:

1   Building relationships through collaboration
2   Building self-esteem through accomplishment
3   Leadership opportunities
4   Building skills
5   Creation of a meaningful place
6   A sense of project ownership through decision making
7   High levels of responsibility and accountability

Next, these seven forms of empowerment are illustrated through student stories that emerged from participant observations, photo analysis, project analysis, and analysis of student feedback from surveys.

Forms of Youth Empowerment through Community-Built Art

1. Building Relationships through Collaboration

Through the Winters High School Mural Project, youth built relationships through collaboration, teamwork, mentorship, and community participation. In his article "Painting Material Culture: Community Art Research in Saginaw, Michigan," Michael Mosher says, "A community mural is democratic politics in the best sense of the word, a process of incorporation of many voices, addressing multiple agendas and needs so everyone benefits" (2012, 44). Youth were able to gain social capital though establishing peer relationships, taking part in leadership roles, and diplomatically making decisions through group discussion. Of the participating youth, 77 percent indicated that they enjoyed working with others on this project, while 74 percent agreed or strongly agreed they would like to work with others on a project in the future, and 56 percent agreed or strongly agreed they would be more likely to participate in a community project in the future.

One important empowering relationship is that of mentorship. Providing an example of excellent leadership offers model behavior for students to look up to. Many students asked me questions about being an artist and a college student. One female student confided in me and asked me for advice. She said she looked to me as a mentor. Of the students surveyed, 62 percent agreed or strongly agreed that they liked having a mural artist as a mentor.

Students indicated that they enjoyed the collaborative aspect of the mural making experience. The following is a selection of their survey quotes about what their favorite part of the mural making process was:

- "Painting and working together."
- "Coming up with the design and being able to incorprate [*sic*] everyones [*sic*] thoughts and ideas."
- "Seeing it come together!"

When asked what the most unique or special aspect of the mural making process was, students indicated the following:

- "Talking about ideas,"
- "Communicating with others,"
- "That we all did something,"
- "Collaborating ideas," and
- "Everybody had a part."

FIGURE 5.5 Students operating and working in the scissor lift

Source: Tiva Lasiter

Additional student comments about working together included the following:

- "It was great working with a small group on the last day, even though it was a challenge with the little time we had."
- "It was a great experience that I will remember doing in high school."
- "It was fun experience, and I had fun working together with my art class."

2. Building Self-Esteem through Accomplishment

One revelatory moment for me was shock followed by satisfaction when one student asked what the mural was going to be of and I replied that it was going to be a student-created design. The students were so happy that they would be entrusted with the responsibility of designing the mural. It appeared that students felt they could do something meaningful and important and emphasized that their opinions do matter.

The students demonstrated tremendous pride for their accomplishment of the completed mural, and from holding important roles in the process. High school students need to be nudged, because they grow when they are out of their comfort zone, and this project took them out of their normal routines.

3. Leadership Opportunities

Students were empowered through participating in leadership opportunities. Developing leadership among community members is crucial to community organizing and to passing on the legacy of engagement to youth (Bobo, Kendall, Max and Midwest Academy 2001). In the survey, 57 percent of students agreed or strongly agreed that they would be more likely to participate in a leadership role in the future after participating in the project. I saw many students develop leadership roles, hold each other accountable, and step up to make the project happen. A few students acted as set-up or clean-up crews, and some students would be my personal assistants, ready to take on various assignments such as washing brushes, setting up ladders, and setting up the paints for use that day.

One student took a role as a team leader and assistant. He took on extra responsibilities and treated it like a job. He had finished his book project and was able to receive extra credit for helping me. Another student took initiative to help plan and organize a pizza party fundraiser at a local restaurant. An additional leadership example is when one student asked her dad if we could use a mechanical lift. He let the students borrow and operate it. This was instrumental in the timely and successful completion of the mural. The student led the process of getting approvals and liability waivers, as well as making arrangements to have the machine delivered, picked up, and secured nightly.

4. Building Skills

In addition to leadership skills, students also gained a diversity of other skills. Students had many choices of how to participate in the mural making process,

FIGURE 5.6 Students consulting each other

Source: Tiva Lasiter

including mural design team, photo documentation, project planning, team leadership, fundraising, contributing themes and ideas, painting, drawing, and participating in evaluation. Students learned how to design a mural; how to paint on a large-scale, non-traditional surface; how to work in collaboration on a large-scale project; and basic point-and-shoot photography skills, including photo composition. Certain students relished in the responsibility of operating the mechanical lift. As one student said in the post-project survey, "i like driving the fork left [*sic*]."

5. Creation of a Meaningful Place

By creating a meaningful place through the expression of a shared identity and experience, students were able to create lifelong memories and leave a legacy of what was important to them. The youth were able to express what matters to them and let that become public knowledge. The youth's voices became publicized and were made vulnerable to being seen and heard. Young people are not accustomed to their opinions and stories being recognized and acknowledged, and this project attempted to validate those stories as important and worthy of being told through a mural.

Student survey quotes about the importance of sharing their ideas and creating place included the following:

- "This was a great project inspiring [*sic*]. Wish it could happen more around our community. Murals add a beautiful touch of art and life to blank canvases."
- "Great experience, definately [*sic*] something i will tell/show my kids."
- "I think the planning and designing was a special aspect because there were so many great ideas and desings [*sic*] we could have used."

When asked what was special or unique about the project, students said the following:

- "seeing our thoughts being included in the mural,"
- "being able to put personal material in the mural," and
- "aggreing [*sic*] on something that everybody will like."

Student surveys also indicated that 71 percent agreed or strongly agreed that they feel the mural has created a place in front of the art building. Sixty-eight percent of students agreed or strongly agreed that they think they will return to the mural in the future, while 72 percent agreed or strongly agreed that the mural leaves a legacy of their classes, and 67 percent agreed or strongly agreed that they would like to paint another mural in the future.

6. A Sense of Project Ownership through Decision Making

By participating in planning and decision making, students developed a sense of ownership of the project. One way we broke up the project was to have certain teams be in charge of specific areas of the mural, with each team captain responsible for encouraging and motivating his or her team, as well as acting as a peer trainer. Many students took ownership of certain areas of the mural or of certain aspects of planning. For example, one student took ownership of the fundraiser in planning the logistics. She acted as party hostess and spread the word about the fundraiser. Because the students felt the project was their own and the success of the project depended on them, they have a sense of ownership of the mural.

One part of the mural did not turn out as planned, but students took it upon themselves to change it, illustrating they felt ownership of the mural and had the skills and initiative to change it. The wind was not originally planned to have student names written in it, but it ended up with a lot of student signatures who were not intimately involved in the entire mural process—they were from another class and were just helping us on the last days of painting. This caused disapproval from a lot of the students who worked hard to perfect the mural and come up with a meaningful design. At the time of the mural completion, school was ending in just a couple of days; we had planned the commemoration event for the mural, and we didn't have the time or ability to change it. Many students were unhappy about the signatures in the wind on the mural. One student survey comment that exemplifies the student opinion about the wind was, "I do not like all the names written in the swirls. It takes away from the connection with the message the mural TRIED to give." Students were invested in the project and they took it upon themselves, with the assistance of their teacher, to paint over the wind and fix the areas that had large signatures on them. This action they took to change the mural themselves and make it how they wanted it shows that the students took pride in the mural, from the design to the execution, and when they weren't happy with the result, they had the leadership ability, the passion, and the skills to make change happen.

7. High Levels of Responsibility and Accountability

The students were empowered through having high levels of responsibility and expectation placed on them and for being accountable for the process and final product. When students have a high stake and high responsibility, they can build skills to become agents of change. Students' level of involvement in the project and their direct involvement with decision making were intrinsically connected to the level of empowerment obtained. Those students who opted out of the process or only took part in some of the painting were not as empowered by the project as the students were who were deeply engaged in the decision making and planning processes for the project.

Conclusion

Through this creative placemaking project, I teamed up with over eighty high school students to transform their school art building into a beautiful gathering place. Together, we created a mural that exceeds the California standards of excellence for visual art. Students were empowered and experienced an increase in community and school pride. They learned mural history and trends through a specially designed mural curriculum. They learned skills—from leadership to large-scale design and non-traditional painting.

This project was possible only through the cooperative collaboration of high school students, their art teacher, principal, and school board, and myself. This project fostered positive relationships between youth and adults and provided new social possibilities for students. The students who participated created lifelong memories and transformed a space by creating a mural that enhances the area and indicates "what happens here inside the art building." The mural created a place to be enjoyed by the entire school and all passersby for years to come.

The following student survey comments indicate deep satisfaction with the project:

- "everything went well, we had alot [sic] of fun making this hopefully next year we could do the whole building."
- "This was a really great project and i hope to do something similiar [sic] in the future."
- "Very fun expercance [sic] and id [sic] like to do it again."
- "i loved it."
- "i realy [sic] liked working on the mural."
- "I would love to make more murals."
- "Fun."
- "It was cool."
- "Awesomeness."
- "it was worth it."

Community participation and engagement in public art making transforms space, creates lasting memories, and changes lives. There is a special kind of joy experienced when working with a group of young people on a community mural. There is joy from working together and from leading youth to create something meaningful for themselves. The young people involved in this project transformed a bleak building at their school into a vibrant entryway that symbolizes the collective experience for students at Winters High. Students were empowered through building relationships and collaborating on teams together, gaining self-esteem through taking pride in their accomplishments, and learning leadership through peer training, team captain experiences, and taking initiative when planning the mural. Participants gained a plethora of skills that will be applicable in life situations.

Students felt a sense of ownership of the mural because it was a meaningful place to them. They had created an amazing place through working together that represented their own collective consciousness. Because students were involved in important decision-making processes, and were given high expectations and responsibilities, they became empowered to be able to make decisions for themselves and take action. They had obtained the agency needed to affect change. When students were unhappy with the final outcome of the mural, they banded together and took action to paint over the wind so that the mural was a closer reflection of their original intention. They also organized funding and volunteers to apply sealant on the mural after they changed it.

Participating in large-scale, community-built art gives youth participants the efficacy to make decisions, to voice their ideas and opinions, to take control of their situation and their environment, to act as a team, and to rally together to take initiative and take action to create change. Students involved in this project learned how to persevere and carry a project with multiple challenges through to completion. The many challenges were part of what made this project such an incredible learning experience for the youth involved, as they needed to learn to make adjustments and remain flexible. I set high expectations for students, and they were motivated to take on high levels of responsibility to meet the challenging needs of the project.

Creating places where members of the community can engage meaningfully with one another is a means in itself of creating viable communities. Through creative placemaking, community members engage in a shared experience and create a beautiful place together. Young people are highly capable and should be engaged in community planning and placemaking. The students involved in this project created a space for themselves to commune and enjoy, fostering positive interactions and relationships, and simultaneously created social change. Youth are empowered by participating in the creative process, and they desire to be recognized and appreciated. Adolescents are often excluded from the picture of community, and their inclusion is paramount to a positive future for all. Communities that include access and opportunities for youth provide for a positive community experience. Community developers and communities working on large-scale public art projects together need to keep tools for empowerment at the forefront of the process. Including young people in community-built public art projects, and encouraging collaborations between community members and artists, has the potential to revitalize communities and give a sense of place and meaning.

References

Baca, J. 2009. "Judy Baca: Public Memory." *Part of a Special Section: Here to Stay: Public Art and Sustainability*, 20(2): 28–9.

Berk, A. 2001. "Are People More Important than Art?" *Artweek*, 32(4): 15–16.

Bobo, K. A., J. Kendall, S. Max, and Midwest Academy. 2001. *Developing Leadership*. Organizing for Social Change: Midwest Academy Manual for Activists. Santa Ana, CA: Seven Locks Press.

Buffington, M. L. 2007. "Art to Bring About Change: The Work of Tyree Guyton." *Art Education*, 60(4): 25–32.

Chin-Newman, C., S. Min, and K. Fleming. 2011. "The Diversity Mural Project: A Partnership Between the University and the Community." *International Journal of the Arts in Society*, 5(6): 105–16.

Clifford, N., S. French, and Valentine, G. 2010. *Key Methods in Geography*. London: Sage Publications Ltd.

Conrad, D. R. 1995. "Community Murals as Democratic Art and Education." *Journal of Aesthetic Education*, 29: 98–102.

Craig, G. 1 January 2002. "Towards the Measurement of Empowerment: The Evaluation of Community development." *Journal of the Community Development Society*, 33(1): 124–46.

Creswell, J. W. 2013. *Qualitative Inquiry and Research Design: Choosing Among Five Approaches*. Los Angeles: Sage Publications.

Garber, E. 2006. "Why Teach Public Art?: A High School Primer." *Public Art Review*, 17(2): 28–9.

Grams, D. 2010. *Producing Local Color: Art Networks in Ethnic Chicago*. Chicago: University of Chicago Press.

Griswold, C. R. 2007. *Chicano San Diego: Cultural Space and the Struggle for Justice*. Tucson: University of Arizona Press. 165–9.

Listen, Inc. 2000. *An Emerging Model for Working with Youth: Community Organizing + Youth Development = Youth Organizing*. New York: Surdna Foundation.

London, J. 1 January 2007. "Power and Pitfalls of Youth Participation in Community-Based Action Research." *Children, Youth and Environments*, 17(2): 406–32.

Mosher, M. 2012. "Painting Material Culture: Community Art Research in Saginaw, Michigan." *Material Culture*, 44(2), 43–60.

Nikitin, C. A. 2000. "Making Public Art Work." *Sculpture*, 19(3): 44–9.

O'Malley, Ed, ed. 10 January 2001. "Content Standards Visual and Performing Arts." *California Deparment of Education*. California Department of Education. http://www.cde.ca.gov/be/st/ss/documents/vpastandards.pdf. Accessed 4 March 2013.

Pigg, K. E. 1 January 2002. "Three Faces of Empowerment: Expanding the Theory of Empowerment in Community Development." *Journal of the Community Development Society*, 33(1): 107–23.

Prigoff, J. 2005. "Museum of the Streets." *Public Art Review*, 17(1): 14–15.

Rice, R. 1999. "Art as Civic Biography: Philadelphia Murals Project." *New Art Examiner*, 26(7): 18–23.

Stephens, P. G. 2006. "A Real Community Bridge: Informing Community-Based Learning Through a Model of Participatory Public Art." *Art Education*, 59(2), 40–6.

Turk, J. 2012. "Collaboration, Inclusion, and Empowerment: A Life Skills Mural." *Art Education*, 65(6), 50–3.

PART II

Culture and Identity

6

COMMUNITY ERUVIN

Architecture for Semi-Public/Private Neighborhood Space

Barry L. Stiefel

The *eruv*—translated from Hebrew as "mixture"—refers to the joining of residents and domains within a limited area. *Eruvin* (plural) are physio-psychological enclosures used by halachic-observing[1] Jews, by making this space semi-private, to enable them to "carry" in the public domain on their Sabbath without violating their precept of prohibited Sabbath "work" from the Fourth Commandment. "Carrying" on the Sabbath includes the picking up of any material object—such as house keys, a book, or even a child—and transporting it across the threshold of the public-private domain boundary. If a family had a young child, a parent—most often the mother—had to remain home and could not attend synagogue services or other activities outside the house on the Sabbath.

Eruvin structures are documented in ancient Jewish texts, though contemporary practices have direct links to the nineteenth century when urbanization led to the proliferation of purpose-built eruvin. Contemporary eruvin often utilize utility poles and wires to create the enclosures. For the rest of society unconcerned with Jews carrying on the Sabbath, these poles and wires blend into the background of an electrified city street. My case study is Charleston, South Carolina, where there are three eruvin for a relatively small Jewish community. Each eruv encloses a different area where groups gather together for religious worship and fellowship on the Jewish Sabbath. How has this come to be for such a small community, especially one where halachic-observing Jews are relatively few in number? Eruvin make for an intriguing case study within the framework of community-built construction and architecture because their socioreligious importance is not the physical structure itself per se, but a symbolic representation of making public space semi-private for the purpose of enabling greater community cohesiveness through the activities that take place within them.

Eruvin are documented in the Talmud, which dates from the early centuries of the Common Era, where they are attributed to King Solomon (Eruvin 21b).[2]

FIGURE 6.1 A postcard depicting a Jewish family walking and carrying things with them to synagogue, early twentieth century, North America

Source: William A. Rosenthall Judaica Collection, Special Collections, College of Charleston Library

Historically, city walls often served as boundaries for eruvin. For instance Charleston, South Carolina's eighteenth century colonial city wall hypothetically could have served as an eruv for the small number of Jews who lived there.[3] Jews have been welcomed and lived in South Carolina since the late seventeenth century, where a Lockean-style freedom of conscience began as part of the English colony's social contract in order to encourage commerce. During the nineteenth century, when advances in military technologies had rendered walls obsolete, the city wall was removed (Marcuse 1997). Napoleon demonstrated this in his conquest of Europe, where he also physically tore down the walls to cities and Jewish ghettos. While the formal end of the ghetto was both literally and physically liberating for Jews, and the removal of city walls enabled greater urban expansion in the age of industrialization, these combined factors created a hardship for halachic-observing Jews to carry things on the Sabbath, since walls also commonly served as eruvin.

Ironically, nineteenth century Protestant missionaries took an interest in eruvin. Some believed that if they could better understand Jewish religious practices, they would be better able to convert them to Christianity. Their accounts from Ottoman Jerusalem on eruvin are informative:

> In conversation with ourselves the Jews attached great importance to the observance of this custom. Some of them termed it "hiring the city," and said that it was done in connection with the laws of Eruv, for Sabbath observances; for that when the city is thus hired as a whole—all within its walls is considered by their law to have become as one house—within which they are then free to pass on the Sabbath from dwelling to dwelling, even though bearing slight burdens, without infringing any of the laws for keeping the holy Sabbath-day. It must be remembered that in Jerusalem the term house does not mean, as with us, a number of rooms all covered by one roof. Every house there is a cluster of rooms, each having its own roof, but all enclosed within a common wall or court; and that in passing from one to the other, it is necessary to go into the open air. Thus, by legal definition of Eruv, Jerusalem, being surrounded by a wall, is regarded as one habitation or house.
>
> *(Schwartz 1868, 47)*

Under Jewish law, eruvin do not necessarily need to be made of solid masonry. According to the rabbis, a "wall can be a wall even if it has many doorways creating large open spaces" (Rozovsky 2014). The key element is the architectural design of the structure. Thus, "the eruv enclosure may be created by telephone poles, for example, which act as the vertical part of a doorpost in a wall, with the existing cables strung between the poles acting as the lintel of the doorframe. As such, the entire 'wall' is actually a series of 'doorways'" (Rozovsky 2014). Other structures, such as fences, will also suffice. When not a solid wall, an enclosing colonnade using the post-and-lintel construction type is paramount because of the doorway interpretation. Within eruv terminology, the "doorpost" is called a *lechi*, regardless of whether it is load-bearing. Furthermore, the lintel—called a *koreh elyon*—must run unobstructed from one lechi pole post to the next and without it being deflected by an intrusive object, such as a tree branch. The koreh elyon also may not sag or sway significantly in the wind. The height of a lechi must not vary much from the top of one pole to the next, with the exception if the eruv terrain travels up or down a hill slope. All *lechai'in* (plural) must stand vertically upright. Lechai'in are usually driven directly into the ground but may be secured or propped up by other objects as long as all of the previous requirements are met. Furthermore, the koreh elyon must rest directly over the pole. It may not be tied around the pole or affixed to the side. Natural topography, such as a deep body of water or cliff, may also form an eruv boundary (Eider 1973; Bechhofer 1998; Mintz 2011).

However, there is an additional caveat regarding the doorway design concept. While the koreh elyon must rest directly over the top of the pole, it does not necessarily have to be attached to the lechi. Thus in Charleston, as well as in many other places, eruvin are sometimes built with already extant utility poles. Where the koreh elyon wire is affixed to the side of a utility pole, a vertical lechi extension is added in order to fulfill the requirement of being underneath. These lechai'in are nailed or tied to the utility post and are about four feet in height in Charleston. The practice of using existing utility poles requires majority consensus, however, since some halachic-observing Jews believe that it is an inappropriate way to construct eruvin. More stringent Jews require the lechi and koreh elyon structure to be constructed or bound together in their entirety. Since Judaism is a religion without a centralized authority, in contrast to the papacy in Catholicism, differences in opinion can coexist. Eruvin in North America, where the entire structure is built completely, average about $40,000—a prohibitive amount for many smaller Jewish communities. These expenditures do not include the annual cost for inspection and maintenance. Startup expenses include the lechi and koreh elyon hardware, permits and safety inspections from the local government, and legal fees (Watkins 2008–13). Using existing utility poles can reduce costs considerably, though the Jewish community is then dependent on where utilities companies have installed their infrastructure.

Occasionally, as in Charleston, South Carolina, eruvin combine topographic/ geographic features with purposely built poles and wires. The various features must be connected together. How this is accomplished is on a case-by-case basis, depending upon the circumstances. For instance, at Charleston's South Windermere eruv, the lechi-koreh elyon system was connected to the natural boundary of Wappoo Creek by building the structure out into the water (circa 1994). Members of the community physically drove lechi poles into the muck of the sloping riverbank by hand with a sledgehammer, a very challenging task where the water was sometimes too deep to stand in. Efforts were further compound by local sport fishermen who mistook the lechi poles for structures to moor their boats. The lechai'in often could not handle the weight of the boats in the current, causing them to become dislodged—temporarily invalidating the eruv until the lechi poles were reinstalled. Signs also had to be made and erected to inform fishermen not to use the poles to moor their boats (Ellison 2014; Rephan 2014).

FIGURE 6.2 A lechi attached to a utility pole at one of the eruvin in Charleston, South
Carolina

Source: Barry L. Stiefel

It may seem odd that the rabbis established regulations requiring that permission
for constructing an eruv be obtained from governmental authorities, even when
officials are not Jewish. The formal granting of permission is often conducted by
contract, usually a lease for some aspect of public property (i.e. utility pole) for

FIGURE 6.3 An example of an attached lechi to a utility pole, where the lechi is aligned underneath the utility wire, which is serving as a koreh elyon

Source: Barry L. Stiefel

a specified period of time with a nominal payment, such as a dollar. Thus non-Jews also play an important part in the aspect of community building with eruvin. In other words, an enclosing structure built clandestinely—either physically or symbolically—is not considered a valid eruv (Lees 2007).

An additional requirement to the establishment of an eruv is that there must be communal food set aside. The food is an additional, shared part of the material culture of the eruv and, according to the rabbis, is necessary for establishing joint semi-private ownership of outdoor space that was once entirely public. Traditionally, all those who were participating adherents to the eruv contributed to the communally set aside food, though there is also a practice of collectively shared financial support for communal food (Bechhofer 1998; Fonrobert 2005). The food is often stored in a communal building, such as a synagogue. In many instances, the food consists of matzo, the traditional unleavened bread eaten during the Passover festival due to its long shelf life. Regular bread as well as other foods could be used, but can spoil, thus becoming unusable for the eruv. Commercially made matzo, such as Manischewitz brand, can last for more than two years if stored properly, though the rabbis have prescribed that the food set aside for an eruv be refreshed at least on an annual basis (The Manischewitz Company 2013).[4]

The construction type described previously is known to have existed in the nineteenth century and earlier. Outsiders to Judaism have commented that these structures are peculiar, as well as the whole paradigm of Sabbath carrying within an

FIGURE 6.4 The designated box of matzo for completing one of the Charleston eruvin, as required by one of the Talmudic regulations

Source: Barry L. Stiefel

eruv, as accounts from more than one and a half centuries ago by Protestant missionaries testify:

> It was here [Safed, Ottoman Palestine] that we first observed the "Eruv" . . .
> a string attached from house to house across a street, or fastened upon tall
> poles. The *string* is intended to *represent a wall* [source's emphasis], and thus by
> a ridiculous fiction the Jews are enabled to fulfill the precept of the Talmud,
> that no one shall carry a burden on the Sabbath-day, not even a prayer-book
> or a handkerchief, or a piece of money, except it be within a walled place.
>
> *(Bonar and M'Cheyne 1843, 57)*

Other early examples include New York's Lower East Side eruv, established in 1905, which was enclosed by an elevated train and the Hudson River. Jewish legal debates regarding its permissibility ensued in response to the creation of this eruv, especially its use of the elevated railroad tracks. Rabbi Joshua Segal published arguments in support of the use of modern urban infrastructure components in *Eruv ve'Hotzaah*, a work that is still frequently consulted. A second eruv on Manhattan was also established in 1949 (Bechhofer 1998; Gurock 2009; Mintz 2011). In The Hague, Jews "constructed" their eruv with the surrounding dikes and the adjacent river, since these natural boundaries met the Jewish legal criteria. The Jews of Venice did similarly, since the city was enclosed by a canal system and lagoon. Most nineteenth and early twentieth century Jewish urbanites were not as fortunate as those living in the Lower East Side, The Hague, or Venice, since they lacked structural or natural features available to serve as their eruvin. Others, such as those living in Amsterdam in 1866; St. Louis, Missouri, in 1894; and Toronto, Ontario, in 1921, had to purposely build structural eruvin, these being the first deliberately built eruvin constructed within these countries (Mintz 2011; Snyder 2013).

Eruvin also require that fewer than 600,000 people, non-Jews included, reside within the enclosure.[5] This number is the threshold for what constitutes semi-private versus public space within Jewish culture, and it is significant when we consider modern urbanization. For instance, during the 1850s, New York's population exceeded 600,000. Thus, the waterways surrounding Manhattan Island could not function as a natural eruv for Jewish residents (Grinstein 1945).[6]

Eruvin can come in all sizes. In 2005, while residing in New Orleans, the author witnessed two Jewish neighbors in the Uptown neighborhood create a small eruv that only enclosed their residential properties. Jewish Boy Scouts also sometimes build temporary eruvin around their campsites so that they may carry things between their tents on the Sabbath ("So That's What an Eruv is" 1992).[7] On the other hand, the Los Angeles Community Eruv has a perimeter length of approximately forty miles and encloses nearly twenty square miles.[8]

Eruvin are visually inspected before every Jewish Sabbath to ensure that they are intact and functional. Usually, an inspection entails those familiar with eruv architecture making a circuit around the eruv boundaries by foot or automobile. Due to its size, the Los Angeles Community Eruv has been inspected by helicopter since its founding in 2002 ("Rabbis in the Sky—Checking the Eruv" 2014). If a break is found in the eruv, usually due to construction or severe weather, every effort is made to repair it before the onset of the Sabbath. If the repair is not made, the eruv is decreed "down" and not functional. Word is spread through local synagogues so that halachic-observing Jews do not unknowingly carry and violate the Sabbath.

Contemporary American eruvin are not without controversy, including conflicts within local Jewish communities as well as between Jewish and non-Jewish groups. In 1999, certain residents in Palo Alto, California, were upset by the proposed eruv desired by Emek Beracha congregation. Residents opposing the eruv's construction, including non-Jews, non-halachic observing Jews, American Atheists, Inc., and others, threatened to sue the municipality for infringement of their California Constitutional rights. These rights protect "free exercise and enjoyment of religion without discrimination or preference are guaranteed" (*Constitution of California*, Article 1, Section 4). The legal question was whether an eruv showed "preference" to a religious group, even if no public money was being spent. If so, was an eruv any more or less symbolic than a public Christmas tree or some other structure or object of similar religio-cultural origin? Christmas trees are frequent community-built projects, so why not an eruv? The city manager and council dropped the matter from the city's agenda in 2000 due to the disturbances the controversy caused and to avoid threatened litigation. Congregation Emek Beracha was thus unable to obtain the necessary permission from the local government to construct the eruv. However, the eruv was re-proposed seven years later and successfully approved with little incident the second time ("The Eruv Question: An Unorthodox Debate" 2006).

Other Jewish communities, such as in Berkeley, California, learned from Palo Alto's experience in wanting to avoid destructive local politics. When they went about creating their eruv in 2005, Berkeley Jews designed the eruv to extend slightly into the adjacent municipality of Albany. Permission to create the eruv thus had to be obtained at the county level, not city. The eruv sailed through the approval process with the Alameda County Board of Supervisors. Local church-state activists and the media did not become aware of the eruv until it was a fait accompli in 2006 (Eskenazi 2006).

Eruvin have been the subject of litigation, most notably in *Tenafly Eruv Association v. The Borough of Tenafly*, which wound its way through the courts between 2000 and 2003. Like in Palo Alto, non-Jews and non-halachic-observing Jews opposed a proposed eruv in Tenafly, New Jersey. However, there was already precedent by the town government allowing other groups to use utility poles and other public structures for private uses. When the town government denied their application, the Tenafly Eruv Association brought a lawsuit, alleging discrimination. Why should others be able to use public utility poles freely and not the Eruv Association? The Third Circuit Court of Appeals ruled in the Tenafly Eruv Associations' favor. The Borough of Tenafly appealed to the U.S. Supreme Court, but its petition was denied. Thus, in a very unusual way, a federal court ordered the local government to permit the eruv construction (Schlaff 2003; Lees 2007).

The Eruvin of Charleston, South Carolina

As previously mentioned, it is unknown if the small number of Jews residing in eighteenth century Charleston, who formed congregation Beth Elohim in 1749, regarded the wall that enclosed their city until the 1780s as an eruv. Indeed, North American Jews as a whole did not concern themselves with eruvin until the late nineteenth and early twentieth centuries. Even then, eruvin could only be found in St. Louis, New York, and Toronto prior to 1970. By and large, North American Jews either did not concern themselves with the biblical precepts of carrying and work or did the best they could with what they had. Consequently, only adult men and older children in halachically observant communities could attend synagogue services on the Sabbath, while mothers generally remained home to tend to young children. Mothers with young children were only able to attend if a babysitter could be found to take their place, since pushing a stroller or baby carriage is also considered a form of carrying.

Prayer books, prayer shawls (*tallisim*, pl.), and other objects for use at synagogue were transported to and from the synagogue before and after the Sabbath. Combination number key boxes and creative means of turning house keys into "garments" (since "wearing" of clothes and some jewelry is not considered carrying) were often used when there was no one staying home with young children. Not until the 1970s did eruvin proliferate across the Jewish communities of North America. Over two hundred eruvin currently exist in North America. The spread of eruvin has been attributed to the effects of the second-wave feminist movement (1960–1980s) on Orthodox Judaism, which took an interest in family issues and the inclusiveness of women in religious ritual that meshed with halacha, causing greater sensitivity to synagogue attendance (Lipstadt 1996; Lees 2007).

As eruvin arose in various North American Jewish communities, interest in constructing an eruv began in Charleston during the 1970s. However, little action beyond conversation happened for a considerable period of time (Radinsky 2014). Talk evolved into action during the early 1990s. A small group of young halachic-observing families began investigating the logistical issues—physical, political, financial, and so on—of what was needed to build an eruv in Charleston. Early key players included Morris Ellison, Nathan Rephan, and Hershel Sarasohn; Rabbi David J. Radinsky; and Rabbi Joel Landau (Radinsky 2014). However, the proposed eruv location was not in the downtown area where Charleston's only orthodox synagogue Brith Sholom Beth Israel (BSBI) is found, but in the suburban neighborhood of South Windermere, west of the Ashley River (Gurock 2004).

During the 1960s, Jewish families began moving to South Windermere, a neighborhood built by Jewish developer William Ackerman outside of downtown (Rosengarten and Rosengarten 2002). These families began a satellite prayer group, called a *minyan*, of BSBI synagogue in the neighborhood circa 1969, which they affectionately called the "Minyan House." Although the participants have changed, these Sabbath and holiday services continue to the present. Many of those attending the Minyan House were, and continue to be, teachers. For instance, Evelyn Sarasohn,

Hershel's wife, worked at Addlestone Hebrew Academy, eventually becoming principal of the school (Minis 1996). BSBI's members residing downtown at the time tended to be older and their children largely grown; they were generally less interested in the technicalities of Jewish ritual observance in contrast to those who settled in the South Windermere neighborhood (Ellison 2014).

In 1991, Morris Ellison and his family relocated from downtown Charleston to South Windermere, where they lived near Rabbi Landau, BSBI's assistant rabbi since 1988. There, the Ellisons and Landaus began to introduce "Shabbat Hospitality," where guests experience a relaxing Saturday afternoon and meal with the company of friends and neighbors. The conversation topic of eruv began to become more frequent and serious because they wanted to make it easier for families with young children to participate in these Sabbath gatherings. As a native Charlestonian who had spent a great deal of time on the local rivers in his youth, Ellison knew the area's topographic features, such as Wappoo Creek and the utility poles and lines along the railroad line and US-17 Savannah Highway, which could be used to establish the structure (Ellison 2014; Rabbinical Council of America 2014). They got together with Rabbi Radinsky and Nathan Rephan to scout out a possible path of eruv delineation.

Following the identification of a potential eruv boundary, Rabbi Hershel Schachter of Yeshiva University in New York, an expert, was consulted on the matter. Permissions were obtained from South Carolina Electric and Gas Company (SCE&G) to use the utility poles. A ninety-nine-year lease was also signed with the City of Charleston for use of the public space within the proposed eruv, for which BSBI was charged one dollar.[9] The agreement, which congregant Charles Karesh helped broker, also fulfilled the requirement of "hiring the city." The major difficulty was explaining to the non-Jewish authorities at the city and SCE&G what an eruv was and why it was important, since many non-Jews had never heard of it. Nathan Rephan and Hershel Sarasohn purchased lumber from Buck Lumber & Building Supply, Inc., and cut the wood to size. Many other volunteers also participated in building the eruv and its subsequent weekly examinations and maintenance. The inspection was done by driving around the eruv's periphery and making repairs as needed, such as along Savannah Highway (Sarasohn 2014). The completion of the South Windermere eruv was first announced in the November–December 1994 edition of the BSBI *Messenger*, the congregation's newsletter. A hotline was established for people to call where they could hear a weekly message regarding the status of the eruv.[10] Hershel Sarasohn often made the recording following his inspection. The local phone company, Bell South, provided the complimentary hotline to BSBI ("Eruv" 1994; Sarasohn 2014). The hotline has since been replaced by e-mail and Internet communication. The South Windermere eruv was a big accomplishment for such a small Jewish community in 1994.

The building of the South Windermere eruv is largely a story about halachic-observing husbands and fathers enhancing the Sabbath experience for their wives and children, as well as themselves, while keeping within their religious precepts. In contrast, Charleston's downtown eruv, which lies east of the Ashley River and surrounds BSBI, was largely the result of a lone and very determined woman. The story of the downtown eruv begins when Jill HaLevi settled in Charleston in the 1990s with her husband, Andrew, in order to begin her legal career and practice. She had completed her J.D. from the University of Michigan and passed the South Carolina Bar exam in 1995. Approximately two years later, Jill was pregnant with her first child and did not want to be confined to the house after her daughter's birth, desiring instead to attend synagogue on the Sabbath as she always had. She both enjoyed attending services as well as the *kiddush* afterwards, a light meal where congregants socialize. Jill and her husband also wanted to remain in their downtown home and not relocate to South Windermere. Jill had resided in Chicago earlier in life, where there was an eruv, though she had not lived within its boundaries. At that time, it was not as much of an issue since she was without children (HaLevi 2014).

Jill contacted Rabbi Radinsky about what could be done to build an eruv downtown. At first, Radinsky did not take her petition very seriously. After all, he and his wife had had seven children and had lived in downtown Charleston for two decades without an eruv, but Jill was persistent. The HaLevis were not only interested in having an eruv, but offered to assist in its development and continued maintenance. Another authority on eruvin, Rabbi Bernard "Barry" Freundel from Washington, DC, was consulted and brought to Charleston to delineate a potential eruv route. Since Jill was an attorney, she petitioned Charleston's municipal government for consent to erect the eruv on the behalf of BSBI. Permission was granted in 1998 when city council passed a resolution, signed by the mayor, Joseph P. Riley, allowing BSBI to

> rent according to Jewish Laws, to Ms. Jill E. M. HaLevi, member of Brith Sholom Beth Israel Congregation . . . [the area] bounded by the Ashley and Cooper Rivers, Charleston Harbour and Mt. Pleasant Street . . . for a period of 99 years at a rental of One United States Dollar . . . for the purpose of carrying on the Sabbath and Jewish holidays.
>
> *(City of Charleston 1998)*

With legal approval obtained, Jill dispatched Andrew and Rabbi Radinsky to build the downtown eruv with supplies purchased at Lowe's home improvement store and primarily using the method of lechi extensions attached to utility poles. The project took several months to complete, due to the complexity of logistics and time constraints from busy life schedules, but not long after baby Noa was born, the downtown eruv was completed.

The area that actually became enclosed was significantly smaller than the dimensions described in the city council's resolution. Originally, the lease with the city included the entire historic core of Charleston, which is a peninsula surrounded by the Ashley and Cooper Rivers. However, when actually built, the downtown eruv was gerrymandered to include only the synagogue and houses of the HaLevis and Radinskys, since most of Charleston's Jews who believed eruvin to be important were living within the South Windermere neighborhood. Small additions were made to the downtown eruv, with the help of Hershel Sarasohn, to include a hotel and a kosher bed-and-breakfast, called the Broad Street Guest House, in order to extend the eruv service for out-of-town guests and tourists. Andrew HaLevi, Amos Lawrence, and Rabbi Radinsky were also responsible for the eruv's weekly inspection and maintenance (HaLevi 2014).

During the early 2000s, another orthodox minyan emerged in the West Ashley area of Charleston, several miles north from South Windermere. This third group met at Charleston's Jewish Community Center (JCC), located on Raoul Wallenberg Boulevard, and they started to come together because some living in that area wanted to encourage observant community members to relocate near the JCC in order to also bolster this institution. Rabbi Radinsky of BSBI had retired in 2004 and had been replaced by Rabbi Ari Sytner (who also left for another position in 2012). In 2005, this group called itself the West Ashley Minyan, or WAM (Gurock 2004; Ellison 2014).

While WAM was unable to persuade BSBI's members to relocate BSBI from its downtown location, some orthodox Jews living near the JCC decided to construct a separate eruv around the JCC neighborhood. A conversation occurred between Randy Cohen, who attended WAM, and South Windermere's Morris Ellison regarding expanding the South Windermere eruv to include the JCC area. Another discussion also took place between Cohen and Synagogue Emanu-El, Charleston's only conservative congregation, to have an eruv enclose these two Jewish institutions so that WAM members could more easily attend life cycle events of close friends and family. However, in the end, logistical issues became too difficult and WAM's eruv came to encircle only the JCC neighborhood. Rabbi Freundel was invited to visit Charleston and consult on the boundaries for WAM's eruv. Eli Hyman provided the use of his boat for inspecting the waterways (Freundel 2014). Permissions from Charleston's city government and SCE&G to use the utility poles were soon obtained (City of Charleston 2012). Randy Cohen, along with B. J. Novit, Jason Berendt, and Travis Gaines went about installing the lechai'in (Cohen 2014). WAM's eruv boundaries include the Ashley River on the north, I-526 on the west, and Ashley River Road and Sam Rittenberg Boulevard on the south and east. In 2012, WAM formally declared itself a new congregation, now called Dor Tikvah, and hired its first rabbi the following year, Michael Davies. William Scheer has also been involved with the weekly inspection and maintenance of Dor Tikvah's eruv since early 2013, when Cohen and his family relocated to Chicago. Dor Tikvah's eruv maintenance falls under the management of the Building and Grounds Subcommittee, which Scheer chairs. On the eve of the 2013 High Holidays, Scheer, Rabbi Davies, and Jonathan Zucker conducted extensive repairs to the eruv (Congregation Dor Tikvah 2014; Scheer 2014).

Rabbi Moshe Davis currently serves as BSBI's rabbi. He has obtained permission from the city for expanding the downtown eruv. Davis believes eruvin are an important accommodation for young families and tourists and their Sabbath mobility, and would like to expand them as much as possible (Davis 2014). The downtown eruv enlargement was highlighted in Charleston's daily newspaper,

Post and Courier, on November 30, 2012, the first time any local media coverage mentioned an eruv in Charleston since it was first established nearly twenty years earlier (Parker 2012). Reporting on the eruv was done in a positive light, in contrast to some contentious instances in California and New Jersey. The eruv in South Windermere was also partially reconstructed by the community in 2015 due to public utility and road construction improvements that took place in 2014, and it was rebuilt smaller in order to ease the task of weekly inspection and maintenance.

Conclusion

Charleston's eruvin have brought people together in very special ways. First, in South Windermere, the residents empowered themselves and approached their rabbi—as well as recruited the advice of outside experts—to both tangibly and metaphysically build a structure that could hold their community, enabling them to have more meaningful relationships on their Sabbath day of rest. Indeed, during the summer of 2011, the author recalls the sense of urgency after an inspection by Rabbi Freundel from Washington, DC, declaring the eruv "down," which lasted for two consecutive weeks. SCE&G had conducted maintenance work of their own on the utility poles along Savannah Highway, which required the eruv to be partially rebuilt. After the second Sabbath had passed sitting at home with our eighteen-month old son, the author's wife made it very clear that something had to be done to ensure that the eruv would be up before the next Sabbath. With this compulsion, Michael Friedman—a sometimes Charleston resident and college student at New York's Yeshiva University—and the author hit the pavement to repair the eruv. With his more intimate knowledge of eruv architecture and my experience with carpentry, we replaced and repaired the needed lechai'in, hiking miles in the hot July sun of Charleston. We carried precut lumber on our shoulders, stuffed our pockets with nails, and strapped hammers to our belts. We saw the remnants of our predecessors who had first built the eruv nearly twenty years earlier and felt a sense of camaraderie with those from the past. The assistant rabbi at the time, Elisar Admon, came by and inspected our work, making a few tweaks with Michael. The following Shabbat the eruv was up, the community was happy, and my wife grateful. Due to the small number of Charleston's halachic-observing Jews, an "all hands on deck" approach to the eruvin is essential. Thus, by building and continually maintaining the eruv together as a community-built structural work, social community building and a sense of togetherness is also regularly strengthened.

Although not having as many halachic-observing families, the downtown eruv with BSBI synagogue at its center has become a symbol of Jewish-style southern hospitality. Tourism is a significant part of Charleston's economy. The kosher bed-and-breakfast has unfortunately gone out of business, but the downtown eruv and a hotel within it enables halachic-observing Jewish tourists to experience an enjoyable Shabbat downtown. Furthermore, the downtown eruv embodies a feminist approach to Orthodox Judaism, embodying the spirit of the quote coined by Laurel T. Ulrich: "well-behaved women seldom make history" (Ulrich 2007). If Jill HaLevi had acted like so many other prior Jewish mothers, resigned to staying at home with young children instead of attending synagogue with family in tow, the downtown eruv would have not been built.

In contrast, WAM/Dor Tikvah and its eruv grew out of community contention and conflict. While fracturing can be divisive, there is hope (the Hebrew translation of *tikvah*). Currently, relations between many members of BSBI and Dor Tikvah are gradually improving. The rabbis Davis (BSBI) and Davies (Dor Tikvah) both came to Charleston after these events occurred, and without a chip on their shoulders, they were able to explore some cooperation between the congregations. Perhaps from an emotional perspective, if not actually physical, an "eruv" to bring together all Jews in Charleston regardless of the number of minyans or congregations will come about. Notwithstanding, what can be seen through the physio-psychological concepts of eruv design is that there is symbolism between material culture and the meaning of community-built work.

Acknowledgments

I am indebted to Rabbi Adam Mintz and Rabbi Moshe Davis for their reviews of earlier drafts of this manuscript, especially pertaining to the halachic issues of eruvin.

Notes

1 *Halacha* is the Hebrew term for Jewish law.
2 The plural form, *eruvin*, is Aramaic, not Hebrew. This is the contemporary usage of eruv lexicon.
3 This is based on contemporary studies of Charleston's urban form and topography. Documentation as to whether or not eighteenth century Jews in Charleston recognized this as an eruv is lacking.
4 Matzo is made of flour and water, similar to hardtack—the infamous bread served on transoceanic voyages of discovery prior to the invention of refrigeration—though the process for making it is somewhat different.
5 The number 600,000 is significant in Judaism because it correlates to the approximate number of Israelite men counted in the census that left Egypt in the Biblical Exodus.
6 According to the U.S. Census, Manhattan's population was 515,547 in 1850 and rose to 813,669 in 1860. Again, this is based on contemporary studies of Manhattan's urban form and topography. Documentation as to whether or not New York Jews recognized this as an eruv prior to 1850 is lacking.
7 The author also witnessed an eruv around a Jewish Boy Scout troop campsite at the 1997 National Jamboree in Fort A. P. Hill, Virginia.
8 The size of the Los Angeles Community Eruv was calculated using Google Maps (https://maps.google.com/). The boundaries roughly correspond to Western Avenue on the east, US-101 on the north, I-405 along the west, and the I-10 at the south.
9 This lease was supplanted by City of Charleston, *Resolution No. 2006–38*, signed September 14, 2006, by Joseph P. Riley, mayor.
10 The telephone number for the South Windermere eruv hotline was 843-723-7038.

References

Bechhofer, Yosef Gavriel. 1998. *The Contemporary Eruv: Eruvin in Modern Metropolitan Areas.* Jerusalem: Feldheim.

Bonar, Andrew A., and Robert M. M'Cheyne. 1843. *Narrative of a Mission of Inquiry to the Jews from the Church of Scotland in 1839.* Philadelphia: Presbyterian Board of Publications.

City of Charleston. *Resolution No. 1998–47*, signed 10 November 1998 by Joseph P. Riley, mayor.

———. *Amended Resolution No. 2006–38*, signed 25 September 2012 by Joseph P. Riley, mayor.

Cohen, Randy. 12 March 2014. Phone interview.

Congregation Dor Tikvah. 2014. *Eruv—Congregation Dor Tikvah.* http://www.dortikvah.org/eruv.html. Accessed 5 March 2014.

Constitution of California. Article 1, Section 4.

Davis, Rabbi Moshe. 18 March 2014. Personal interview.

Eider, Shimon D. 1973. *A Summary of the Halachos of the Eruv.* Lakewood, NJ: Feldheim Publishers.

Ellison, Morris. 16 February 2014. Personal interview.

"Eruv", November-December 1994 / Kislev 5755. *Brith Sholom Beth Israel Messenger,* 48(2): 4. BSBI Collection, Box 22, Folder 13, Special Collections, College of Charleston, Charleston, S.C. Eruvin 21b.

"The Eruv Question: An Unorthodox Debate." 2006. *Palo Alto History.com.* http://www.paloaltohistory.com/the-eruv-debate.php. Accessed 1 February 2014.

Eskenazi, Joe. 17 February 2006. "Wire to Wire: Religious Boundaries Ease Shabbat Restrictions in Berkeley area." *J Weekly.com.* http://www.jweekly.com/article/full/28452/wire-to-wire/. Accessed 1 February 2014.

Fonrobert, Charlotte E. 2005 "The Political Symbolism of the Eruv." *Jewish Social Studies,* 11(3): 9–35.

Freundel, Rabbi Bernard "Barry". 14 March 2014. Phone interview.

Grinstein, Hyman B. 1945. *The Rise of the Jewish community of New York, 1654–1860.* Philadelphia: Jewish Publication Society of America.

Gurock, Jeffrey S. 2004. *Orthodoxy in Charleston: Brith Sholom Beth Israel and American Jewish History.* Charleston, SC: College of Charleston Library in Association with Brith Sholom Beth Israel.

———. 2009. *Orthodox Jews in America.* Bloomington: Indiana University Press.

HaLevi, Jill. 14 February 2014. Personal interview.

Lees, Susan H. 2007. "Jewish Space in Suburbia: Interpreting the Eruv controversy in Tenafly, New Jersey." *Contemporary Jewry,* 27: 42–79.

Lipstadt, Deborah E. 1996. "The Impact of the Women's Movement on American Jewish Life: An Overview After Twenty Years." In *Studies in Contemporary Jewry: Values, Interests, and Identity: Jews and Politics in a Changing World,* Peter Y. Medding, ed. New York: Oxford University Press, 86–100.

The Manischewitz Company. 2013. "FAQs." *Manischewitz.* http://www.manischewitz.com/faqs.html. Accessed 1 March 2014.

Marcuse, Peter. 1997. "Walls of Fear and Walls of Support." In *Architecture of Fear,* Nan Ellin, and Edward J. Blakely, eds. New York: Princeton Architectural Press, 101–12.

Minis, Wevonneda. 20 July 1996. "Addlestone Hebrew Academy Principal Evelyn Sarasohn: Lifelong Educator was Born to Achieve, Encourage Excellence." *The Post and Courier.* E1 and E3.

Mintz, Adam. 2011. *The History of City Eruvin, 1894–1962.* Ph.D. diss. New York University.

Parker, Adam. 30 November 2012. "A Rabbi's Challenge: Davis Joins BSBI Synagogue in Time of Outreach, Growth." *Post and Courier.* http://www.postandcourier.com/article/20121130/PC1204/121139930. Accessed 5 March 2014.

Rabbinical Council of America. 2014. "Rabbi Joel Landau: Israel Up Close Productions, Israel," *Rabbinic Profiles.* http://www.rabbis.org/news/article.cfm?id=105609. Accessed 1 March 2014.

"Rabbis in the Sky—Checking the Eruv." 2014. *Los Angeles Community Eruv.* http://www.laeruv.com/eruv-guide/rabbis-in-the-sky-checking-the-eruv/. Accessed 1 February 2014.

Radinsky, Rabbi David J. 13 February 2014. Phone interview.

Rephan, Nathan. 27 February 2014. Phone interview.

Rosengarten, Theodore, and Dale Rosengarten. 2002. *A Portion of the People: Three Hundred Years of Southern Jewish Life.* Columbia: University of South Carolina Press in Association with McKissick Museum.

Rozovsky, Lorne. 1993–2014. "What is an Eruv?" *Chabad.org.* http://www.chabad.org/library/article_cdo/aid/700456/jewish/What-Is-an-Eruv.htm. Accessed 13 March 2014.

Sarasohn, Hershel. 23 February 2014. Personal interview.

Scheer, William. 13 March 2014. Phone interview.

Schlaff, Shira J. 2003. "Using an Eruv to Untangle the Boundaries of the Supreme Court's Religion-Clause Jurisprudence." *Journal of Constitutional Law,* 5(4): 831–99.

Schwartz, C., ed. 1868. *The Scattered Nation; Past, Present, and Future.* Vol. III. London: Elliot Stock.

Snyder, Saskia Coenen. 2013. *Building a Public Judaism: Synagogues and Jewish Identity in Nineteenth-century Europe.* Cambridge, MA: Harvard University Press.

"So That's What an Eruv is." September 1992. *Scouting: A Family Magazine Published* by the Boy Scouts of America, 80(4): 93.

Ulrich, Laurel T. 2007. *Well-behaved Women Seldom Make History.* New York: Alfred A. Knopf.

Watkins, Yaakov "Jim". 2008–13. "What's an Eruv?—Or . . . You want to do WHAT?!" *Eruv.org: Definitive Eruv Information and Global Directory.* http://www.eruv.org/. Accessed 3 March 2014.

7

COMMUNITY-BUILT AND PRESERVED MATERIAL CULTURE

Square-Log Cabins in the Village of Mont-Tremblant, Quebec

Mariana Esponda Cascajares

Square-log cabins, which were historically built by groups of settlers in the Laurentides of Quebec, are now being preserved and adapted for new uses by their contemporary communities. Despite the changes, the overall historical character of the cabins is still evident, the old coexisting with the new. Preservation of these log cabins is important not only because of their technological aspects, but also because of the collective memory and its powerful connections with the environment that is expressed through the cabins' material culture (Mackie 1997). The Laurentides are a mountain range in southern Quebec, Canada, north of Montreal and the St. Lawrence River, running from the Mille Îles River to the north of Mont-Laurier, from east to west, the territory between Terrebone and Argenteuil (Laurin 1989). The Laurentides are shaped by gneiss and granite, incredibly hard bedrock that are almost as old as the Earth, spanning across an area of 2.2 million hectares (Potvin 2003). The region is one of the oldest mountain ranges in the world, shaped by the glaciers, full of rivers and lakes—close to ten thousand—and covered by dense forest (Lesieur et al. 2004). The Laurentides consists of two distinct subareas, the Basses Laurentides and the Hautes Laurentides. Raoul Blanchard (1877–1965) described the region as a vast labyrinth of hills and valleys (Blanchard 1953). The Euro-Canadian settlements, in contrast to the Montagnais First Nations tribe, were built near the waterways during the nineteenth century. In the twentieth century, the area also became a popular tourist destination with a cottage and lake culture in the summer and downhill and cross-country skiing in the winter, most significantly near Mont-Tremblant in the 1930s (Tremblant through the Years 2015).

Forests have always played a major role in Canadian culture. Since the Algonquin community inhabited the Laurentides area, the white pine was an abundant resource with many purposes: spiritual, cultural, and medicinal. The white pine provided shelter (the first tipi was not built with skin but with branches), transportation (the canoe and the paddle), and food. The log cabins of the eighteenth century were also built with white pine. White pine is a softwood, which is easy to work and does not split as easily as other types of wood. With the extensive logging in the nineteenth and twentieth centuries, white pine experienced a decline (Uprety and Adsselin, and Bergeron 2013). Most of the better quality logs, with diameters of 12–14 inches, were shipped to Europe. Consequently, most of the cabins in the Hautes Laurentides during the late nineteenth century were built with smaller diameter logs of white pine, between 6 and 10 inches. Other type of wood were spruce and fir. The remaining log cabins in the village of Mont-Tremblant are the product of their history, the community, and the values that keep changing with age. As such, these examples need to be understood as the process of adaptation through use and time. Hence, preservation needs to be viewed as an evolving narrative. This research explores this narrative by analyzing the natural, sociocultural, economic, and technical aspects of these cabins in respect to the people who built, maintained, and continue to use them over time.

History of the Foundation: Village of Mont-Tremblant

Father Antoine Labelle (1833–91) is considered to be the founder of the settlements in the vast lands of the north, today referred to as the Hautes Laurentides, earning him the title "King of the North" (Laurin 1989, 15). In 1869 and 1870, Labelle lead an expedition to the Vallée de la Diable, but found the territory too inhospitable with its interminable hills and valleys. During these expeditions, Labelle, with the support of native peoples, encountered the Rivière Diable and Rouge, as well as the highest peak in the Laurentides—Tremblant Mountain, "the mountain of the spirits" for the Algonquian people (Laurin 1989, 13).

Labelle's first objective was to halt the emigration of Québécois south into New England, by creating better living conditions in Canada (Saint-Jovite Centenary Album 1978). In 1871, he developed one of the first northern routes, and in 1874 built a covered bridge in the old De Salaberry and Grandison cantons, what is today the village of Mont-Tremblant. The first pioneers established settlements in the west of the Rivière Diable that same year. In 1877, there were forty-four pioneers, but only eleven stayed permanently. The remaining pioneers, motivated to find less rocky land, moved further away (Sock 2014). Between 1874 and 1881, more than 200 families travelled north and established settlements in Wolfe, Salaberry, and Grandison cantons (Lauren 1989). Meanwhile, the Vallée de la Diable was opened to colonization, with economies based on agriculture and forestry. In less than a decade, all arable lands in Salaberry, some 45 percent of the territory, had been allocated. (Prévost-Lamarre 1941). Labelle was a visionary and sought the construction of a railway line into the Laurentides to encourage the area's economic development. The railroad tracks were built up to Saint-Jovite in 1892, and then extended to Lac Mercier in 1904. While Labelle was colonizing the Vallée de la Diable, a parallel Anglo-Protestant colonization movement was developing to the north of Argenteuil, reaching Arundel and Saint-Jovite, which encountered the Francophone settlements (Shurtleff and Morison 1967; Lauren 1989).

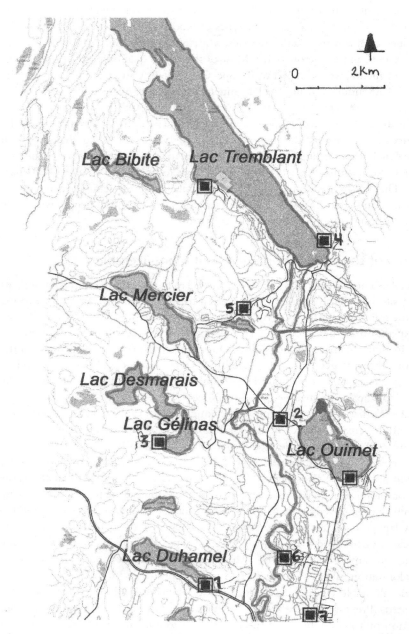

FIGURE 7.1 Aerial view with the existing square-log cabins (marked with squares) in Mont-Tremblant, Quebec

Source: Mariana Esponda

In 1877, Father Labelle observed that "most of the landscape at the time was covered by a tall, dense forest" (Archambault 2009).[1] An area of old Salaberry township (today Mont-Tremblant) experienced a forest fire fifty years ago, facilitating the clearing of the forest for the construction of settlements (Saint-Jovite Centenary Album 1978). In addition, part of this land was a vast plain, with few rocks (La maison québécoise. début XIXe–début XXe siècle 2015). The land was fertile due to the presence of limestone and ferruginous soil. Colonization spread west toward Lac Long River, and the main village began to take form in 1875. In the process, the villagers felled trees to clear space for farming, constructing their log cabins and bridges, heating, and cooking (SOPABIC 2004).

Architecture Composition: Building Typology and Human Environment

The vernacular architecture in Quebec is the result of an adaptation of ancestral French domestic models, as the original design was adapted to new climatic and material constraints. In the seventeenth century, house forms followed a pattern imported from France (Traquair 1947; Kalman 1994; Contal and Revedin 2011). But the hostile winters forced the settlers to resort to a new kind of thinking, and house design evolved rapidly. The orientation, materials, construction techniques, and forms of the new houses responded specifically to the local culture and colder environment (Weber and Yannas 2014). Designing in response to the climate influenced the roof angle, the number and orientation of doors and windows, the volume and dimension of the habitable space, the arrangement of the interior space, and the choice and use of materials (Lessard and Marquis 1972).

A detailed study of the first log square cabins in the village of Mont-Tremblant between 1874 and 1910 reveals that the pioneers chose the location by studying the natural environment, in order to make the most of the building in a Canadian winter. The first interesting aspect of the log cabins is their site locations. Although moderate and significant slopes characterize most of the terrain's topography, the cabins were constructed in areas of flatland. Second, the cabins are oriented in such a way to maximize sun exposure, and thus heat and light, for the better part of the day. The sun rises on one corner of the cabin, and throughout the whole day, the cabins have sunlight. Only the north facade is not exposed to the sun. Third, the houses are close to a small brook or creek, ensuring access to running water throughout the winter. This habitat was ideal for farming, fishing, and hunting, which meant that different food sources were close to the homestead. After finding an ideal site, settlers had to follow government rules in order to lease the land, requiring a minimum of one hundred acres at thirty cents per acre. Then the settlers had to build a house with minimum dimensions of 16 by 20 feet. Finally, they had to farm the land and clear ten acres of trees every year. In the beginning, the main types of trees were white and red pine, spruce, and hemlock. During the

FIGURE 7.2 Thibault log cabin built in 1874. The cabin shows a very strong relationship with the landscape that ties the concepts of placemaking and material practice as fundamental to ensure the "permanency" of architecture. This image was taken circa 1976.

Source: Denis Archambault

winter, they would fell trees and in the spring use the axe to square the timber for purposes of making square-log cabins, which can be better insulated (Mann and Skinulis 1979; Archambault 2009).

The function and organization of the square-log cabins in Mont-Tremblant correspond to the town's socioeconomic structure and its relationship with environmental resources. Cabins were built with local materials, primarily wood. They typically consisted of wood walls made by horizontal square logs connected on the corners with dovetail connections (Rempel 1980). The chimney and foundation were built with local fieldstones, bonded together with lime mortar. As general knowledge, they knew that it was important to build on dry-set foundations to avoid rotting the first course of logs, but many cabins were built directly on the ground. This may be due to the fact that some cabins were erected on a minimal budget, within a short time frame (Archambault 2014–2015).

The colors of the windows and doorframes are noteworthy on the square-log cabins. For generations blue, yellow, and red were used most frequently. These combinations of colors are associated with the symbols of French Catholic culture in Quebec. The final coating of the cabin walls were completed with a white lime wash paint (*chaux*), a lime-and-water solution that gives wood a white-washed look. It was applied for practical purposes: to control rot, deter insects, protect the walls, and brighten interiors. The windows were usually small and few in number since glass was expensive to import and precious heat could easily be lost in winter through large openings. Later, internal wood partitions would be added to divide the interior space into rooms. Most of the log cabins were small, about 225 square feet, and the ceiling heights were low to be more efficiently heated during winter. There was a pitched roof, with the main rafters resting on a ridge beam and several small joists supporting the roof. The roof's underside shows the typical curve *coyau*—a character-defining element of the typical Québécois house (Log Homes 2015).[2] The roof pitch is positioned perpendicularly to the ground slope in order to allow snow to settle on top of it, as a form of insulation. Roofs were originally covered with overlapped cedar shingles, which provided protection from the rain and snow while also facilitating air circulation. The interior layout aimed for natural air movement. The east and west facades have symmetrical windows to allow cross ventilation. In the south facade, a side room, called a summer kitchen, was added. This annex helped enhance the energy efficiency of the cabin, making it possible to keep the air cool during the hot summer.

Square-Log Cabin Case Studies

From the hundreds of log cabins that were built by the settlers in Saint-Jovite at the end of the nineteenth century, very few are still located in their original place. Prime surviving examples include the Thibault, Bréard, and Lafleur cabins. Other log cabins have been refurbished with new additions and other changes, such as the Maison Paquin. Starting in the 1960s, several cabins were relocated to different locations, including Clagett's Cabin, Jewelry Plourde, and Refuge des Draveurs. The importance of these seven log cabins is examined through their historical, natural, sociocultural, and economic aspects. Exploring how these cabins change over time reveals how the sociocultural values associated them have evolved.

1. Thibault Log Cabin, Lac Duhamel (1874)

One of the earliest log cabins built was by Guillame Thibault in 1874. He settled near Lac Long, today called Lac Duhamel. Thibault leased two lots for a total of 88 acres (Archambault 2009). This well-built structure measures 25 by 25 feet square and housed a family with fourteen children. Thibault squared the logs and cut the dovetails on the cabin so that water flowed away from the building. Second, he tilted the walls slightly inward at the top, like a house of cards, to make it stronger and avoid water infiltration. Third, five wood beams, at both ends, shaped in 45 degrees intersect the walls for supports. Finally, Thibault inserted two-inch-long wooden pegs every two feet into the wall logs to secure the position of the timber.

The cabin remained in Thibault family's possession until 1937, when Armand Labelle bought it, changing ownership again in the 1960s, when Zelia Dufour bought the cabin. After 140 years, the cabin is still in good condition. The main changes observed on the exterior are the roof (material finish and new lucerne dormer windows) and a new 1960s addition built on the south facade, which serves as a summer kitchen. The cedar roof was replaced by metal in the 1930s, most likely when Armand Labelle bought it. In the 1960s, when Zelia Dufour inhabited the

FIGURE 7.3 Dovetail connection, detail; Thibault log cabin

Source: Mariana Esponda

cabin, a new metallic layer was added to the roof and the color was changed to black. The interior is almost the same, except for a change to the kitchen sink (in both location and material), the incline of the stairs, and the extra room added to the south side.

FIGURE 7.4 Beam to wall connection, detail; Thibault log cabin

Source: Mariana Esponda

2. Lafleur Farm, Village of Mont-Tremblant (1865 and 1960)

This log cabin stands out in the village for its large size (21 by 35 feet), its two main volumes, the surrounding landscape, sun exposure, and central location. Jean-Baptiste Lafleur and Éliza Paquette settled in Mont-Tremblant around 1877 with their thirteen children. Fascinated with the proportions of Lafleur structure, Mary Ryan bought it and moved in as of the early 1960s. The Ryan family was one of the more prominent families in the village, thanks to the establishment of the ski station on Tremblant mountain, having connections with artists, political figures, and other important people (O'Rear and O'Rear 1954). The Ryan family set an example, followed by other community members, who desired to preserve and live in similar log cabins.

The interior and exterior walls were completely covered by many layers of various materials, added to reduce air drafts. Mary Ryan tore off the layers and found what she was looking for: an original log cabin wall. After the layers were removed, the cabin walls began to crumble, and thus the adventure in restoring the original wood structure began. The process included numerating the logs, disassembling the structure, cleaning the logs, and reassembling all components back into their original placement. In order to show the "soul" of the log cabin, Mary Ryan decided to leave both the interior and exterior walls exposed. She retrofitted the interior space in a contemporary fashion. The main room, 21 by 21 feet in size, has an open kitchen with a long island, dining table, small chimney, and new stairs to the second floor, previously only accessible by ladder. The thin proportion of all the structural wood beams is noticeable. Mary Ryan incorporated lucerne dormer windows in the roof. The original cedar shingles were replaced fifteen years prior by Burke Smith after a fire caused by creosote from the chimney (Smith and Smith 2015).

Following her passion for recovering log structures, Mary Ryan went to Orleans Island in Quebec City and bought another log structure (20 by 16 feet in size). It was assembled next to the original log cabin and was turned into the residence's living room. This log structure and the original differ in log size and wood type. The logs from Orleans Island are a foot wide of white pine instead; the original Lafleur cabin has 8- to 9-inch logs. The finish of Quebec City logs is more carefully crafted; the incision is a little bit curved, marking the "trace" of the type of the axe used. In the Quebec City structure, the mortar mix between the logs is two inches larger. Mary Ryan incorporated bay windows into the west facade, although this type of window does not belong to historical Quebec architecture. In addition to the main log cabin and the structure moved from Orleans Island, this property has an original blacksmith shop from Saint-Jovite. This simple log structure—with dovetails connection—was the place where horseshoes were forged. It was transported in one piece in the late 1960s, placed behind the cabin, and used as a garage.

FIGURE 7.5   Lafleur Farm. The left side is the original log cabin (built in 1867). The right side was transported from the Orleans Island, Quebec City, and was assembled in the 1960s. The small structure behind the house was the old blacksmith shop that was transported in 1960s from downtown Saint-Jovite.

Source: Mariana Esponda

3. Bréard Cabin, Lac Gelinas (1898)

Looking for better living conditions, Georges Bréard, a shipbuilder, arrived in 1898 to build the first log cabin in Lac Gelinas (before Lac Claire) with his wife Julie and son Stanislas. Bréard chose one of the few flatlands in the area to build their home. Even though it was well oriented, close to a waterway, the soil was not well suited for agriculture. The small cabin (15 by 20 feet) is full of life and stories. In the 1920s, the Bréard family decided to rent out the cabin to generate more income during the summer months. They built a small addition onto the east facade that includes a summer kitchen with a stove. Some of the carpentry details illustrate the precarious living conditions of the original residents. The square logs and dovetail connections were cut by axe; the finish is rough because of the deep axe cuts. The spruce logs range in size from 6 to 8 inches. Some logs still have the round edge of the tree. In order to provide protection from the cold weather, a kind of caulking called oakum, or *étoupe*, was used, made of tarred rope fiber. A thin tree branch and several layers of newspaper were placed along the logs, since the perception of wood as a finishing material has changed over time. It is still possible to read some stories on these old newspapers.

The exterior has not changed much, except for the addition of a small roof extension above the main door and the roof's finish material. During the 1950s, the owners moved the square-log cabin approximately 32 feet next to a new house on the same lot. The log cabin was used as a garage. But in the early 1960s, they decided to relocate the cabin back to its original location (Royer 2015). Some of the logs were replaced. The new logs are distinguishable because they are smaller in size and do not have the same patina. During the reconstruction, they found that the two bottom logs had rotted, so they replaced them with a two-foot-high concrete beam. Currently the log cabin is being used as a warehouse. The cabin shows a fair amount of degradation and is in need of preservation maintenance; however, it is one of the last remaining cabins whose exterior lime-washed coating has survived and still has some traces of the interior coating.

In the 1960s, the Canadian conservation movement became increasingly concerned with architectural heritage preservation. During that time, there was a synergy between preservation and community planning. Diverse groups advocated for stopping the destruction of irreplaceable structures, and in many instances, they preserved structures by moving them from their original location. An important revival of log cabin building happened in the village of Mont-Tremblant, spearheaded by families such as the Ryans and the Clagetts and by local heritage enthusiasts, such as George Kelleger. The nostalgia for the log cabin and its associations with wilderness and recreation played a role in the promotion of tourism in the region. Log cabin building in Canada became associated with a rustic aesthetic, often applied to private recreational retreats. In general, the impact of the back-to-the-land revival encouraged a greater engagement with the natural environment and an interest in preserving log cabin construction, and by extension, the Canadian frontier identity (Mills 1994).

4. Clagett's Cabin, Hotel Quintessence
(1885, 1960, and 2002)

This square-log cabin was built as a home for the settlers in 1885 in Saint-Jovite. In 1960, the Clagetts, an American family, bought a property on the shores of Lac Tremblant for their summer residence. The Clagetts moved an old cabin from Cap Street, in downtown Saint-Jovite, to their land in 1962, and used it as a guesthouse near the Canadian wilderness. In 2000, the Clagetts sold their property to a luxury hotel, Hotel Quintessence. Sean O'Donnell, one of the new owners, wanted to turn the log cabin into a special "Québécois" featured hotel. For a second time, the structure was disassembled, moved, and reassembled. In its final position, nestled in the woods, adjacent to the main building, it now has a better view and more privacy. In 2002, when a concrete foundation was built for the cabin, in addition to repair work to the cedar roof shingles, window replacement, and an interior renovation. The romantic refuge has two rooms: the main room has a queen-sized bed, cast-iron pedestal tub, and a rebuilt brick chimney. The second, smaller room contains the bathroom. The cabin is shaped with tight-fitting dovetails. One can easily perceive the rough finish made by the axe in the spruce logs. The logs are 8 to 9 inches in width and held together with a mortar mix. Clagetts's cabin shows how historic architecture can be reused to generate an income (De Bellefeuille 2014–2015). This log cabin is used year round and is booked almost 90 percent of the time (Mont-Tremblant 2015).

5. Jewelry Atelier by Carole and Alain Plourde
(1850 and 1980)

This square-log cabin, originally built as a post office in the 1850s, was moved in 1980 from another town, Saint-Andre Avelin, near Montebello. Carole and Alain Plourde were passionate skiers who loved the landscape of the region. They were fascinated by other log cabins in the village, such as the Lefleur Farm and the building by Lac Ouimet, owned by Dr. Curtis. Alain explains, "We decided to look for one, bring together all the log pieces and make their own living in the village" (Plourde and Plourde 2014). He remembers well when Jill Gean Gras, the person responsible for the reconstruction, showed them the puzzle of the log pieces. This wood structure is not only used as a home, but the basement is used as their jewelry store. The log cabin design is used in their business logo, creating an associated identity. The Plourdes have appreciated the aesthetic and historical qualities of the cabin as well as its financial benefits.

One characteristic that stands out in this building is the log size that is nearly a foot thick. The logs are bigger than the ones typically used by the settlers in Mont-Tremblant. Another interesting aspect is the angle of the roof. The roof from the original log home was ruined, so they saw this as an opportunity to look for another style. They recycled the roof from a barn, and the new angle provides more space on the second floor. The cabin has the same orientation as the old post office, so the ageing (from the weather and the heat) on the logs continues in a similar pattern. The layout for the cabin consists of one open space. The exterior does not have any coating, as is usually the case with the adaptive reuse of log homes since the 1970s. Rather than try to construct an idealized version of the past, the Plourdes are adapting the building to their needs. In 1992, the Plourdes built an extension onto the back of the cabin for an elevator.

Grassroots Efforts in Preservation

In the last decade, an effort has been made in the village of Mont-Tremblant by property owners to preserve their cabins using creativity, a planned budget, and their own set of requirements. Villagers have restored log cabins from the town and other areas in the Laurentides. They have adapted existing structures and added extensions to accommodate new uses. As Mathieu Régnier explains, "the challenge for many owners wishing to renovate a heritage residence has been to combine modern comfort while at the same time preserving the historical aspect of the building" (Régnier 2013). Some projects have placed greater emphasis on the conservation of the log cabin, while others have altered the historic character.

1. Thibault Log Cabin Restoration (1874 and 2003–5)

The cabin belonging to Denis Archambault—from the first case study described in this chapter, the Thibault log cabin from 1874—is an excellent example of a grassroots effort to preserve the material culture of an original square-log cabin. In 2007, after their restoration work was completed, Archambault won the first prize for heritage architecture from the Council for Culture of the Laurentides. This log cabin has been under his family's ownership since the 1960s, but he became the owner in 2003. This restoration required the use of the same traditional methods. The main damage was caused by ants at the bottom of some square logs, located on the north, south, and west facades. In 2005, Richard Arbic was responsible for the new extension on the south facade. Arbic explained that the main challenge was recreating the original dovetails and finding suitable wood pieces. For the three new walls, he recreated the same height and width on each square log. The logs were reused from another cabin from Saint Michel de Bellechasse, Quebec (Arbic 2015). During the process, Arbic used traditional craftsman techniques and materials, except for the tools that were contemporary.

During the restoration, Arbic discovered that the mortar mix between the logs contained sawdust. Another original feature that was revealed is the wood pegs in the roof structure. Arbic believes that this was probably a local characteristic of the Laurentian dovetail cabin construction. The original wood beams from the roof are in very good condition, despite the weight of the snow and their age. The inspection revealed that the beams did not have any mechanical damage or decay. To build a new roof on the extension, Arbic followed the original construction system: the same roof angle, connections, and sections of the wood beams. Only the external finish was modified; the new finish was selected to match both roofs.

Another modification is found in the inclination of each log in the wall. The original logs were tilted two to three inches, but they were not tilted in the new extension. The inclination is a unique character-defining element of the original, which they wanted to respect. By not tilting the new logs, the new extension is slightly distinguishable from the original, keeping the old and new distinct, which was one of the principles in the restoration of Thibault's cabin (Andy 2015; Martel 2015). During several different site visits, which took place during the summer and winter of 2014, the author observed that the inside temperature was adequate: on a hot summer day, the indoor temperature was cool; meanwhile on a cool and humid fall day, the indoor temperature was comfortable, even without a mechanical system's help. The windows—with their small size—have performed well over the years, controlling heat dissipation providing cross ventilation, and minimizing wood decay. This cabin design has adapted well to the harsh Quebec environment.

New Shed, "The Love Shack" (2007)

Denis Archambault decided to build a small shed following the same principles that were discovered during the restoration of the Thibault log cabin. The smaller cabin, 12 by 18 feet, was executed by the same master builder, Arbic, but with the help of an apprentice, Serge Barbe. The aim was twofold: to learn more about square-log techniques and to translate the traditional knowledge into a shared skill for future preservation and construction. Archambault also participated in the learning process on how to cut the dovetails. The small building is located on the same land as the original Thibault cabin, but not with the same orientation. Most of the wood is recycled from other dismantled cabins, but the logs were not tilted. The roof uses cedar shingles, as was done by the settlers.

Another Square-Log Cabin, Lac Narcisse (2010)

Following his passion for local wood construction, in 2010, Archambault decided to build another square-log cabin on a new property near Lac Narcisse. This time, Barbe had to use all of his acquired knowledge. This new cabin follows the exact window and door proportions as the original Thibault cabin and is similarly oriented. The size is smaller, 15 by 18 feet. Dovetail connections join the logs. The spruce logs were recycled from other dismantled properties. To build the chimney, they collected the stones from the lakeshore. The roof has cedar shingles, but the *coyau* is longer than in a traditional roof, in order to better protect the cabin from the sun.

6. Refuge Des Draveurs, the Golf Course Le Maître de Mont-Tremblant (1850 and 2007)

This square-log cabin from the 1850s (according to local records) is another interesting example of how community decisions can have significant impact on the values—historical, sociocultural, economic, and sustainability—associated with old buildings, even when they are neglected, small, and ordinary (Vellinga 2015). This small cabin was saved from destruction in 2007, moved from Saint-Eustache, Quebec, and then relocated to the golf course Le Maître, Mont-Tremblant. Pascal De Bellefeuille, director of sales and marketing for Le Maître golf, explained that it was the club community that made the decision to invest in a heritage building. It was not an easy or a fast solution, but the rationale was that this kind of practice reinforces the cultural identity of a place and a community. Now, the building has evolved from being a settlers' cabin to a clubhouse along the river, where the children play during the summer. It has a playroom, meeting room, and changing room, with bathrooms for the beach. It is called the Refuge des Draveurs (Refuge of the Log Drivers), inspired by the nineteenth century history of the Edmonds family owned farm and the river where lumberjacks used to float timber to the mills in the springtime on the Rivière Diable (Roy and Bonnette 1989; Brisebois 2010). De Bellefeuille explained that when "we had restored a lumber cabin, we tried to bring together the contemporary reality and the legends of Quebec; it is now part of the history of the site and lives in the memories of all residents and visitors of Le Parc de la Diable" (De Bellefeuille 2015). The Refuge des Draveurs log cabin certainly tells a story not just about the past but also about the current people and place. A specific challenge in this adaptation was to only use building materials that were traditional in order keep the character authentic. Windows from the original cabin were missing. Instead of making new ones, they decided to recycle old windows from a hotel that was demolished forty years earlier, which had been saved in an antique shop.

This adaptive reuse not only assigned new life to a building that was abandoned for years, but it also served an educational purpose. Children and their families are more aware of their cultural heritage because the building is part of their daily life. They can then experience the walls of a heritage log cabin without being in a museum. The last lesson learned: heritage can be a cost-effective tool. According to De Bellefeuille, "Let's give a financial value to our heritage!," so that people will invest in the memory of sites like the Drapeur log cabin (De Bellefeuille 2015). The cabin functions as a semi-public space where members of the community can benefit from this amenity next to the Diable River and beach.

7. Maison Paquin (1871 and 2016)

The last example in Mont-Tremblant is the Maison Paquin log cabin, a product of a grassroots effort. In March 2010, Louis Beaudoin bought the building as an adaptive reuse project. The initial idea was to make a small commercial space and

FIGURE 7.6 Refuge des Draveurs. This small cabin was saved from destruction in 2007 and retrofitted as the clubhouse for the kids at the golf course Le Maître, Mont-Tremblant. The main goal was to reinforce the cultural identity of a place and a community.

Source: Mariana Esponda

art gallery, reusing original furniture and architectural elements. Unfortunately, the main building, storage addition, and jewelry section in the mansard part were in poor condition. During the demolition in September 2011, a square-log structure in the jewelry section was discovered (De Bellefeuille 2015). This log cabin, as many others in the valley, was hidden behind clapboards in order to give a more refined appearance and provide better insulation and maintenance. A stonewall was added in the late 1940s. After a specialist evaluated the building, the parties involved agreed that it was important to keep the old structure. At the same time, Societe du Patrimoine du Bassin inférieur de la Rouge et de la Chaîne géologique du Mont-Tremblant (SOPABIC) and the Mont-Tremblant Historical Society investigated the heritage significance of the cabin and discovered pictures of the structure from the late nineteenth century (Légaré 2011). After several meetings between the city and owner, they agreed on some changes to the project. The log cabin would be rebuilt on the same site and be integrated as an attraction in the new contemporary building, in order to best reflect present values. The owner also exchanged land with the city so that public space could be integrated into the project. Currently, the project is still on the drawing board and the timbers are in storage. Hopefully the story of the Maison Paquin will continue and a new chapter will be written soon.

Conclusion

Through the different preservation cases from the village of Mont-Tremblant, I explored not only the physical aspects of the square-log cabins, such as the use of traditional building materials, craftsmanship, and construction techniques, but also the sociocultural values linked to living conditions, a sense of place, and collective memory of the community. Undoubtedly, these wood structures from the nineteenth century represent material and social constructs, local values, expressions of Canadian identity, and environmental and economic functions. Historic buildings are reminders of local history, but what happens to these places depends on the contemporary cultural ideas and values from the contemporary community. The story of the grassroots effort by Denis Archambault to preserve the Thibault log cabin reasserts that historic buildings contain a narrative about the past and people through time. Archambault recounted:

> One day when I was about five, I asked my grandfather why he was working so much on the house. He was working more than the neighbors on their properties. He took me in the old house, brought me in his arms and asked me to put my hand on the inside beam. He then asked if I felt the axe traces. I said yes and then he said, "This shows that someone really worked hard at building this house, you should never forget this."
>
> *(Archambault 2014–2015)*

In the village of Mont-Tremblant, there are no protective ordinances or laws protecting the historic log cabins. Once the value of a building is identified, the people involved take on the project of preservation on their own accord. The awareness of this type of vernacular architecture requires a mode of engagement from the community, creating continuity with the past through the process of adaptation over time and use. Cultural heritage is a complex set of qualities with significance for individuals, communities, and society as a whole. To preserve vernacular buildings as part of our living cultural heritage, it is often necessary to perform adaptive re-use.

Vernacular buildings work with climate, rather than against it. The remaining log cabins show how settlers respected and responded to the harsh Quebec environment, living in harmony with it. In order to maintain thermal comfort, they employed knowledge of traditional construction technologies, such as natural and cross ventilation, building orientation, and day lighting. The efforts to preserve historic cabins, as covered within this study, are best practice examples pertaining to both material and craftsmanship authenticity, with the Thibault cabin preservation project being an extraordinarily exceptional case study. The success of these adaptive reuse projects could lead to many other restoration projects in other villages. Le Refuge des Draveurs, the Clagett's Cabin, and Plourde's jewelry store are examples of the appreciation of historical and aesthetic values, and how they can provide financial and sustainable benefits (Carroon 2010; Van Hees, Naldini, and Roos 2014; Todorovic 2015).

The log cabins of Mont-Tremblant, spanning from ones built by the settlers in the nineteenth century to those relocated and repurposed in the 1960s, contribute to the character of the landscape, and their relationship between environment and people. They reflect the current needs of the society while still allowing the values of the past to be communicated through the remaining structures (Gourbiliere and Joliet 2007). This demonstrates how contemporary values have evolved through time, and how sustainable community development is needed for future generations. Everyone involved in Mont-Tremblant's preservation movement provided invaluable time and resources, especially in terms of the material culture of the village and the sense of place, and respected in the fragile nature of these log structures. The community has maintained the integrity of the original material and construction processes, while minimizing the cost of maintenance, perpetuating the rich heritage of the Laurentians.

Acknowledgments

This research is based on the collection of oral histories of the people who built, lived in, and/or restored the log cabins. Special thanks to the people of Mont-Tremblant and owners of the square-log cabins who kindly opened their doors and hearts to share many details that represent the cultural identity of the Laurentides: Denis Archambault, Pascal De Bellefeuille, Louise Royer, Renée Girault, Jane and Burke Smith, and Carole and Alain Plourde were especially helpful in this respect. I am also grateful to the master builders that allowed me to apprentice in this savoir faire on square-log technique: Richard Arbic, Yves Andy, and Michel Martel.

Notes

1 Extract from a letter by Father Labelle to Monseigneur Duhamel in October 1877, where he describes the selected land. Archambault, *In Une belle histoire des pays d'en haut*. Number 2. *"les bois sont mêles, élevées, sans branches exceptées a la tête"* (personal translation), 2009.
2 The *coyau*, or the sprocket, is a triangular piece of wood or a bent structural element that, placed on the rafter base, extends the roof over the eaves walls, protecting them from rain, snow, and ice. The drip mold can then throw off rainwater away from the face of a wall. This creates an elegant and distinctive curvature on the roof, which is prominent on houses in Quebec but small and almost inexistent on French homes. *La maison québécoise.* début XIXe–début XXe siècle. http://www.culture-patrimoine-deschambault-grondines. ca/la-maison-quebecoise.php#t2.

References

Andy, Yves. 24 January 2015. Personal interview.
Arbic, Richard. 7 January 2015. Personal interview.
Archambault, Denis. 2009. *In Une belle histoire des pays d'en haut*. Number 1, 2, 3 & 4.
Archambault, Denis. 25 August 2014, 20 September 2014, 8 January 2015, 12 April 2015. Personal interviews.
Blanchard, Raoul. 1953. *Province De Québec: L'ouest Du Canada Français*. Montréal: Beauchemin.
Brisebois, Robert. 2010. *Les Chemins Du Nord: Roman Historique*. Montréal: Hurtubise.

Carroon, Jean. 2010. *Sustainable Preservation: Greening Existing Buildings*. Hoboken, NJ: Wiley.

Contal, Marie-Hélène, and Jana Revedin. 2011. *Sustainable Design Ii: Vers Une Nouvelle Éthique Pour L'architecture Et La Ville. Arles*. France: Actes Sud.

De Bellefeuille, Pascal. 7 December 2014, 12 and 24 January 2015, 16 February 2015. Personal interviews.

Gourbiliere, Claire, and Fabienne Joliet. 2007. "Emblematic Landscape of Lac-Tremblant Nord: Natural Scenic Area and Cultural Heritage Asset." In *Encyclopedia of French Cultural Heritage of North America*. http://www.ameriquefrancaise.org/en/article-380/emblematic %20landscapes%20of%20lac-tremblant-nord:%20%20natural%20scenic%20area%20 and%20cultural%20heritage%20asset. Accessed 29 January 2016.

Kalman, Harold. 1994. *A History of Canadian Architecture*. Toronto: Oxford University Press.

"La maison québécoise. début XIXe–début XXe siècle." 2014. *Culture et Patrimoine Deschambault-Grondines*. http://www.culture-patrimoine-deschambault-grondines.ca/la-maison-quebecoise.php#t2. Accessed 25 January 2015.

Laurin, Serge. 1989. *Histoire Des Laurentides*. Québec: Institut québécois de recherche sur la culture.

Légaré, Colet. 16 November 2011. "Quel àge avait la maison paquin." *Info du Nord Tremblant*.

Lesieur, D., P. Lefort, Y. Bergeron, and È. Lauzon. 2004. *Reconstitution de l'historique des perturbations naturelles et de la composition de la forêt pré-industrielle au sud de Val-d'Or*. Rapport de la Chaire industrielle en aménagement forestier durable soumis à Domtar.

Lessard, Michel, and Huguette Marquis. 1972. *Encyclopédie De La Maison Québécoise*. Montréal: Éditions de l'homme.

Mackie, B Allan. 1997. *Building with Logs*. Willowdale, ON: Firefly Books.

Mann, Dale, and Richard Skinulis. 1979. *The Complete Log House Book: A Canadian guide to Building with Logs*. Toronto: McGraw-Hill Ryerson.

Martel, Michel. 16 January 2015. Personal interview.

Mills, Edward D. 1994. *Rustic Building Programs in Canada's National Parks, 1887–1950*. Ottawa: National Historic Sites Directorate, Parks Canada.

"Mont-Tremblant." 2015. *Quintessence Hotel*. http://www.hotelquintessence.com/en. Accessed 15 January 2015.

O'Rear, John, and Frankie O'Rear. 1954. *The Mont Tremblant Story: Including Skiing the Mont Tremblant Way*. New York: A.S. Barnes.

"Log Homes." 27 May 2015. *National Research Council Canada*. http://www.nrc-cnrc.gc.ca/ eng/solutions/advisory/codes_centre/faq/log_homes.html. Accessed 10 January 2015.

Plourde, Alain, and Carole Plourde. 12 December 2014. Personal interview.

Potvin, Denise. 2003. *Mont-Tremblant: Au Coeur Des Laurentides*. Outremont, QC: Trécarré.

Prévost-Lamarre, Cécile. 1941. *Par Monts Et Par Vaux À La Suite Du Roi Du Nord*. Saint-Jérôme, QC: Éditions de l'Avenir du Nord.

Régnier, Mathieu. June 2013. No. 137. *Des fondations en héritage*. Le flèche, QC: Le magazine del Laurentides, 32–3.

Rempel, John. 1980. *Building with Wood and Other Aspects of Nineteenth-Century Building in Central Canada*. Toronto: University of Toronto Press.

Roy, Odile, and Michel Bonnette. 1989. *Les Revêtements De Bois*. Québec: Ville de Québec.

Royer, Louise. 6, 11, 15 and 22 January 2015, 3 February 2015, 3 April 2015. Personal interviews.

Saint-Jovite Centenary Album. 1978.

Shurtleff, Harold R., and Samuel E. Morison. 1967. *The Log Cabin Myth: A Study of the Early Dwellings of the English Colonists in North America*. Gloucester, MA: P. Smith.

Sock, Sandra. 2014. "The Laurentides: A Very Concise History Part 1 & 2." In *Laurentian Heritage WebMagazine*. http://lauretian.quebecheritageweb.com. Accessed 12 December 2014.

SOPABIC. 2004. *Cent vingt-cinquième anniversairede la Paroisse de Saint-Jovite—1929–2004.* Mont-Tremblant, QC: SOPABIC.

Smith, Burke, and Jane Smith. 15 January 2015. Personal interview.

Todorovic, Nicolá. 25 January 2015 and 20 June 2015. Personal interviews.

Traquair, Ramsay. 1947. *The Old Architecture of Quebec.* Montreal: The MacMillan Company.

"Tremblant Through the Years." 2015. *Mont Tremblant, Quebec.* http://www.tremblant.ca/75/tremblant-through-the-years/index.aspx. Accessed 20 January 2015.

Uprety, Yadav, Hugo Asselin, and Yves Bergeron. 2013. "Cultural Importance of White Pine to the Kitcisakik Algonquin Community of Western Quebec, Canada." *Canadian Journal of Forest Research*, 43(6): 544–51

Vellinga, Marcel. 2015. "Vernacular Architecture and Sustainability: Two or Three Lessons." In *Vernacular Architecture: Towards a Sustainable Future*, Vegas Mileto, Garcia Sorriano, and Cristini, eds. London: Taylor & Francis Group, 3–8.

Weber, Willy, and Simon Yannas. 2014. *Lessons from Vernacular Architecture.* New York: Routledge.

8

CONSTRUCTING AND PRESERVING HISTORY THROUGH COMMUNITY ART PROJECTS

Anastasia L. Pratt

According to the Association for Public Art, public art is distinguished by

> the unique association of how it is made, where it is, and what it means. Public art can express community values, enhance our environment, transform a landscape, heighten our awareness, or question our assumptions. Placed in public sites, this art is there for everyone, a form of collective community expression. Public art is a reflection of how we see the world—the artist's response to our time and place combined with our own sense of who we are.
>
> *(What Is Public Art 2014)*

Moreover, it is

> part of our public history, part of our evolving culture and our collective memory. It reflects and reveals our society and adds meaning to our cities. As artists respond to our times, they reflect their inner vision to the outside world, and they create a chronicle of our public experience.
>
> *(What Is Public Art 2014)*

All around the world, artists have installed mosaics and murals as works of public art. Sometimes working within the confines of a commission and sometimes working as part of a larger community collective, they have planned and executed mosaics of a variety of sizes and shapes.

This chapter will explore one such project, the *Clinton County History through the Eyes of Its Children* mosaic. Although this project is unique, its role within the larger world of mosaics, public art installations, place-based education, and public history is not. I will show how this mosaic, like so many others, brought community members together to create an accounting of local history and a representation of

FIGURE 8.1   The *Clinton County History through the Eyes of Its Children* mosaic, installed
on the side of the Clinton County Government Building, in Plattsburgh,
New York, in 2009

Source: Anastasia Pratt

identity. The mosaic asks—and answers—questions about who can and should be
included in accounts of local history, while at the same time it highlights absences
in the historic record.

Clinton County History through the Eyes of *Its Children,* a Mosaic Project

Over the course of 2008 and 2009, students in the fourth, seventh, and twelfth
grades, from every school district in Clinton County, New York (the northeastern-
most county in the state), worked with their social studies and art teachers, the Clinton County historian, and three artists to create a mosaic that would showcase the
county's history. From researching the history of their school and region, to proposing images and then making tiles based on those images, the students were actively
involved in a project that created a 38 by 9 foot ceramic tile mosaic, which now
graces the side of the county's government center. The idea for the installation came
from Sandra McClatchie Morse, a retired kindergarten and first grade teacher, who
hoped that the county's four hundredth anniversary commemoration of Samuel de
Champlain's (1574–1635) arrival in this region would include a joint community
and school project. Knowing that both had been involved in other school-based art
installations, Sandy contacted Bucky Rogers Seiden, another retired teacher, and
Sue Burdick Young, a professional potter, to develop a proposal for funding. That
request brought the women in touch with me, as Clinton County historian, and
together we created a project plan for a project that would supplement New York's
curricular guidelines for local history and art.

Our plan was to create a visual timeline of the county's past, beginning before
European contact and continuing until 1880. Each portion of the timeline would

illustrate life in the area, with images of animals and plants situated near images of people, workplaces, transportation methods, battles, and scenes of everyday life. As time progressed, the scenes would represent significant changes, with nature giving way to industry and the Battle of Plattsburgh (1814)—which took place during the War of 1812—fading as the Underground Railroad and abolitionist movement took center stage. Moreover, each of the eras would include items of local interest, with students from the various schools assigned portions of the timeline that most closely fit their district's history. For example, Northern Adirondack Central School, located in Ellenburg, would work on the pre-European and First Nations components of the timeline, since that district includes a significant First Nations community, while the Plattsburgh school district would focus on the Battle of Plattsburgh, which occurred within blocks of the current school.

Once county funding and legislative approval were secured—but before total funding of more than $50,000, gathered through individual and corporate donations, as well as grants, for the project was in place—we sponsored a professional development workshop at the North County Teacher Resource Center, inviting social studies and art teachers from across the county to attend and learn more about the project. We provided attendees with proposals for the project, curriculum maps to explain how this project could supplement the state requirements for seventh grade students, and research materials to supplement the teachers' local history collections. With a basic agreement in place, I started to visit every school district, speaking with students about the project and local history. In every instance, I shared a PowerPoint presentation focused on the school's specific portion of the timeline. The images within the presentation were designed to offer a historically accurate representation of the era to spark questions about life in the past, and to inspire the students to create drawings that might be used for the mosaic. Within a month, I had received drawings from every school district.

At that point, the supervising artists, Bucky Seiden and Sue Young, returned to work, looking over every student's drawing and identifying portions that could be transferred to tiles most easily. We photocopied those portions of the larger illustrations (since deposited at the archives of the Clinton County Historian's Office), and the artists arranged their chosen images into a mock mosaic to be sure that everything would fit together in a clear visual narrative. They then began to visit all of the schools, teaching students to roll, cut, and tool clay slabs; to transfer their images onto the slab; and to texture and cut background tiles with a series of tools. Students learned about ceramics throughout this experience, finding that tiles need to dry for a week before they are bisque fired in preparation for glazing, and discovering that ceramic glazes, which often appear gray, require careful attention during application and another round of firing to create the highly impermeable and permanent tiles.

Understandably, the process of creating the tiles was time-consuming. However, by the end of the 2008–9 school year, all of the tiles had been created and the artists were ready to begin the installation. Working from a community room in the government center, Sandy, Sue, and Bucky laid out every tile on a grid and then transferred those tiles to the exterior brick wall that had been specially cleaned and re-pointed in preparation. With the help of local art teachers and artists, as well as family members and friends, the students finished the installation in time for an unveiling ceremony on August 12, 2009.

The finished product includes thousands of tiles created by seventh grade students at the Au Sable Valley, Beekmantown, Chazy, Northern Adirondack, Northeastern Clinton, Peru, and Saranac Central Schools, as well as the Plattsburgh City and Seton Catholic Schools. Fifth grade students in Colleen Anstett's class and students in Jerry Seguin's high school art club—both at Northern Adirondack Central School—also contributed tiles, with the largest pieces (a First Nations woman and child, Samuel de Champlain with two of his guides, the county map, and a ship) coming from the studios of Sue Burdick Young and Bucky Seiden. At the end of the installation, Sandy Morse expressed her pleasure, saying,

> I love the fact that the large images of the mural not only emphasize important aspects of our history, but are also designed to draw people in from a distance. Once closer, the view will discover life events in our County's history in all the wonderful tiles created by the students.
>
> *(Pratt 2009, 7)*

Bucky Seiden added,

> This project has provided the children and all of us who have participated in this incredible adventure, with a truly hands-on journey through our history. We have connected with our past in ways which have . . . enriched our knowledge and our spirit.
>
> *(Pratt 2009, 7)*

Mosaics and Murals

Those connections to the past, drawn through the creation of public art, tie this project to countless other mosaic and mural installations around the world. Some of those projects, like the *Four Seasons* mural in Battery Park City, lower Manhattan, New York, combined a specially designed curriculum with after-school workshops to allow 600 students to create a large-scale ceramic tile mosaic. Other projects, like the Verona Road Mosaic Project in Madison, Wisconsin, called for children and their parents to volunteer to create and design silhouettes to be incorporated into the final installation. *The Story Wall*, an eighteen-meter-long mosaic in Ipswich, Australia, combined the talents of an Aboriginal artist, Nathan Manu; a mosaic artist, Denise Chard; and the students of Blair State School to celebrate "story, art and culture through collaboration"(Fullarton 2014, 13). Another international project, The Guernica Children's Peace Mural Project, began in Tallahassee, Florida, in 1995:

> [Children] created a moveable canvas mural on the theme of peace, which was the size of Picasso's *Guernica*. This was then taken to Japan where children

responded and painted another similar sized mural on the same theme. This process of exchange has mushroomed to include seven more countries.

(Clements 2008, 30)

Still other projects bring many community members of all ages together to effect community change. The Mural Arts Program in Philadelphia, for example, began as part of the Philadelphia Anti-graffiti Network in 1984 and was reorganized in 1996 to focus on creating murals to serve as

the visual products of a powerful and collaborative grassroots process in communities. The mural-making process gives neighborhood residents a voice to tell their individual and collective stories, a way to pass on culture and tradition, and a vehicle to develop and empower local leaders

(City of Philadelphia Mural Arts Program 2014)

Finally, some mosaics and murals, like the seventy-foot-long *Warrensburgh—A Town in Harmony with Its Past*, focus on the history of an area, offering a visual interpretation of the history that community members share. Both art forms—the mosaic and the mural—have long histories. Murals, which are generally large-scale paintings, "are presumed to be the oldest human art form, as cave paintings at numerous ancient human settlements suggest, and can be found all over the world" (Jonsson 2014). Artists like Diego Rivera, Jose Clemente Orozco, and David Alfar Siqueriros used the form to make political statements and, in doing so, inspired countless artists hired by the Works Progress Administration during the Great Depression. Now, murals most frequently serve to bring communities together, often designed according to community needs and executed by community members under the guidance of an artist. In fact, the community mural is "a larger than life representation of a community's histories and hopes" (Chicago Public Art Group 2014).

Mosaics, on the other hand, began as early as the fourth century BCE, in ancient Greece, and were created to beautify the environment. Described as "one of the cornerstones of classical art or the art of antiquity" (Mosaic Art and Art History 2014), mosaics are created through the assemblage of small stones and shells or pieces of ivory, glass, ceramic, or other materials. Throughout the Roman Empire, mosaics adorned the walls and ceilings of important buildings, often showing scenes from mythology or focusing on hunting or beautiful women. Different images and patterns were used throughout the Byzantine Empire and the Iberian Peninsula, with Islamic mosaic and tile art taking on a Moorish tinge. After a decline in popularity during the Middle Ages, mosaics enjoyed a resurgence in the nineteenth century. According to Mickey Goodman, "Today's mosaics are less figurative and more likely to feature texture, mixed materials and brilliant color manipulation. They are also bound to reflect a record of a people" (Goodman 2005). A global phenomenon, mosaics enjoy popularity around the world. The long-lasting nature of the installations certainly recommends them. However, when it comes to public art installations, mosaics are particularly useful because they lend themselves to

FIGURE 8.2 The *Warrensburgh—A Town in Harmony with Its Past* mural, located on the side of the Warrensburgh Historical Society building

Source: Anastasia Pratt

community participation and, due to their durable nature, continue to engage community members over many generations.

Although mosaics and murals are not interchangeable forms, the two media share many of the same goals and ties to the community. Karen Heid describes their social beauty, writing:

> Mural art often attracts public attention to social issues and, in that invitation, they engage people in conversation, and challenge them to understand the community in which they live. Murals can have a dramatic impact on the attitudes of passers-by, especially when those murals are located in areas where people live and work—offering an increased aesthetic to the otherwise mundane daily lives of residents. Through viewers' reactions to, and interactions with the art, the mural becomes a vehicle for encouraging people to know themselves and others in more powerful and meaningful ways.
>
> *(Heid 2012, 32)*

Understanding the Community through Art: Place-Based Learning

Mosaics like *Clinton County History through the Eyes of Its Children* offer viewers a new way of understanding their communities. Beyond sharing a timeline of historical events, the mosaic highlights the variety of life found in this place over several hundred years. First Nations life, for example, appears in a variety of tiles. Some literally illustrate recorded history, with two native guides bringing Samuel de Champlain onto the lake that was later named for him in a canoe. Other tiles give a sense of what life must have been like for those who lived in this area before European colonization and in the early days of settlement. A beautiful native woman, with her child on her back, offers a historically accurate look at the clothing worn by First Nations women of this region and a sense of how women cared for their children.[1] Tiles that recall the various plants and animals from this area surround the people. Those tiles represent robins, blue jays, blackbirds, and crows, but they also remind us of the presence of owls, snow geese, and cardinals. The tiles show brown bears, raccoons, squirrels, coyotes, and wolves, as well as corn, apples, and potatoes. Along with the fish, shown in the river and lake, all tiles combine to offer a glimpse of local life. In the hunting scenes, themselves reminiscent of the oldest murals and mosaics, most of which focused on hunting and gathering activities, we see how the first inhabitants of this area found and prepared their food. We also see how clothes were made and washed, how shelters were erected, how social order and history were maintained (particularly through the presence of totems and other native symbols), and how entertainment was derived from various sporting activities.

Other portions of the mosaic pay special attention to the hundreds of fish species that have lived within Lake Champlain and its tributary watershed. These tiles, which run the length of the mosaic, underscore the portions of local life that have maintained consistent over time. Although the methods of fishing have changed, the activity ties together generations of Clinton County residents, who look to the lake for sustenance and perspective. While that consistency floats beneath, the scenes on the land show changes in technology and in the scale of human life. From the relatively sparse human population of the earliest years, we travel into scenes that show increased human presence. Buildings become more common, with some of the most historically significant structures, like the Old Stone Barracks, the Israel Green Tavern, the Blockhouse, and the Turner Mansion, summoned through children's drawings. So, too, do people. In the central and right portions of the mosaic, we see children playing, women teaching, and men working in the fields and factories. We also see enslaved men, women, and children making their way to freedom in Canada on the Underground Railroad.

These portrayals, beyond offering a sense of the past, occasionally preserve for future generations the visual presence of buildings that would be lost otherwise. Take, for example, the case of the Israel Green Tavern. Built around 1795, the tavern stood on the corner of Bridge and Green Streets in Plattsburgh. It was the site of a victory celebration at the end of the Battle of Plattsburgh, as well as the setting for various local meetings and presentations. Unfortunately, the Israel Green Tavern burned down in 1868. Although it was replaced by a brick structure—the O'Neil Packing House, itself iconic for later generations—the tavern is, in essence, preserved for the community through this mosaic representation. Similarly, the mosaic's portrayal of the Old Stone Barracks offers a vision of the structure's origins. Built in 1838, the structure was designed to house enlisted men at the Plattsburgh Barracks. Originally situated on the lot with a similar structure designed for use by officers—who were assured a lake view by the placement of the buildings—and a horse stable, the barracks was a hub of activity. Yet, generations of Clinton County residents and visitors know the building only as an abandoned block, a building that was gutted by the Air Force in an effort to preserve the historic exterior.[2] *Clinton County History through the Eyes of Its Children* shows a much more vibrant barracks, with an army band playing and troops lined up for parade review. Again, bringing this image to the public preserves the reality of an historic building through its reuse as a kind of canvas for public art.

From the start, the creation of those meanings occurred through collaboration, interaction, and place-based education. Rather than simply dreaming up images, students throughout Clinton County based their drawings and tiles on the stories they heard from local historians, parents, and grandparents. Students researched elements of local history that most interested and inspired them, seeking information along with legend and folklore. That process of creation immersed the students in their place. Perhaps for the first time, children learned that the places where they live and attend school are part of a larger historical narrative, that they are historically and culturally significant. Further, they learned to connect the history of their place with the larger histories of New York State, the United States of America, and the world.

Students at the Peru Central School, for example, learned about the Union, an area between Peru and Au Sable. Settled by Quakers, the Union and the town of Peru were created formally in 1792. From the time of its establishment, the Union served as a hub of abolitionist and anti-slavery activity. In fact, throughout the early nineteenth century, Quakers from Peru, Keeseville, Au Sable, and Champlain served as conductors on the Underground Railroad. Opening their houses and barns to those seeking freedom, these local men and women took an active role in ending slavery in the United States. Their stories and those of the men, women, and children escaping from slavery bring to life the history that students read about in textbooks. With the exposure to stories of local residents like the Keese family, the Smiths, and the Moores—all active in the Underground Railroad—students are able to draw connections between their place and the American history they learn, contextualized within a small rural place like Clinton County, New York.

Similarly, students at Seton Catholic and the Stafford Middle School (Plattsburgh City School District) were able to learn about the significance of Lake Champlain and Plattsburgh within the American Revolution and War of 1812, especially the Battle of Plattsburgh. While history textbooks and state-approved curriculum programs emphasize the great importance of the Revolutionary War, they rarely focus on local connections to the war. Yet, the Battle of Valcour, which occurred on Lake Champlain in October 1776, was incredibly important to the war, leading to the British retreat north for the winter and to the eventual victory of the colonists the next spring. Similarly, the Battle of Plattsburgh, which actually refers to both a land and a naval battle, led to a British defeat and retreat that tipped the tide in favor of the Americans.

For students who live and attend school in Plattsburgh, learning about this history was revolutionary. The children could visit a local building that came under attack during the Battle of Plattsburgh and see the cannon ball still embedded in the wall, as well as walk over the bridge dedicated to the men who fought valiantly to prevent the British from taking control of the city. They could read the stories of the students at the Plattsburgh Academy who were considered too young to join the New York State Militia and the local men who were considered too old or disabled to join. These boys and men, with the help of relatively few regular military troops, held off the British during the land battle. Their history, told as stories, makes the textbook version all the more powerful. In fact, those connections of local history to the larger past, of individuals to the histories of their place, are the most powerful results of the *Clinton County History through the Eyes of Its Children* mosaic. Creating this mosaic gave the students a sense of history; in turn, they offered a visual representation of local history to every person who walks by the mosaic.

Public Art and Historical Meaning

Pierre Nora, in his 1989 essay "Between Memory and History: *Les Lieux de Mémoire*," explains the constant tensions between history and life, arguing that "memory is life . . . history, on the other hand, is the reconstruction, always problematic and incomplete, of what is no longer" (Nora 1989, 8). His theorizations, *lieux de mémoire*, "originate with the sense that there is no spontaneous memory, that we must deliberately create archives, maintain anniversaries, organize celebrations, pronounce eulogies, and notarize bills because such activities no longer occur naturally" (Nora 1989, 12). Thus, Nora asserts, "the quest for memory is the search for one's history" (Nora 1989, 13). To that notion, Chris Healy adds that monuments are "spaces where the possibilities between history and memory can be acted out, spaces that denote sites of history and can connote environments of memory" (Healy 1997, 26).

Every bit as durable and long lasting as monuments, mosaics like *Clinton County History through the Eyes of Its Children* do this work. They create spaces for discussions of history, for questions to be raised, and for memories to be formed. Certainly the students who created this mosaic, now more than seven years older, have a different relationship with the installation than they did when they were sitting in classrooms learning about local history and creating ceramic tiles. Now they can point to the mosaic and say with confidence, "I made that." Their ownership of the project ties them more firmly to the county's past, and the mosaic offers others a chance to learn about the past as well. The students can also explain the mosaic, both as a work of art and as a work of history, to those around them, showing their increased visual and historical literacy. Even those who were not involved in the creation of the mosaic can learn from it. An interpretive panel on the site offers a broad-strokes explanation of the content of the mosaic and the history of the area. Website and archival materials are available to visitors who move from the mosaic into the Clinton County

Government Building and the Historian's Office. The power of the installation is that as a work of art it effectively shares stories—the mosaic gives "a visual voice to a particular community" (Chicago Public Art Group 2014).[3]

At a certain level, though, no additional information is required to find meaning in the mosaic. If, as Paul Clements argues, "the primary concern and function of public art is to enable wider access to culture, and participation by all members of society" (Clements 2008, 21), then the mosaic's very existence is meaningful for people who live in or visit Clinton County, New York. Those who stop and look at the mosaic can immerse themselves, even for just a little while, in an accounting of the county's past, of its collective memories; even those who simply pass by cannot help but experience a flash of that collective past. That experience of the past is essential, as it helps us—as a community—define ourselves.

One of the major questions that arose from the creation of this mosaic was, "Where are the women?" Very few of the accounts of Clinton County's past included women. The most complete history of the county, Duane Hamilton Hurd's *A History of Clinton and Franklin Counties, New York* (1880), goes into great detail about the settlement of the county, from Samuel de Champlain's arrival in 1609 to subsequent generations of land grants. The development of churches, businesses, and volunteer organizations are all explained thoroughly, with listings of those who served as pastors, managers, and leaders included. Yet the few women who are included in that accounting of the past are referred to principally as the wife or daughter of a man who is named—not according to their own accomplishments.

Despite their absence in the historical record, women are represented in the mosaic. Students created tiles to show ordinary life, which involves men and women, children and adults. Thus they helped correct the historic record through their tiles. The community at large, then, can see a more balanced representation of itself and add to the stories of its past. One of the most delightful results of the mosaic's unveiling was the increased contribution of stories, photographs, and documents to the Clinton County Historian's Office, the Clinton County Historical Association, and all of the local history museums and societies. After seeing a portion of our past, it seems, residents wanted to ensure that future generations had access to the materials to construct the next century of the county's history.

Conclusion

While a large-scale project like *Clinton County History through the Eyes of Its Children* is not possible for every school or municipality, the principles of collaborative public art and place-based education are. Occurring through the immersion of students in "local heritage, cultures, landscapes, opportunities and experiences, using these as a foundation for the study of language arts, mathematics, social studies, science and other subjects across the curriculum" (What is Place-Based Education 2015), place-based education "fosters students' connection to place and creates vibrant partnerships between schools and communities. It boosts student achievement and improves environmental, social and economic vitality" (Place-based

Education Evaluation Collaborative 2010). On the local level, immersion in one's place can lead to any number of projects. Students, with the help of artists and historians, can certainly create mosaics like the one described here. However, they can also take on oral history projects, dramatic performances, and environmental stewardship.

When place-based education is combined with a public-art project, the results can be astounding. According to the Chicago Public Art Group (2014), "Community-generated public art builds social capital, the sense of connectedness among members of a community. Public art projects can transform bland public spaces into visually exciting places that encourage civic dialogue." Further, "collaborative public art projects create opportunities for intergenerational work and communication, for youths to contribute positively to their local environment, and for individuals to use their creative talents for the public good." Olivia Gude and Jon Pounds explain,

> the goal of community dialogue for a public art project is not to come up with a single, simple narrative statement. Through the dialogue, participants identify images and concepts that make up the complex, crisscrossing ideas that are in play at a given time and place.
>
> *(Chicago Public Art Group 2014)*

Clinton County History through the Eyes of Its Children transformed a brick wall into a story of the past, creating a site-specific work of art. It connected people of several generations—the oldest contributor, a local historian, was ninety-two; the youngest, a fourth grade student at NACS, was nine. It shows the past from multiple perspectives, correcting omissions in the historical record and showing daily life from the perspective of young people who live in the places pictured. Pedagogically, it offered students a chance to "understand the ways in which the spaces they inhabit shape the intellect and spirit of human beings" and to "recognize that places in the 21st century are created (preserved or manufactured) by human choice and effort" (Gude 2014). Most importantly, it offered the community a chance to "come together to research the past, reflect on the present, and imagine their future" (Chicago Public Art Group 2014).

Notes

1 Ray Fadden, Tehanetorens, founder of the Six Nations Indian Museum in Onchiota, New York, worked with artist Sue Burdick Young to verify the clothing, decorative elements, and comportment of the figure. More information about the museum can be found at its website, http://www.sixnationsindianmuseum.com.

2 Locals recently learned that the building was purchased by the Valcour Brewing Company, which plans to restore the building according to the State Historic Preservation Office guidelines.

3 Christina Ralls, in her 2009 essay in the *Public Historian*, explains, "Art, though underutilized, can be an effective tool for sharing previously untold stories and documenting personal recollections" See Christina Ralls (November 2009), "One Mosaic, Many Voices: A Reflection on the Baltimore '68 Mosaic Monument," *The Public Historian* 31(4): 55.

References

Chicago Public Art Group, 2014. "Community Public Art Guide: Making Murals, Mosaics, Sculptures, and Spaces." http://www.cpag.net/guide/. Accessed 31 December 2014.

"City of Philadelphia Mural Arts Program." 2014. http://muralarts.org/about/history. Accessed 31 December 2014.

Clements, Paul. 2008. "Public Art: Radical, Functional or Democratic Methodologies." *Journal of Visual Arts Practice*, 17(1): 19–35.

Hurd, Duane Hamilton. 1880. *A History of Clinton and Franklin Counties, New York*. Philadelphia, PA: J.W. Lewis and Co.

Fullarton, Lee. 16 July 2014. "Story Wall Inspires Great Art." *Ipswich Advertiser*, p 13. EBSCO, Points of View Reference Center (apn.VJ25QA05).

Goodman, Mickey. November/December 2005. "Tile: Mosaics: History's Reporter." *Veranda*, 19(6): 114 and 266. EBSCO (18784028).

Gude, Olivia. 2014. "Psycho-Aesthetic Geography in Art Education." *Chicago Public Art Group*. http://www.cpag.net/guide/5/5_pages/5_1.htm. Accessed 31 December 2014.

Healy, Chris. 1997. *From the Ruins of Colonialism: History as Social Memory*. Cambridge: Cambridge University Press.

Heid, Karen. December 2012. "Peace by Piece." *Ceramics Monthly*. 60(10): 32.

Jonsson, Eric. 2014. "A Brief History of Murals and Mural Painting." http://www.jonssonsworld.com/A_Brief_History_of_Murals_and_Mural_Painting.htm. Accessed 31 December 2014.

"Mosaic Art and Art History." 2014. http://www.arthistory.net/artstyles/mosaic/mosaic1.html. Accessed 10 December 2014.

Nora, Pierre. Spring 1989. "Between Memory and History: Les Lieux de Memoire." *Representations*, 26: 7–24.

"Place-based Education Evaluation Collaborative." 2010. *The Benefits of Place-Based Education: A Report from the Place-Based Education Evaluation Collaborative*. 2nd ed. http://tinyrl.com/PEECBrochure. Accessed 18 December 2014.

Pratt, Anastasia. 12 August 2009. *Clinton County History through the Eyes of Its Children: A Mosaic Project*. Clinton County, NY: Commemorative Booklet.

Ralls, Christina. November 2009. "One Mosaic, Many Voices: A Reflection on the Baltimore '68 Mosaic Monument." *The Public Historian*, 31(4): 54–9.

"What is Place-Based Education?" 2014. http://www.promiseofplace.org/what_is_pbe. Accessed 11 January 2015.

"What is Public Art?" 2014. http://associationforpublicart.org/public-art-gateway/what-is-public-art/. Accessed 10 December 2014.

9

YELLOW-STAR HOUSES

A Community-Generated Living History Project in Budapest

Ildikó Réka Báthory-Nagy

In the middle of Europe, the small country of Hungary, a former German ally, not only lost World War II but also had to account for more than 400,000 victims of the Holocaust. The systematic and organized deportation of Jews started in the countryside and then moved into the city of Budapest. On June 16, 1944, the mayor of Budapest issued a decree that set aside almost 2,000 apartment buildings, into which 220,000 marked persons were obliged to move. They were forced to wear a yellow Star of David on their clothing, leave their own apartments by midnight on June 21st, and move into one of the designated apartment buildings in the city also identified with a yellow star. They are called the "yellow-star" houses.

This network of yellow-star houses was unique in the history of the Nazi-perpetrated Holocaust in Europe. The houses served the same purpose as the ghettos, a preparatory stage for deportation. For half a year, everyone passing by could see precisely who the persecuted Jews were, and where they lived. In the following months, thousands of them died on death marches, thousands were shot to death, and thousands more died during the siege of Budapest. In Budapest at that time, an astonishingly large number of apartment buildings bore the yellow star. Of these, 1,600 former yellow-star houses are still remaining, but barely a trace of their past role remains in public memory (1600 egykori csillagos ház előtt emlékeznek a 70 évvel ezelőtti kényszerköltöztetésekre 2014).

To mark the seventieth anniversary, the Hungarian government announced 2014 as the Memorial Year of the Holocaust. Several centralized events were launched, organized by national institutions—though they were largely judged as having contradictory messages and were met with much public disapproval. As a counterpoint to the centralized governmental program and official narrative, many non-governmental organizations, including the Open Society Archives (OSA), organized events and set up websites to call attention to the until-now invisible network of yellow-star houses (Kalas 2014). This project resulted in an extraordinary alternative narrative generated by thousands of residents across the city who came together, many for the first time, to examine and discuss extremely painful events from the past. OSA provided the concept and framework, but the community generated the images and stories.

OSA, part of Central European University, was established in 1995 and has one of the biggest repositories of paper and digital documents of the Cold War Era and also on the history of human rights. The archive is not only a collector but also a driver of scientific research, forming and implementing new research and evaluation methods. OSA is also a mentor to and leader of the civic community in many areas. The obscure history of the yellow-star houses was thrust into the spotlight in 2015, when a massive trove of census documents that had been hidden in a wall—the information that provided the very basis for determining the yellow-star houses—was found totally by accident in the course of the renovation of an apartment in downtown Budapest (OSA Launches Yellow-Star Houses Website and Public Program 2014).

A Day in a Yellow-Star House, Then and Today

In the spring of 1944, the mayor's Habitation Office and the Ministry of Internal Affairs identified the buildings and the method of moving and collecting Jewish residents. By that time, each Hungarian citizen had a certificate of origin that was required by the anti-Semitic laws established between the wars. Therefore it was clear who they were, where they lived, and what they had. In June 1944, the families declared to be Jewish were required to pack and move their personal belongings into their new homes in five days.

The houses soon became packed and overcrowded. Multiple families, sometimes between twenty to thirty persons, shared an apartment. On many occasions, housemates had been strangers to each other prior to the move. There was insufficient space and furniture for everyone. Some had to sleep under the piano or by the kitchen stove. Jews were not permitted to have visitors or to talk through the windows. Every day there was a headcount and curfew. They could leave the house only once a day for a couple of hours. Jews could only buy food from certain stores (Frojimovics and Komoróczy 1999). In case of bombing, there was a separate place for them in the cellar shelters. The control and organization of the people's life was in the hand of the superintendent, who was supposed to administer the rules and prosecute people who disobeyed. Even in these conditions, there were few conflicts among the families.

Of the original yellow-star house residents, some survived the Holocaust, returned, and still live in the same apartment building. Some survivors were simply unable to face the painful memories of the same place and did not return. Most of the extant yellow-star houses are still used as apartment residences. Certain neighborhood shops and local institutions are still remaining. Many of the houses have tenants who are survivors of the Holocaust, moved into the house after the war, and do not know about the history of their house. Many of them do not want to know. Katalin Berger-Frankel, who moved to Budapest after the war into a former yellow-star house, indicates:

> 'I am afraid of the past. I have spent the last seventy years with trying to forget the past. Imagine, the best period of my life, when I was a young woman, I have spent it in a concentration camp and then, after the war, with my broken, ill and hopeless family. I do not want to remember.'
>
> *Stated by the Holocaust survivor Katalin in an interview*

This is a common attitude—many survivors are unwilling to relive the past. Some of the people in the postwar generations are interested in learning but are unable to ask about it, being shut out of this past. Some of the younger generations are also afraid of the past, often due to fear of an unsavory history. Others are afraid of the present, since passive anti-Semitism is still an underlying part of society. In this context, an average intellectual person with a typical interest in social or historic issues might reject participation in a project pertaining to the Holocaust since it might reveal an unwanted part of the past.

Generations of Silence

Until recently, Hungarian society has not spent much effort reflecting on its association with the Holocaust. After World War II, the first priority was to rebuild the country, to restart the economy, and to punish war criminals. During the communist dictatorship, the official version of the history and also the protocol of reminiscence was idealized and disfigured by the then-prevalent ideology. According to this ideology, there was no intention to start a conversation on the role and feelings of the society on the Holocaust or the maltreatment of Jews. There was no intention to start any kind of common dialogue—which would have referred to an undesirable imperialist and capitalist society. A whole nation grew up socialized not to talk about this history.

Since the collapse of the communist regime, Hungarians have still been unable to face collective or individual culpability in the Holocaust. There is a common agreement on the guilt and responsibility of the Nazi regime as well as the Hungarian Arrow Cross party, which was allied with the Nazis. There were several cases at the national and international level, in which actors of the Hungarian Holocaust were sentenced, convicted, and penalized. But we have yet to question the responsibility of society as a whole—that is, the massive number of bystanders who stood by, silent and frozen without trying to prevent the massacre. Historians revealed plenty of facts, proving that the Hungarian government and also numerous residents not only served the ruling authority of German invaders but were also keen on serving well, even when it was unnecessary.

One example is the network of yellow-star houses, a Hungarian intervention to make deportation more effective. Numerous documentary pieces, diaries, and also significant historical publications provided information about how people lived during the German occupation (Somorjai 2015). We know many details about the everyday life and also many details about the personal struggles of the non-persecuted. As a Hungarian, I wonder: Did my grandmother or grandfather know what was going on? How did they feel about it? How can we live with that today? The documentary movie *Once They Were Neighbours* (2005) by Zsuzsanna Varga tried to answer similar questions by reporting the reminiscence by non-Jewish neighbors of the historic events of the Holocaust in Kőszeg, a small Hungarian border town (Varga 2005). The Christian witnesses of the past events describe and tell the story through their own testimonies. Many of them still struggle to define their personal role and responsibility, even struggling with understanding their own anti-Semitism.

Time is short for comforting the survivors, due to their age. Today's politicians also have an agenda, distorting the history of the Hungarian Holocaust in order to gain political power in the present, especially by romanticizing the role of the anti-Semite Governor Miklós Horthy. According to András Lénárt, passive anti-Semitism is still endemic in contemporary Hungarian society. From this social and political context, it is hardly encouraged to ask the jarring questions. This is why there is so little reflection on Hungarian participation in the Holocaust. We cannot continue without confronting the past, without honestly discussing Hungarian society's role in the Holocaust, in order to work out a process of healing and reconciliation from this shared social trauma.

The Project Envisioned

In January 2014, OSA launched a series of community formed and supported memorial events that could serve to confront Hungary's shared past with dignity and honesty—including the yellow-star houses project. The project's aim was not only to display the history of the Holocaust in Hungary but also to remind today's society of the tragedy. As everyone is a survivor of the Holocaust in one way or another, it is essential to face up to the responsibility of the national political position and also society of the time. One of the main goals of the project was to strengthen one's shared moral responsibility toward both the past and the present: "we want to emphasize the historical and moral indefensibility of the recurring mantras of post-Communist right-wing historical revisionism: the contemporary glorification of the interwar period, the trivialization of the role of anti-Semitism" (Yellow-Star Houses 2014), as the project's founders described it.

The basic idea of the project was to promote an open and inclusive preparation process for a commemoration event, while supporting and gathering the works of voluntary participants. During preparation, local communities would democratically form in the interest of discovering new information about the past. The focal point of the project would be commemorating the event through community-driven investigations of what had been hidden since 1945. As the collection of data was an additional goal of the project, personal reflections, documents, and photos were gathered and published using a variety of digital media (Somorjai

2015). Even with a clear vision of goals and framework, organizers felt they were making a stab in the dark. How many people could be engaged? How many of the engaged could be really activated? Could dignity and honesty be managed through such an event?

Structure of the Project: Realization

OSA provided the infrastructure of the project through social networking and digital media. First, a team of professionals in OSA collected facts and documents, creating an "archive of the past" for the project. Among the first steps, the archive launched a dedicated yellow-star houses website in January 2014. All information was published on the website in Hungarian and English (Jones 2014). One of the results of the data analyzed was the interactive map of the yellow-star houses (Figure 9.1), which presented how numerous the buildings are in the city.

The map shows the location of the buildings and what they look like today. It is supplemented with numerous documents, including the relevant decrees by the Fascist regime, a list of houses, a timeline, glossary, and recollections. The website even offers a collection of masterpieces of Hungarian Holocaust literature, composed of poems, essays, and diaries (Jones 2014). Using the navigation tools, visitors can view the buildings at street, district, and city levels. As an interactive site with user-driven content, visitors could submit their recollections or personal stories.

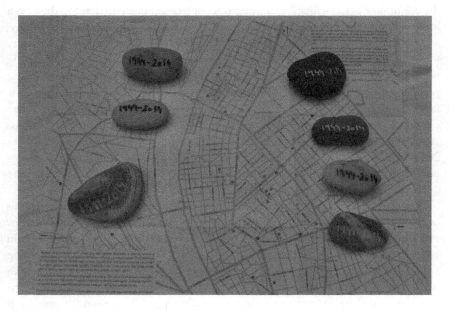

FIGURE 9.1 A printed map of the yellow-star houses

Source: Andrea Gallé

Meanwhile, organizing a Facebook group and an associated event started the oral history information collection and community building (Jones 2014). An international community of collaborators was formed in order to search for new information from abroad, giving an interface for personal documents and reflections to be shared (A. L. B. 2014).

As active data collection started, so did recruitment for community involvement. First, the communities of each former yellow-star house were informed about the project and the opportunity to get involved. The buildings were marked with a sticker of a yellow star, similar to seventy years ago. The star marker indicated to the public the house's historical role, and an information panel placed inside the house explained the details of the project and the possibilities for involvement. OSA invited the current residents of the former yellow-star houses to organize a collective memorial event on June 21, 2014, on the seventieth anniversary. The number of voluntary organizing communities increased daily. After registering, the house could join the project, and residents were invited to develop their own event and research their addresses' own role in the past (OSA Launches Yellow-Star Houses Website and Public Program 2014).

The project's success can be attributed in part to its balance of organization and spontaneity. OSA determined in advance when and where events would take place, which gave the project the necessary foundation to be successful. But it was the voluntary organizer communities who worked out the details of events. The network of former yellow-star houses provided the physical and geographic setting. OSA organized all events for one single day, June 21st. All other details were left to the communities to facilitate. Communities got free assistance to develop their own localized program. Reading aloud the text of the original yellow-star house decree, a short musical performance, singing, reading aloud a literary text, holding a few moments of silence, or placing a simple commemorative plaque on the building were some of the numerous suggestions. The hodgepodge of events included drama performances and the singing of the anthem of the European Union by a voluntary chorus, accompanied by the Budapest Festival Orchestra led by Adam Fischer, a famous conductor whose family were among the Holocaust's victims. Famous artists and actors were involved in many places where events occurred (Krezinger 2014). The date of June 21st also coincides with the annual "Night of the Museums" festival, and some prominent museums and cultural institutes integrated the commemoration into their program.

The important role given to each volunteer to inform, gather and organize his or her own community established trust in the project; it would be something for everyone. One volunteer from each house undertook the role of the manager in order to involve other residents, keep contact with OSA, conduct research, develop and execute the program, organize participants and visitors, and document what was accomplished. Social media and personal communications helped the communities find their audience and partners for the events. The event was free from formal ceremony, so was rather small, simple, and personal—a memorable event for all involved.

FIGURE 9.2 A yellow-star house commemoration in a courtyard with a reading by actor
József Székhelyi

Source: Ildikó Réka Báthory-Nagy

The Community the Project Formed

As weeks went by, more and more people entered the Facebook group, registered
on the website, and showed willingness to participate in the project, resulting in
an unexpectedly large number of people coming from all varieties of nationalities,
religions, ages, and educational levels. The project reached survivors and former
residents of the yellow-star houses across the world. The Facebook group was (and
still is) supporting the dissemination of subjective personal histories. The interface
was like a developing book of family legends and also served as a practical guide for
the local organizers (Jones 2014).

OSA organized meetings to support community volunteers with preparation
by giving social and technical help. These meetings, called "residential assemblies,"
were the forums where the executive board of the project shaped the methodology
of the work, adapting to the changing environment. For example, support staff and
volunteers not only learned how to perform historical research and event planning
better, but also how to discover their personal roles in "Budapest 1944": participants took on roles as members of a post-Holocaust society, as residents of former
yellow-star houses, and as volunteers for memorial events (OSA Launches Yellow-
Star Houses Website and Public Program 2014).

Volunteers came from many different social classes, ages, and nationalities; they had a variety of personal motivations and drives. Experiences included the reviewing of movies, documentaries, books, and photographic exhibitions, and visiting museums. Impacts through these documentary experiences still kept participants as passive outside observers, however with many expressing thoughts such as, "Horrible what happened, but it has nothing to do with me." In Budapest, everyone underwent the Holocaust in one way or another. Each family has its own part of the period, its own tragedies and hidden history. The tragedy exists, even if we do not know how we are affected. There were two major groups of volunteers active in event organizing. The victims' survivors formed one group, along with other Jewish families who faced personal tragedies in the past. The other consisted of curious non-Jews who desired commemoration. The mixture of the two kinds of volunteers resulted in outstanding programs, artworks, and discussions, creating a community of our own. There was one common purpose—do something to end the antipathy.

A Memorial of Community-Generated Visual Art

Several art pieces were presented exclusively for this event: sculptures, concerts, music pieces, paintings, films, and other visual expressions. Performances supported the speeches and discussions to start collective conversation on Holocaust remembrance. As a one-day event, it gave an opportunity to introduce temporary art performances and exhibits of various kinds. Presentations of dramatized moments from the past and present Jewish life were common. Concerts, recitations of Hungarian poetry masterpieces, as well as reflections by ordinary people made up the programs. Some houses showed a short film on the site, mixed with archival pictures on exhibit. Other houses placed a memorial relief sculpture or plaque on the wall.

Artists came from many countries: Hungary, Poland, Ukraine, Germany, the United States, Italy, Portugal, and Spain. The message that the artists shared was universal, emphasizing personal participation. Many artworks were meant to reflect on Jewish tradition. Traditional music was one of the more common tools to support commemoration events. Soloists, duets, and ensembles of all kinds played classical, contemporary, and traditional music, including vocal and acoustical pieces. Recitations of historic documents and Holocaust poems, combined with klezmer melodies, created a striking contrast when performed for the audience.

The events were also an opportunity to explore Jewish cuisine. Several sites offered cooking demonstrations by community members and tastings of traditional dishes. An innovative approach to understanding everyday life in the former ghettos was to taste the foods of the time. Starving housewives at the Auschwitz concentration camp reminisced about delicious homemade meals and former family dinners. It became their habit to share recipes to take the edge off their appetite. One of them noted the recipes on small pieces of paper, using pencil parts. This collection of recipes was found and published in a book. It also served as a basis for an alternative theater production by Golem Theatre. Other yellow-star house commemorations involved cooking some dishes. At one event, they offered food created by a well-known gastro blogger Zsófia Mautner to the visitors, and the food was accompanied by a historical piece performed by well-known Hungarian actor and editor Róbert Alföldi.

An Ongoing Documentation

Pictures of dozens of historic documents and photographs were collected and offered by OSA for informational purposes at many yellow-star house sites. Exhibitions of prints, hung on the dilapidated interior walls of courtyards and staircases, captured the attention of visitors. Some sites have not been changed since 1944, without a single renovation to the buildings or courtyards. Placing historic photographs on a wall dating back to the same period created an authentic effect.

Photographers, such as a reporter for the Hungarian online portal *Index*, János Bődey, made a documentary report of former yellow-star house residents, taking pictures in the houses where they once lived. In Bődey's report, he presented a collection of photos of mortified but peaceful elderly people and their tragic personal histories. The pictures by Bődey used light, shadow, and symmetry to emphasize the emotion of the depicted story. The report was acknowledged and rewarded by Hungarian and World Press photo exhibitions.

Photographs and films had two primary intentions: to represent the current condition of the buildings and to find connections to past events or persons through the use of period materials, people, music, and other cultural artifacts. Many short movies were made to re-create the march, the moving-in, or the daily life of the yellow-star house inhabitants. One such short firm shows a nine-year-old boy repeatedly running down an old rickety staircase.

Uncle Bandi's Street: Video Projection at Dohány Street 57, 59, and 61, by Daniel Besnyő and Dénes Beviz

This video projection was presented in the Jewish Quarter of Budapest, very close to the renowned Dohány Street Synagogue. The screen of the movie was the facade of three former yellow-star houses. The three large Beaux-Arts style residential buildings of the quarter became giant screens for dramatic effect. Uncle Bandi, a 105-year-old Jewish man, who was born and lived his entire life in this house, briefly explains his personal history. While listening to the faint and hoarse autobiography of an elderly man, the audience is invited to learn about the life saga of the storyteller. The story is illustrated with oversized moving and expanding quotes and images of the period. Heightening the drama, a five-times larger than life marching queue of foot soldiers appear on tripled screens, wobbling and waving down from the facade to the street, giving the Nazi salute of *sieg heil*. To make the trauma tolerable, in several points, photographic imagery went into pieces, turned over into vortices, and floated out into space. At the end of the film, only a granulose screen remained, with the white background noise of television static. Due to the temporary film art exhibit, three completely mundane urban buildings gained significance for a short period of time, attracting the attention of passers-by.

The Commemoration in Our House

The house where I live is situated in the thirteenth district of Budapest. Our quarter, called Újlipótváros (New Leopold City), is located in the north part of the metropolis, next to the outer ring road, built along the Danube River. This is the youngest part of the city center, having been developed at the end of the nineteenth century when industrial factories and mills were built. By the end of the nineteenth century, many mills were closed, and new development trends reached the area: streets were designed with geometrical order and residential blocks were developed, all guided through a master plan. The urban character of the quarter is based on the plan of 1888 and the zoning regulations of 1928. Five-story tall tenement houses with closed staircases were built, all in the same architectural manner. Buildings were placed next to the streets, fully occupying the street side of the lot, completely framing the block by buildings, creating a high urban density. In most of the blocks, a relatively large open space was left in the middle for a yard, often containing a hidden garden, giving a great contrast to the busy street life.

The architectural character of the neighborhood is a mixture of Beaux-Arts, Art Deco, and Bauhaus styles. Újlipótváros is highly supported by urban infrastructure and social amenities. Craftsmen's workshops, restaurants, cafés, shops, boutiques, and art galleries have occupied basements and street-level spaces of buildings. Many of the businesses have been continuously present since the end of World War II. This quarter of nearly 40,000 inhabitants was always a district characterized by upper middle class people, many of them Jews. During World War II, many buildings were among the *protected houses*, which were used by different European embassies. Jewish residents of these houses were relatively hidden and had more of a chance to escape to safer countries. Swedish ambassador Raul Wallenberg, Italian Giorgio Perlasca, and the Swiss consul Carl Lutz played significant roles in assisting hundreds of Jews to escape and survive. Names of streets and local institutions commemorate their humanity. Due to the population, yellow-star houses were also densely a part of the urban fabric. The former yellow-star house where I live is nothing out of the ordinary: an average five-story, eclectic-style residential tenement from the 1930s with twenty-two apartments and a courtyard in the back.

When I first saw the yellow-star sticker placed by OSA on the gate, I was shocked. It made me recall documentary movies of the Holocaust, and it inspired me to search for its meaning. Getting to know the program, I registered and became the volunteer organizer of our building's participation. First I made a poster announcing my commitment and invited the neighbors to discuss the topic and the possibilities of our collective participation.

The yellow star sticker from OSA and my poster were immediately removed. This began my determination. I stood for a moment and revised my thoughts on how to continue. I started informal conversations on the staircase with neighbors so that I could gather information about the building and its formal residents. I found out there are still three Holocaust survivors living among us in the building. Although none of them were taken away from this location, I wanted to get their approval for my commitment and the proposal for the commemoration. All three

survivors supported me in this undertaking, but none of them wanted to participate. According to organizers from other buildings, this was a common attitude of
survivors. They do not want to be in the spotlight, nor do they want to remember.
I accepted their wishes, which gave me more courage to continue.

Seven of us from the building came together for the task. However, I was the
one with a strong vision of the program. The others only wanted to participate in
preparation and documentation. As Dóra Patakfalvi, a young journalist and one of
the organizers from our building, explained:

> It was not a question for me to participate. . . . I felt from the very beginning,
> I do want to be in such a community event, which appropriately commemo-
> rates my house's survivors and deported residents . . . There was only one
> fact [that] counted: seventy years ago thousands of people were stigmatized,
> spoiled and deported to death in my country, in my city, in my street and—in
> my house. Commemoration is the only tool in the hand of a human to use
> after decades, to fall into silence for some minutes in honor of victims and to
> extend a hand to the survivors.

My neighbor, Katalin Szentmiklósi, turned out to have a very special personal history related to the Holocaust. She was born in 1944, and afterwards, her parents
were taken away. She never got the chance to know her parents. The pictures she
showed me, taken shortly after her birth on a balcony, were all that she had. The
picture (Figure 9.3) showed a young couple with a small baby with bright and

FIGURE 9.3 The Szentmiklósi family picture, circa 1944

Source: Katalin Szentmiklósi

shiny eyes on a face full of hope and happiness. Her mother was a Transylvanian Jew and her father a Swab from Baranya County. Her father did not let his wife be taken away alone; he followed her to defend her. They both felt they were Hungarians.

We decided to develop our program around her family picture and the story of her personal tragedy—to never to know one's parents. Our proposal was to point out the responsibility of everyone to refuse political orders at appropriate times.

Katalin, who had lately her seventieth birthday, indicated:

> Yes, I AM affected—like each of us in this country. You might don't know about it . . . My personal goal was to open one's eye and not let them be led like sheep, but to act like an individual. Not to be ashamed having one's own ideas and to recognize the persuading purpose of politics! That's why I participated!

She continued:

> We have already heard plenty of sad stories and, yes, I understand everybody who wants to tell and cry. But much more important to have a common message for the future generation: think and make individual decisions!
>
> You know, if I think of the time before this madness had been started . . . here in Pest Swabs, Jews, Slovaks and other nationalities lived and worked together, none of them had a thought not to be Hungarian. . . . They built the country. For example, the medicine factories made some industry world famous. Then they built our loved capital Budapest. If we think of the construction of Andrássy Avenue or the quarter of Újlipótváros where we live now, all were born and became famous by the needs of Swabish and Jewish industry makers. In that context, it is incomprehensible how they could be made to be each others' executioners!

To develop our short program, we decided to be personal, talk less, listen and ask more, show pictures, and develop a temporary art piece. The two-hour long program consisted of reciting aloud the former decrees, projecting historic pictures on the wall of our staircase, and showing a short film in one of the apartments, illustrating everyday life at the yellow-star houses. The main element of the program was the short speech by Katalin and the explanation of her family picture.

My personal motivations to become an organizer of such an event were multifold. First of all, I believed it important to learn about and teach others about this tragic period in Hungarian history. Second, I sought the opportunity to instigate a community conversation on a topic causing such frustration, even today. I imagine that the silent will begin to talk. In order to facilitate conversation, we furnished the courtyard as a living room, with chairs from our dining rooms and living rooms in order to create a comfortable setting for the people willing to speak with us. Third,

I, as a member of TÁJÉK Land Art Group, planned to develop an art piece together with my neighbors. We titled the art piece *Blank Line*.

Blank Line: A Participatory Art Piece

A dotted line of pebble stones, collected from the Danube River by hand, each washed and precisely placed, mark where thousands were executed. The yellow stars and black signs on the stones mark the period between 1944 and 2014.

Neighbor and voluntary organizer Dóra Patakfalvi remembered:

> The preparation itself made a deep impact on me. As the stones started to form a row in our courtyard the atmosphere became more and more intimate. And when it reached the street through the open gate, [people] could not pass without stopping and staring at it. Then I thought our commemoration overreaches our residential community.

The line of stones, beginning at the staircase, leads the way from the building out to the street. The stones are a dotted line to the courtyard, the actual site of the commemoration held in the building. The present residents of the house placed the stones in the courtyard, which attracted the attention of passersby and provoked acknowledgement of the event. The line of pebbles is straight but uneven, suggesting a line of hopeless and exhausted people of different ages and conditions, forced to march to an unknown destination.

Zsuzsanna Berman-Bagonyai, a local resident of the quarter, described her reaction to the art installation:

> First I saw the row of stones in front of the building, leading to the courtyard. Then I saw the handwritten year numbers on the stones: 1944–2014. Then I noticed there are hundreds of marked stones. All washed and marked one by one. It was very touching to see the commitment of the organizers, the emotional energy they put in the project, the attention they put on every detail of the scene. . . . It was symbolic to see children playing with the stones—who received the best example of remembering and making others remember.

At the end of the commemoration program, participants were invited to take a stone home as a souvenir of the experience.

About eighty visitors came to see our program, many of them from our neighborhood, including secondary school students, grandparents, and parents with children. Some visitors came from other countries. Just before starting our program, an elderly man and his wife stopped in front of the open gate. He turned to me and started to talk the most natural way I have ever heard: "Good evening! My name is John Kessler. I came from Israel to be here at today's events. I was a child in this

FIGURE 9.4 Marked and washed pebble stones from the Danube

Source: Andrea Gallé

yellow-star house in 1944. I spent a couple of months here and then was taken away . . . Oh . . . but I don't remember the building." He stared at the facade and, again, the courtyard. After a couple of seconds of shock, I started to explain that the gate was replaced and now it has a totally different character. I started to explain how the surroundings had changed, trying to comfort him while bringing back

FIGURE 9.5   *Blank Line* art installation facilitated by TÁJÉK Land Art Group

Source: Gábor Báthory

his memories. He was continuously staring at the courtyard's yellow brick paving, which remained from the initial construction of the building, the pavement that was there in 1944. After some seconds of silence, I invited them to come inside for a while. They excused themselves; being very tired, they decided to go back to their hotel. They waved and slowly walked away.

FIGURE 9.6 Children collect marked stones from *Blank Line*

Source: Andrea Gallé

Dóra Patakfalvi commented:

> The most touching moment for me was when an old man, a survivor told
> his story of deportation. Ware Wagen, Auschwitz, Doctor Mengele—we were
> numbly listening how these common words were sounding through our

courtyard. After a while I could only stare at my chair where the man sat. The
chair I had brought down from my kitchen one hour earlier. . . .

Attila Győr, an architectural historian, shared this reflection:

I always look at the buildings. I have to look at buildings as part of my work.
Some other times I look at them for the love of it. I have observed and taken note
of them. A building consists of stones, shaped nicely or less nicely. . . . Rarely
houses start to talk. Interesting. Basically everything is interesting—who lived
there, how tanks got through the gate, why it was reconstructed, how old the
fig tree is and so. . . . These are all included in the house and [are] interesting
because they are part of it. Small marked pebble stones . . . lead out to the street
from one of the yellow-star houses. The house could not hold them, these had
to reach out. These could not be held. I don't remember how the building
looked . . .

Reflections and Outcomes on a Community-Made Narrative

More than 7,000 volunteers participated and generated their own memorial project
in over 130 locations across the city. The people of Budapest and their guests—
which included former and current yellow-star house residents, elderly and young,
survivors and their families, friends and neighbors, housekeepers and shopkeepers,
theater groups and musicians, actors and actresses, dancers and singers, poets and
writers, architects and landscape architects, historians, civic groups and public figures,
cultural institutes, and foreign embassies—held commemorations to remember this
tragic and shameful chapter of Budapest's past. An online television channel streamed
footage, and voluntary photographers recorded the events. Over 7,000 volunteers
for a community project is an extraordinary level of participation. That this was realized through the power of community and the finance of each participant, without
national institutional or financial support, made the project even more significant.
The continuously growing project and the memorial day gained wide international
coverage; it was published in several important journals, blogs, and websites (A. L. B.
2014; Walker 2014). One of the organizers and the head of the archives, István Rév,
highlighted the project results as the story of the yellow-star houses became an integral, undeniable, and permanent part of the city's history and memory:

Budapest came alive with commemorative events planned and held by the
people of this city. . . . It is up to us to remember, to understand and to comprehend the past: this is our shared moral, civic and human duty. Our shared
history, and thus this city, are ours.
(OSA Launches Yellow-Star Houses Website and Public Program 2014)

For me, the event was an endless conversation, where special and meaningful communication occurred—a dialogue where information flowed forward and

back, like on opposite lanes of a highway, with one lane having the reflections of the past and in the other the monologues of the present. It was not casual small talk, although some minced words at certain moments. Perhaps some conversations are still too difficult to have due to shocking details, confronting and owning up to the past. "The past was never so real. Never so close to me before," said Dóra Patakfalvi. By taking part in such a participatory event, the community and individuals experienced a great benefit. From the contribution of participants, new documents of the yellow-star houses and numerous personal stories of the families lived were published. The Facebook group has networked with families of survivors, sharing the details of their former lives in the yellow-star houses (Jones 2014). Living in one of the yellow-star houses today, I realize that my home has the same courtyard, staircase, and apartments that provided the setting of these tragic events in 1944. This experience was the moment when I felt I became involved in the history and tragedy of my community's past.

Dedicated to Katalin Frankel-Berger

Acknowledgments: I would like to thank all organizers and participants who I have contact with for their help and encouragement putting together this article, along with our community reflections: Gábor Báthory (husband, artist and artisan), Katalin Szentmiklosi (neighbor, doctor of chemistry, voluntary organizer), Dóra Patakfalvi (neighbor, journalist and voluntary organizer), Marcsi and Imre Horvath (neighbor, voluntary organizer), Andrea Galle (neighbor, voluntary organizer), Katalin Frankel-Berger (neighbor, Holocaust survivor), Zsuzsanna Noth (writer, participant), Zsuzsanna Bagonyai-Berman (participant), Noémi Lapsansky-Lovag (participant), and Attila Gyor (participant, architectural historian).

References

A. L. B. 19 June 2014. "Hungary's history: Remembering the Yellow-Star Houses." *The Economist*. http://www.economist.com/blogs/easternapproaches/2014/06/hungarys-history. Accessed 1 December 2015.

Frojimovics, Kinga, and Géza Komoróczy. 1999. *Jewish Budapest: Monuments, Rites, History*. New York: Central European University Press.

Jones, Gwen. 21 June 2014. *Csillagos Hazak, 1944–2014*. http://www.yellowstarhouses.org. Accessed 1 December 2015.

Kalas, Györgyi. 2 April 2014. *Index*, Sárga matricát kapnak a csillagos házak. http://index.hu/kultur/2014/04/02/sarga_matricat_kapnak_a_csillagos_hazak/. Accessed 1 December 2015.

Krezinger, Sonja. 14 February 2014. *Metropol*, "Csillagos házak: Budapest szembenéz a múlttal." http://www.metropol.hu/cikk/1146345-csillagos-hazak-budapest-szembenez-a-multtal. Accessed 1 December 2015.

OSA Launches Yellow-Star Houses Website and Public Program. 2014. http://www.osaarchivum.org/press-room/announcements/OSA-Launches-Yellow-Star-Houses-Website-and-Public-Program. Accessed 1 December 2015.

"*1600 egykori csillagos ház előtt emlékeznek a 70 évvel ezelőtti kényszerköltöztetésekre.*" 20 June 2014. http://444.hu/2014/06/20/1600-egykori-csillagos-haz-elott-emlekeznek-a-70-evvel-ezelotti-kenyszerkoltoztetesekrol. Accessed 1 December 2015.

Somorjai, Laszlo. 4 April 2015. *ATV*, "Tények, sorsok, csillagok" Dokumentumkönyv a csillagos házakról." http://www.atv.hu/belfold/20150403-tenyek-sorsok-csillagok-doku mentumkonyv-a-budapesti-csillagos-hazakrol. Accessed 1 December 2015.

Varga, Zsuzsanna. 2005. *Once They Were Neighbors.* Budapest: Metafórum.

Walker, Jennifer. 15 December 2014. *BBC Travel.* "A rare look into Budapest's Yellow Star Houses." http://www.bbc.com/travel/story/20141212-a-rare-look-inside-budapests-yellow-star-houses. Accessed 1 December 2015.

Yellow-Star Houses. 2014. *Introduction: Budapest 1944–2014: The Yellow-Star Houses.* http://www.yellowstarhouses.org/historical_background/introduction. Accessed 23 February 2016.

PART III

Local Control of Place

10

BUILDING INFORMAL INFRASTRUCTURES

Architects in Support of Bottom-Up Community Services and Social Solidarity in Budapest

Daniela Patti and Levente Polyak

In many European cities, as a consequence of the past decade's various waves of economic and political crises, the public sector has gradually withdrawn from maintaining certain infrastructure and services. In some cities, citizen organizations and activist groups have engaged in replacing the services that are no longer offered by governmental bodies. In parallel, many architects, planners, social activists, and cultural and social professionals also recognized that traditional funding and organizational models had lost their capacity to provide small-scale, community-oriented urban projects. These citizens started developing alternative formats to help citizens access services.

The growing need for self-sustaining, alternative community infrastructure and services also had a significant impact on architecture and planning. Recognizing the direct social utility of their skills in community-initiated development projects, architects and planners have claimed new roles in assisting these projects. They have emerged as the protagonists—in the role of mediators, organizers, advocates, and technical experts—of a new movement focusing on social engagement and small-scale interventions by matching local resources with community needs. This movement rapidly made its way into the mainstream architectural discourse, being featured in major exhibition spaces and magazines, as well as being incorporated into and often instrumentalized by large-scale urban development programs.

This process unfolded in a particular way in Budapest, Hungary, where budget cuts and reformulated policy priorities have undermined a variety of important social services. Bottom-up community infrastructures of various kinds have emerged, relying upon private or commercial support or volunteer community capacities. In this chapter, after examining the impacts of austerity on public services within cities and the subsequent emergence of community-based architecture and planning, we will analyze the process by which bottom-up community services have gained an increasingly important role in the Hungarian capital. We primarily focus on two cases: VALYO, an informal and itinerant public space project along the Danube riverbank, and Művelődési Szint, a cultural center established as an adaptive reuse of an underused department store.

Austerity and the Changing Face of Urban Development

The neoliberal transformation of urban economies and governance, together with the economic crisis of 2008, has forced countless European cities to undertake austerity measures and give up many of the benefits of the welfare state. National austerity policies to reduce budget deficits and cut spending had particularly severe impacts on cities in Europe, where tax rates are much higher than in the United States and citizens had long been accustomed to the state providing a wide range of social support mechanisms:

> The property boom of the early 2000s appeared at first to revive urban fortunes, but even during relatively good times, municipalities deferred important physical and social infrastructure investments to engage in riskier economic development projects and keep taxes and/or fees low. Now with a prolonged period of slow growth, declining revenues and a new round of central–state austerity measures, many municipalities are in a downward spiral from which there seems little prospect of emerging.
>
> *(Donald et. al. 2014, 11)*

Budget reductions forced both state and municipal organizations to accept "significant reductions in welfare benefits and a shifting of responsibility for certain social services to the local level, both of which will have major impacts on the poor and economically vulnerable, especially children" (Donald 2014, 10). This shift found many local communities unprepared, as in most welfare states, post-war governments' extraction of public tasks from community organizations made community services and infrastructures completely dependent on the state (Blond 2012).

The reconfiguration of public services and infrastructure in urban austerity regimes also has an undeniable effect on urban spaces: decreasing municipal budgets in many cities results in the decay or abandonment of important community facilities and public spaces. Cities are forced to privatize their most important revenue streams, including land and property sales, user fees, and contracted-out service management, and left with "a rump of functions that have failed the profitability test for privatization, the residualized local public sector will likely face intensifying management and financing problems" (Peck 2012, 648), especially with the widespread loss of property tax revenues (Tabb 2014, 92).

Decay and abandonment did not only occur in the public sector. As a consequence of the explosion of the private real estate bubble, a significant surplus in office and residential buildings emerged, even in the cities with the most dynamic economies:

> Given downturns in speculative investment on the one hand, and the turning screws of government austerity on the other, many cities are bearing the

physical scars of disinvestment, disuse and decline; in vacant and abandoned spaces of private rescission and public retreat.

(Tonkiss 2013, 312)

While "maintaining properties or dismantling them so they are not used by junkies and other non-desirables further inflicts cost on neighborhoods" (Tabb 2014, 92), municipalities have been reluctant to look for forms of cooperation other than privatizing properties or out-contracting services to private companies.

In this context, many civic groups, social initiatives and cultural, organizations set out to create spaces and services on their own. These initiatives became proactive forces in shaping the city by creating new public spaces and launching new social services, thereby establishing a parallel civic infrastructure.

Design between Finance and Communities

Architectural design has been instrumental in both the structural transformation of municipalities and in the setting up of alternative community services and infrastructure. With the regular tax revenues declining, municipal budgets became increasingly dependent on the revenue generated by the taxes and other fees paid on building permits. Instead of predicating decisions on aesthetics and functionality, architecture in this context prioritizes financial considerations, aiming at attracting investors with disregard for what kind of users might be attracted. The architects' role was reduced to "enticing investors with ingenious combinations of office storeys guaranteed to generate money for the cultural facility located on the ground floor" (Vanstiphout 2014a, 59), to "performing an endless variation of style" and "inexpensively providing aesthetic form while the building and planning process is relegated to the developer" (Illner 2014, 54).

Even before the 2008 economic crisis, many in the building construction sector warned of the increasing marginalization of architects' roles in urban transformation: Responding to the rise of star architecture's pure formalism, many theoreticians argued for the "expansion of the architectural field," with a new focus on professional practice as a means "to create the basis for an architecture that realistically confronts the present global political, social, and economic reality" (Vidler 2004). A few years later, many young architecture firms emerged to embody these practices:

> Architecture will cease to exist if it refuses to engage with the main developments in society and makes no attempt to come up with answers.... Design research can be pro-active in developing a critical awareness regarding commissions. This would necessitate the development of parallel routes, offering opportunities for experiment. It would also require thinking more widely, to dare to consider fashion, interior design, architecture, urban design and landscape design as an integrated whole.
>
> *(van Boxel and Koreman 2007, 36)*

The restitution of the sociopolitical role of designers required the progressive transformation of the architectural profession itself. In 2007, Michelle Provoost and Wouter Vanstiphout traced the first signs of this transformation by describing a new wave of architects and urban practitioners as the Ditch School of Urban Design:

> These practices don't wait for a client or a commission—they forge ahead on their own and find other ways to finance the project. . . . These offices, groups, and artists have abandoned the idea of the conventional architects' office or urban planning department and have blurred the boundaries between urban planning, urban design, art, and social work. . . . Their interventions can be physical objects but even then are more importantly tactical manipulations of political landscapes. By succeeding in building something, these groups change the political status quo in such a way that more things become thinkable and doable.
>
> *(Provoost and Vanstiphout 2007, 38)*

The economic crisis provided a wake-up call. Originating from the housing bubble and heavily affecting the construction industries, it led to a significant shrinking of the labor market for architects and planners. It also changed the view of the profession; the devastating effect of the recession on the construction industry made architects painfully aware of the unsustainability of previous funding mechanisms and development processes. Finding themselves in the midst of landscapes of unfinished construction, vacant complexes, and fragmented public spaces; a generation of architects began to think critically about the speculation-based economy. They began to take into account the limitations of the shrunken market and notice the opportunities of the urban areas neglected by the official planning mechanisms.

These architects paid more attention to the needs of local citizens, preferring small-scale, community-oriented, and often temporary interventions over large-scale construction projects. They increasingly chose communication campaigns, performances, participatory processes, temporary installations, or in-between use programs to intervene in the built environment, rather than the more conventional approaches. For this generation, the task of architecture has become less about producing pretty objects and more about creating spatial impacts. Against the economic downturn and the new backdrop of repressive policies, many young architects declined to join the state machine and began to turn toward new roles and engagements, joining artists and activists to strengthen emerging bottom-up social and cultural infrastructures. These architects, often organized in collectives, have engaged in spatial experiments, looking at the possibilities of public space or helping the design and construction of new community spaces.

Pedro Gadanho describes the new aspiration of design collectives: "In an atmosphere of social guerrilla practice, architects will take to the streets to achieve more with less than ever. What was once a formal mantra for modernism [Less is more.] will now simply be a radical survival tool" (Gadanho 2013). Acknowledging the pioneers of temporary and mobile architecture from the past, contemporary experimenters recognize that light structures are more responsive to change than solid edifices and more likely to bypass regulations. The construction of outdoor and indoor public spaces such as festival installations, co-working spaces, community gardens, or sport fields constitutes the core of these practices, should they be temporary or permanent.

Designers' desire to improve and establish spontaneous public spaces also contributes to the rise of a new genre of architecture offices. These offices function as collectives whose work focuses on the construction process rather than the final product of the architectural intervention. Collectives like the Berlin-based Raumlabor and the Paris-based Exyzt have become regular guests of temporary festivals all across the world. Their interventions often have an empowering capacity, helping participatory design processes unfold, like in the case of the constructions of Exyzt in Madrid's Campo Cebada or in Lisbon's Terras da Costa. As importantly, these acts of community-driven design and self-construction inspire younger collectives, such as the Collectif Etc. in Saint-Étienne, Orizzontale in Rome, or VALYO and Studio Nomad in Budapest, to provide professional support to communities with limited resources.

In recent years, architectural projects concentrating on deteriorated public spaces, vacant lots, empty buildings, or temporary situations ascended to the mainstream discourse by being selected for prestigious architectural exhibitions. A few years after the Actions: What You Can Do With the City exhibition presenting ninety-nine bottom-up architectural initiatives at the Canadian Centre for Architecture, Europe's leading institutions were suddenly flooded with exhibitions displaying various forms of community architecture and urbanism. Exhibitions such as Hands-On Urbanism at the Architekturzentrum Wien, Re: Architecture at the Pavillon de l'Arsenal in Paris, Spontaneous Interventions in the American Pavilion of the 2012 Venice Biennial of Architecture, or Reactivate! at Bureau Europa in Maastricht are all manifestations of a movement that redraws the boundaries of the architectural profession.

Despite the enthusiasm it generated, the emergence of participatory architectural practices and community-built public spaces has been an ambiguous process. On the one hand, community building played an important role in helping bottom-up social and cultural infrastructure (community centers, cultural venues, social kitchens, youth clubs, drug prevention offices, public spaces, etc.) unfold by providing "local services and spaces that substitute or compensate for absent or inadequate public provision" (Tonkiss 2013, 318). On the other hand, they have been integrated into private development projects as well as municipal planning schemes, as "cut-price locational boosters," as "part of a wider 'neoliberal strategy' for outsourcing municipal services to (unpaid) private actors, [where] the distance between seedbed and sell-out becomes very tight indeed" (Tonkiss 2013, 318).

Accommodating originally subversive and community-oriented processes, commercial developers, housing corporations, and municipalities instrumentalized "placemaking, urban farming, community architecture, and narrative design as integral parts of their methodology. Again the architects pushed into the role of pill sweeteners, grease on the wheels of much larger deals in which they have hardly any position" (Vanstiphout 2014b, 8). The political and economic transformation of the past decade also transformed the architectural profession. It also raised many questions about the role of architects and designers in community development: How can they be involved in a planning and design process early enough to avoid its instrumentalization? How can they ensure that community involvement results in community control of not only the built objects but also the destiny of spaces? How can they become developers and financiers of community-built projects?

Budapest: From Parallel Cultures to Hegemony and Austerity

Budapest emerged from decades of Communist dictatorship with unsustainable welfare services and outdated social and cultural infrastructure. In the last decades of the regime in the 1970s and 1980s, a large segment of avant-garde culture, including theatre, cinema, literature, and contemporary art, existed in a separate yet parallel sphere from officially supported culture. Sometimes tolerated, but more often prohibited by the Communist Party's censors, independent productions often found refuge in semi-public and semi-invisible spaces at the periphery of the system's horizon.

Some of the most important cultural spaces in post-1990 Budapest emerged from these parallel cultural infrastructures. Trafó, one of the most dynamic cultural venues in Budapest, was the first institution in the city to grow out of an informal cultural space. The industrial art nouveau electric transformer station, situated on the edge of the city's historical core, had been abandoned for more than forty years when the French anarchist artist group Resonance discovered it in the early 1990s. They transformed it into a squat that hosted a variety of cultural events, performances, concerts, and presentations throughout the summer of 1991. In the following years, it served as a storage space for theatre and music groups for several years. In the mid-1990s, using funds remaining from the cancelled 1994 World Exhibition, the Municipality of Budapest bought the building to transform it into a well-equipped contemporary art center. The Trafó House of Arts opened its doors in 1998 and quickly became an important Central European center for contemporary theater, dance, and music.

Other initiatives had shorter lives. In 2003, a group of young architects and cultural producers initiated Tűzraktár in an abandoned medical equipment factory on the same street as Trafó. The group rented the 7,000 m² building from its owner for a year at a very low rent, promising the owner the valorization of the building by increasing visibility through cultural events. Tűzraktár opened with minimal architectural intervention in June 2004, and it was an immediate success; thousands of people invaded the factory's empty spaces and courtyards during the first days. Tűzraktár's operation had to be suspended due to its popularity; the building and its temporary commercial spaces had suddenly become very attractive, and the commercial activities gradually overshadowed the cultural functions.

Commercialization became the fate of many other initiatives in downtown Budapest. In the mid-2000s, cultural and alternative functions planted into abandoned buildings gave birth to a peculiar style, with pubs, protocol visits, and fashion shows, retaining the image of pioneer occupation while creating established institutions and commercial enterprises (Lugosi, Bell, and Lugosi 2010).

With the significant economic, political, and social changes of the past decade, the parallel cultural and social services and infrastructure have resurfaced in Hungary. The recession prompted successive governments to reorganize their welfare infrastructures: the country went through an Excessive Deficit Procedure imposed by the European Union, forcing cuts on state and municipal budgets and reducing spending on social, cultural, and educational services. Together with the budget cuts, an aggressive nationalization process by the new government (elected in 2010) engaged in reallocating resources and centralizing social, cultural, and educational funding.

While the crisis diminished the opportunities of private funding for cultural spaces, events, and social initiatives because private companies could not afford to offer sponsorship anymore, it allowed the government to centralize power and to monopolize cultural and social funding, as well as architectural operations. In the years between 2010 and 2015, the conservative party's absolute majority in the parliament as well as in the government enabled the "streamlining" of decision-making processes both in issues of public spending and urban development. While many educational, cultural, and social institutions were left impoverished or shut down, a large part of public budgets was channeled into prestigious and large-scale development projects in major Hungarian cities, including the renovation of central streets and squares in Budapest or the construction of new soccer stadiums across the country. By moving development areas out of the control of local municipalities, the government imposed its decisions with striking efficiency and practically without opposition.

Social Infrastructure and Public Spaces

The ambition to create a parallel social infrastructure that is organized by communities, funded by private individuals and organizations, and operates independently from state institutions and municipal bodies has been recurring in recent social initiatives in Budapest. The centralizing of cultural funding together with budget cuts at national and local administrations resulted in a gap in cultural and social services.

In late 2013, the Budapest Municipality began to deny permission for charity organizations distributing food in centrally located public spaces, arguing that they cause nuisances for residents. The new policy, aimed at pushing poverty out of the city center, exacerbated the impacts of the economic crisis on vulnerable groups. Opposing these measures, that same year, Heti Betevő (Weekly Bread) grew out of the cooperation of private individuals and restaurants in a highly commercialized inner district. Funds for food are crowdfunded with the help of moneyboxes installed in a number of restaurants. Since its launch in December 2013, it has inspired many similar initiatives across the city and the country, and Heti Betevő is a highly successful program that has managed to collect enough money to cover 250 meals every Sunday—all of which are served at the crumbling tables and benches of the centrally located but exceptionally neglected Klauzál Square in Budapest's historic Jewish Quarter.

The program not only acts as a parallel social service in an area abandoned by the state and the city; it also transforms the sense of space: acting illegally, Heti Betevő gives new life to a square, expanding the notion of public space, turning it into a space of exchange and solidarity that exists outside the over politicized, official welfare structure. In this way, architecture plays a marginal role of in Heti Betevő's venture. Its organizers transgressed the rules of the square and expanded its accessibility and inclusivity. While Heti Betevő challenged the imposed rules of public space by expanding its function, other initiatives have created sociable spaces by changing a place's form through architecture.

Among these, some of the most visible and popular spatial experiments were conducted by the Budapest-based collective VALYO (Város és Folyó, City and River). VALYO aims to make the Danube, which cuts the city in two, more accessible and more connected to the urban tissue. Not waiting for public competitions and large investments, the group's architects, designers, and event organizers used low-cost street furniture and installations to turn the underused riverbanks into high-quality public spaces. They also initiated a mobile sauna that allowed people, by appointment, to experience specific views of the river while enjoying the heat in a retrofitted van. The interventions attracted strollers and picnickers as well as evening gatherings, concerts, and screenings. As Gergely Kukucska, one of VALYO's architect members, describes the initial moments of the area's regeneration,

> For us, personally, it was very important to create community activities at the riverbank. We spotted a sympathetic location that wasn't used by anyone, and we designed a bench to be installed there. We got funding, we built it, and we finished the final touches at the location, with the help of passers-by. We inaugurated the space with a community event that gave us a lot of energy and pushed us forward. This is how we created the VALYO-riverbank.
>
> *(Kukucska 2015)*

First they used pallets to build furniture, until realizing how expensive, impractical, and difficult to move they were. Then they began to work with traditional wood, developing a new furniture family that, after being refined, replaced the first benches at the riverbank. The new furniture, combined with events, turned out to be a successful placemaking tool:

> We decided to organize a temporary festival, we borrowed an unused kiosk and this created a very intimate space, which felt like being at home at the riverbank. Then the place became increasingly known, we had to pay more and more attention to security and safety, and we began disturbing the neighbors, the residents of the hotels, the boats, and the other side of the river.
>
> *(Kukucska 2015)*

FIGURE 10.1   Self-built furniture on the Danube bank

Source: VALYO

FIGURE 10.2   Placemaking at the Danube bank

Source: VALYO

VALYO's intervention indicates a new relationship between civic actors and municipalities. Staying within the limits of legality, the collective's experiments reveal the potentials of the riverfront. Their success puts pressure on the municipality to engage with more innovative tools of placemaking, including actors that are more rooted in local and cultural communities. However, the group's achievements have also brought about the closure of the riverbank experiment: "The place started to outgrow itself. This is when we decided to discontinue the festival—in the same time when the city also decided to make more profit from the area" (Kukucska 2015).

Urged by the increasing visibility generated by VALYO, the municipality organized an urban design competition to rethink the use of the riverbank, which is currently dominated by traffic arteries, tourist boats or restaurants, and other elements that do not effectively promote the enjoyment of the local community of the riverfront. The competition forced VALYO to compete with financially much more powerful actors for redesigning the area. Furthermore, by attracting mainstream design and planning players in the formerly neglected riverbank area, the competition threatened to alter the intimate, inclusive, and accessible character of the space:

> I don't know how good a tendency it is that you point at a place; it starts working, serves a social group, and then begins to outgrow itself, but can't lead to a consensus that could be the basis for a well-working public space. Instead, someone else arrives and takes it over. It would be great to create spaces that are sustainable and aren't limited to making money. It's very difficult to reconcile social and communal functions with a commercial activity.
>
> *(Kukucska 2015)*

Due to the visibility and success of its public space interventions, VALYO received invitations by municipalities to get involved in the Budapest Municipality's "TÉR-KÖZ" ("Common-space") funding scheme that aimed at creating collaboration between public administrations and non-governmental organizations (NGOs). Through negotiations with public officers and workshops, they organized for municipalities; however, members of VALYO gradually grew suspicious of the prospect of cooperation with authorities:

> There are simply realizable, quasi-community initiatives, that municipalities begin to support when they realize that with a little effort, they can use them as spectacular tools to generate political advantages. The problem is that these initiatives lose their sense through political instrumentalisation.
>
> *(Kukucska 2015)*

Throughout the various cooperation processes, VALYO members realized that the larger the processes they enter, the more chance there is for the marginalization of their role in the planning and design process—the less control they have on the destiny of the spaces they created and the way they appear in the public imagination. The quest by VALYO's members to find a sustainable role in the creation of new public spaces raised many questions about the possibility of a relative independence from power in the spaces built by communities:

> I start believing that these processes can only achieve their goals if they're illegal. If critical groups can organize interventions without connecting to

municipal developments; or municipalities have to be so enlightened that to see more than their exclusive political and economic benefits in these processes. Or people have to recognize that they can influence their environment. If reflexive communities reach a critical mass and set themselves to defend their values, political and economic interests can also be shaped, consolidated.

(Kukucska 2015)

VALYO's conclusions correspond to the phenomena happening in many different European cities, like the Campo de Cebada in Madrid, or EcoBox in Paris, where the real challenge is not only to design and build new spaces but to avoid instrumentalization by commercial or political actors and keep community control over the transformation of urban space: "If we start thinking about alternative urban development, we can't just patch holes and repair failures. We have to think at another scale" (Kukucska 2015).

Public Functions in Private Spaces: The Case of Művelődési Szint

The desire of social and cultural actors to create independent spaces in Budapest led to many experiments. The right-wing takeover in national and municipal politics resulted in a series of repressive policies aiming at eliminating the strongholds of the progressive cultural scene. In 2011, within a few months, some of the leading alternative cultural centers operating in formerly vacant, municipally owned properties were shut down. The closing down of these cultural venues and the quick commercialization of other formerly available vacant spaces left cultural communities uprooted and looking for alternative solutions to establish new collective spaces and to transfer its belongings, equipment, and furniture.

In the quest for new cultural spaces and infrastructure, the question of vacant lots and empty buildings came to the forefront of public discussions. The recession, combined with many building types becoming obsolete and no longer able to respond to contemporary needs, as well as with the mismanagement of real estate properties owned by private as well as public owners, has emptied a significant proportion of the city from its previous functions and use. While the homeless rights organization "Right to the City" had already been campaigning for creating access to unoccupied residential buildings, in 2012, the Hungarian Contemporary Architecture Centre (KÉK) expanded the discourse to non-residential properties, advocating the community use of vacant buildings and storefronts, as well as vacant lots. This was the situation that influenced the mood of the alternative cultural community in the city just before the space that would become known as Müszi was established.

It wasn't just the architectural community that was exploring alternative use of abandoned spaces; members of the theatre community were doing the same, sometimes with help from local authorities. For example, the theatre association Füge Productions collaborated with the Budapest Municipality to turn an abandoned school building into a 6,500 square meter cultural incubator. But it was the theatre

FIGURE 10.3 Workshop spaces in Müszi

Source: Levente Polyak

collective, Harmadik Hang (Third Voice), that chose another path to create its own space and establish Művelődési Szint, otherwise known as Müszi (Cultural Level).

Müszi was born from the ambition to revive the tradition of the "house of culture," a community space for a variety of activities, an open-for-all public space where consumption is not required. As Julia Bársony, founder of Müszi, explains:

> In the winter of 2011 all the alternative cultural institutions of Budapest got shut down, those that did not only give space for entertainment but also for creation and artistic work. This is when we also lost our building that we used for 5 years as artist studios and wood workshops. I was teaching a theatre class at the university and we were approaching the end of a seminar, before the rehearsals in December and the performance in January, when we found ourselves on the street.
>
> *(Bársony 2015)*

While searching for available spaces, Julia ran into the vacant third floor of a socialist-style department store, right at Blaha Lujza tér, one of the busiest squares of Budapest's historical center:

> We found this space when it had already been empty for 6 years. The owner didn't really want to rent it out: it was complicated to adjust the building's

infrastructures and provide a staircase to the floor, especially since the rooftop bar occupied all of them. I got in touch with the owner and told him that we would like to use the space for 6 weeks, but we have no money. He told me that we could use it if we cleaned it up. We moved in, cleaned up in 3 days and began to work.

(Bársony 2015)

After the preparations in December, the performance took place in January 2012, lasted five days, and attracted over a thousand spectators. It brought a lot of visibility to the previously unknown third floor of a well-known building: "Suddenly everyone discovered this space, everyone felt that something is beginning here" (Bársony 2014). The owner of the building, who liked the group's presence, offered them a rental price. The collective decided to move ahead with renting the space of 2,800 square meters. Realizing that they had nothing to lose, they negotiated a progressive rental agreement, starting with only the utility costs for half a year, then half-price for another six months, then full price.

For the group, to find a privately owned space was crucial to avoid political pressure, as they estimated that, paradoxically, it was only possible to create an independent public space in a privately owned space:

From the beginning, we were in a political situation where we decided to go ahead with developing Müszi because we don't see the possibility that the theatre we're doing would receive any subventions in the coming years. We had to create the circumstances within which we can work. We wanted to build a theatre for ourselves, and we built it, even if we haven't really been able to harness it. . . . When we came here, we decided to stop applying for grants, in order to avoid supporting the system with paying application fees, and to avoid time limits as well as accountancy and reporting obligations towards the institutions. In this way, the whole project can develop in its natural pace. . . . It was important to reassure ourselves, because we wanted to create long-term possibilities. For instance, we installed an intercom in order to oblige the authorities to announce their visit. We knew from the beginning that we needed to create an independent and safe place, in all senses.

(Bársony 2015)

Müszi's business model is based on the recognition of the large demand for affordable workspaces both within the fields of art and activism. Looking for tenants, Müszi made a call for applications, where the criteria for selection included the candidates' activity, their willingness to contribute to the community, and their capacity to pay rents. Through the application process, Müszi organizers got familiarized with precise needs of the prospective tenants, and this informed the design of the whole floor. The space's structure had continuously evolved throughout the construction, reflecting the changing needs:

> We knew that we needed to make as much space available for offices and artist studios as possible. And we also knew that artists and NGO workers needed small spaces as they couldn't afford large ones. In the meanwhile, we also wanted to create spaces for events: for performances, presentations, and dance—we were thinking in mobile spaces.
>
> *(Bársony 2015)*

The first task in the construction process was to transform the floor into an inhabitable space, by using what they had at hand, materials, and volunteers:

> We began by collecting all available materials from the recently closed venues (Tűzraktér, Merlin, Sirály, Gödör, Kossuth Mozi), as well as from a nearby Chinese restaurant. In parallel, we left flyers everywhere announcing that we're looking for furniture, we received many of them. Besides this, we had all the sceneries of Harmadik Hang's theatre pieces, the collection of 8 years' work. And there was a double ceiling, made of wood, covering the entire floor area. We used these to build walls later.
>
> *(Bársony 2015)*

To a large extent, prospective tenants did the first phases of the construction work. To motivate the volunteers, Müszi accommodated many of their ideas in the organization of the new spaces. It was the volunteers' informal expression of needs that determined how many originally previously unplanned services, like a playroom for children with toys and art materials, was able to take shape.

The construction was helped by a young architecture collective, Studio Nomad, which was already part of the performance inaugurating the space. In this sense, the performance already anticipated how the space could be used. The relationship between design and construction was not conventional: "they first had to build each structure, to test the chosen material in the given space, and to draw the plans only afterwards as we had no materials to waste nor teams to build according to plans" (Bársony 2015). Müszi's interior organization was also largely determined by regulations, particularly the requirement of fire safety:

> It would have been very expensive to upgrade the space from being a department store's display level: we adapted to this function and use the floor as a continuous space, even if partitioned into smaller volumes. You can dismantle the interiors with a screw-driver, because everything is built like a scenery: none of the walls reach the ceiling.
>
> *(Bársony 2014)*

Despite the presence of the architects, the decisive logic of the construction process was not so much architectural as theatrical: the cooperation model established in theatre pieces and performances informed the launching of Müszi not only as a cultural venue but also as an indoor public space:

> At the core of developing Müszi was the community, and the good coop-
> eration with people. The reason why I became the engine of this process
> lies probably in my 20 years experience in theatre, from building sceneries,
> through team work to the distribution of tasks. And all we did was always
> motivated by artistic ambitions where practical considerations were in the
> foreground, and never money.
>
> *(Bársony 2015)*

After a months of construction, Müszi opened its doors in September 2012, with a total of 2,800 square meters. Since then, the financial model of the space, based on renting out artist studios and NGO offices in order to support the public space maintenance and its activities, has been established, and Müszi began to expand to new floors.

In 2014, Müszi adopted the names of public spaces renamed in the past years: symbolically accommodating public spaces from the pre-2010 era signals an ambi-tion to become a city in the city, a genuine public space. In addition to its public functions, the space also started to offer social services, solidarity rent, and short-term shelter for those in need. Müszi's long-term ambition is to become a node in an emerging network of independent cultural and welfare providers:

> The next task is to create our social net. Not only to explore the services
> of Müszi, but also to be able to direct people to the services present in the
> neighborhood, to distribute clothes to the homeless, as well as hot tea in win-
> tertime. We envision this as part of an independent social welfare network, as
> part of an independent reality.
>
> *(Bársony 2015)*

This statement signals the ambition of social service providers and cultural pro-ducers to gain independence from the public sector, both in terms of funding and in terms of accountability. Paradoxically, many actors see the real potential of self-organization and community-led development unfolding in private spaces and premises: "private is the new public," goes the claim.

Designing Frameworks for Social Services

Although relatively modest in scale, the examples of Müszi and the VALYO-riverbank signal a new tendency in architects' engagement with community pro-jects. The role of design and building in this context goes beyond the traditional tasks of architects: by taking the initiative at transforming a part of the Danube riverbank, or by helping a client in exploring a building's opportunities, VALYO and Studio Nomad both took on the role of protagonists, not waiting for com-missions but engaging in "unsolicited" architecture projects. The experience of collective building highlights the capacities available in communities: moving these architectural engagements beyond mere design, the process of building generated a community around these spaces in the first place, before they were established as locations for cultural events.

As the previously described projects demonstrate, citizen-initiated social services—assisted, shaped, or established by collective design and building practices—do constitute a growing segment of the new political and economic realities of our cities. This segment is not invisible to decision makers: in many European cities, they influence municipalities, inspire policymaking, and result in enhanced partnerships—or, in negative cases, serve as justification for outsourcing work and responsibilities that should have been provided by the municipal authorities. Even in Budapest, where initiatives like Heti Betevő, Müszi, and the VALYO riverbank are deliberately created outside the formal cultural and planning frameworks, bottom-up initiatives are often cited as models to inspire and influence public administration to rethink public spaces and vacant properties. For example, the aforementioned short-lived "TÉR-KÖZ" funding scheme of the Budapest municipality's planning department was shaped to some extent by bottom-up initiatives in that it subsidized civic-public cooperation in regenerating vacant buildings and potential community spaces.

To avoid instrumentalization, these initiatives need to arrive early enough in a planning and design process: instead of playing a mere executive role, designers need to act as mediators, positioning themselves in the center of interactions of stakeholders. To reduce their submission to external goals, they need to become developers or financiers of community-built projects. By having an overview of the entire development process, they can capture the values they create and avoid being exploited by stronger actors. By utilizing collective involvement in the building and management of new community services and infrastructure, they can assure their leadership in respect to not only the physical form but also the destiny of the new spaces they create.

These ambitions inherently link Budapest practitioners to their counterparts in other cities, looking for more significant, relevant roles for designers, architects, and planners:

> The real ambition right now is for architects not to satisfy themselves and their constituency with immediate physical or communal interventions, but rather to penetrate into mechanisms of power, money, policymaking, and knowledge that actually form the basis for the transformations of our cities and communities.
>
> *(Vanstiphout 2014b, 8)*

References

Bársony, Júlia. 2015. Interview on 9 January.

Blond, Phillip. 2012. *Radical Republic: How Left and Right Have Broken the System and How We Can Fix It*. New York: W. W. Norton & Company.

Donald, Betsy, Amy Glasmeier, Mia Gray, and Linda Lobao. 2014. "Austerity in the City: Economic Crisis and Urban Service Decline?" *Cambridge Journal of Regions, Economy and Society*, 7(1): 3–15.

Gadanho, Pedro. 2013. "Back to the Streets: The Rise of Performance Architecture." http://www.domusweb.it/en/op-ed/2011/09/21/back-to-the-streets-the-rise-of-performance-architecture.html. Accessed 25 September 2013.

Illner, Peer. 2014. "For Me, Myself and I: Architecture in the Age of Self-Reflexivity." In *Real Estates*, Jack Self, and Shumi Bose, eds. London: Bedford Press, 51–6.

Kukucska, Gergely. 2015. Interview on 7 January.

Lugosi, Peter, David Bell, and Krisztina Lugosi. 2010. "Hospitality, Culture and Regeneration: Urban Decay, Entrepreneurship and the 'Ruin' Bars of Budapest." *Urban Studies*, 47(14): 3079–3101.

Peck Jamie. 2012. "Austerity Urbanism." *City: Analysis of Urban Trends, Culture, Theory, Policy, Action*, 16(6): 626–55.

Provoost, Michelle, and Wouter Vanstiphout. 2007. "Facts on the Ground. Urbanism from Mid- Road to Ditch." *Harvard Design Magazine*, 25: 36–42.

Tabb, William K. 2014. "The Wider Context of Austerity Urbanism." *City: Analysis of Urban Trends, Culture, Theory, Policy, Action*, 18(2): 87–100.

Tonkiss, Fran. 2013. "Austerity Urbanism and the Makeshift City." *City: Analysis of Urban Trends, Culture, Theory, Policy, Action*, 17(3): 312–24.

van Boxel, Elma, and Kristian Koreman. 2007. *Re-Public. Towards a New Spatial Politics*. Rotterdam: NAi Publishers.

Vanstiphout, Wouter. 2014a. "The Self-Destruction Machine." In *Real Estates*, Jack Self, and Shumi Bose, eds. London: Bedford Press, 57–66.

———. 2014b. "Dark Matter. Ditch Urbanism Revisited." *Harvard Design Magazine*, 37: 6–11.

Vidler, Anthony. 2004. "Architecture's Expanded Field." *Artforum International*, 42(8): 142–7.

11

THE MAIN STREET APPROACH TO COMMUNITY DESIGN

Jeremy C. Wells

The historic preservation movement in the United States is perhaps most visible in the historic downtowns that are increasingly desirable as places to live, work, and recreate. The National Trust for Historic Preservation (the Trust)[1] has played a central role in this phenomenon by formulating a widely-emulated method for downtown revitalization known as the "Main Street approach." Through this method, hundreds of communities have been empowered to address issues of disinvestment, decay, and ambivalence that have contributed to the decline of their downtowns by leveraging the power of historic resources and placemaking. The Main Street approach avails community volunteers a unique opportunity to envision and implement a wide variety of downtown design projects, from public art to streetscape redesigns and master plans. This chapter will explain how communities empower themselves through Main Street programs and the influence volunteers have over design projects that impact their downtowns. I will also discuss some of the controversial aspects of the approach, including charges of "Disneyfication" leveled against these programs and issues unique to volunteers in these programs, as well as the reasons why their efforts sometimes fail.

Much of the perspective that I offer in this chapter comes from my experience serving as the Main Street manager for Quakertown Alive!, an accredited Main Street program in Quakertown, Pennsylvania. As the second manager, I helped the program move from its inception to its growth phase. While I worked in the program in 2005 and 2006, I came to realize that there was a strong relationship between the overall success of a Main Street program and how closely the program followed the official guidelines published by the Trust. In Pennsylvania, the Pennsylvania Downtown Center (PDC), an accredited Main Street coordinating program, provided all of the official Main Street training in the state. While at Quakertown Alive!, I regularly attended PDC training sessions and yearly conferences and was able to meet many of the other Main Street managers and program volunteers in the state. I also frequently attended the Trust's yearly National Main Streets Conference, which allowed me to share ideas with Main Street managers and volunteers from across the country. My experience serving on the board of the Old Allentown (Pennsylvania) Preservation Association, one of the country's first "Elm Street" programs,[2] helped me to better understand the relationship between residents' buy-in and the success of Main Street programs. In addition, my work as a design committee volunteer in Main Street programs in Washington State and Missouri provided insight in my future work coordinating the efforts of community volunteers.

Most published material on the Main Street approach and its programs is purely descriptive in nature and does not adequately address the complicated bi-causal relationship between successful Main Street programs and successful downtowns, as Kent Robertson (2004) found. Since the publication of Robertson's article, the situation has not changed substantially. Germane to the present inquiry, there also does not appear to be any refereed, published research on community design and the Main Street approach. As part of the official accreditation process for Main Street programs, the Trust's National Main Street Center requires programs to submit statistics on the amount of dollars spent on physical improvements, number of buildings rehabilitated, and the net gain in jobs and businesses in the Main Street program area every year.[3] Proponents then use this data to defend the overall validity of the approach while leaving unanswered questions in terms of the relationship between individual statistics and specific Main Street program activities. Each program is free to define a method for how it collects these figures, which raises concerns of internal validity in the overall methodology used to collect this data.

Because of a lack of research that establishes a clear causal relationship and direction between the creation and growth of a Main Street program and the overall "success" of downtown revitalization, the validity of the Main Street approach is instead substantiated through the deep personal experience of those involved in the programs and tends to be accepted *prima facie* (Dane 1997). A study conducted for The Center for Rural Pennsylvania, which surveyed Main Street managers, did find a positive correlation between these managers' perceived self-effectiveness in implementing the officially sanctioned Main Street approach and the overall success of the program (Kimmel and Schoening 2011, 12). It is not clear from this study if this self-evaluation was actually assessing the effectiveness of the program, its ability to adhere to the official Main Street approach, or the overall effectiveness of the Main Street manager. The Trust's claim that the Main Street approach has led to qualitative and quantitative improvements to historic downtowns seems reasonable, however, even without definitive empirical evidence, considering an ample supply of anecdotal evidence from hundreds of programs during its 40-year life-span.

The Main Street Program and Community Design

The Trust created its Main Street approach in the late 1970s and early 1980s in an effort to save struggling historic downtowns from disinvestment and obsolescence.

It is unique in its emphasis on grassroots efforts led by passionate community volunteers that create and run an organization, restructure the local economy, promote the downtown, and design and preserve places. These volunteers are often involved in implementing public art and building and landscape design projects in order to create a better sense of place that "communicate[s] qualities like safety, vitality, and uniqueness" (Lawniczak 2009b, 111).

From three pilot communities in 1976, there are now over two thousand Main Street programs across the United States (Loescher 2009a). The program was inspired, in part, by the "Magdalen Street experiment," in which the British Civic Trust restored the storefronts of Magdalen Street in Norwich, England, in the late 1950s (Civic Trust 1967). While the revitalization efforts in Norwich were only narrowly focused design principles and as such had limited success (Dalibard 1985, 50; Banks 1988), in the United States, the Trust emphasized issues of organization, promotion, and economics in addition to design in a comprehensive "Main Street approach" to revitalization.

The Trust describes the Main Street approach as a holistic process that engages stakeholders, such as residents, municipalities, and allied community organizations, in an effort to revitalize distressed downtowns. It is overt in its aim to have community stakeholders become directly involved in using heritage as a tool for economic growth (Bull and Girard-Ruel 2009, 3; Loescher 2009b, 11). The Main Street approach is founded on the core ethic of historic preservation/heritage conservation and these four points, which must be addressed concurrently (Dono and Glisson 2009):

Organization: This indicates coordinating the efforts of all stakeholders toward a common goal and forming and sustaining the organizational structure and funding to support the program.

Promotion: Marketing and tourism efforts are initiated and carried out with the goal of selling a positive image of the downtown. Special or regular events are particularly encouraged, along with traditional marketing efforts.

Design: This is the multifaceted approach aimed at improving the appearance of the downtown, starting with saving historic buildings from demolition, removing later layers of change, and then rehabilitating them. Design also focuses on the appearance of window displays, store interiors, and landscape features such as sidewalks, lighting, and streets.

Economic Restructuring: In this area, market surveys are conducted to produce an inventory of the economic and physical assets of the downtown, which are then used to encourage the growth of economic activity in order to attract a wider customer base.

There are also eight guiding principles—be comprehensive, take incremental steps, self-help, build partnerships, identify and capitalize on existing assets, focus on quality over quantity, slow change, and gradual implementation—that direct Main Street programs in their implementation of the four points (Loescher 2009b, 11). Each year, the Trust and many statewide coordinating agencies certify programs that adhere to the Main Street approach. Most Main Street programs are non-profit organizations and, as such, can solicit funding from members as well as through grants. Paid staff are usually limited to one full-time "Main Street manager," with the majority of activities being carried out by volunteers from the community. A few Main Street organizations are affiliated with a municipality or a chamber of commerce.

Volunteers who comprise the Main Street program's board of directors and committees typically receive training from the Trust's National Main Street Center or from a statewide or regional coordinating program, such as the Downtown Pennsylvania Center, Main Street New Mexico, or the Boston Main Streets Foundation.[4] The Trust publishes and distributes training handbooks for each of the four points, providing direction on the purpose of the committee and its activities, the responsibilities of individual committee members, the role of the committee's chairperson, staff responsibilities, and developing work plans. Some coordinating entities have expanded on the Trust's official material and offer additional training, such as Pennsylvania Downtown Center's quarterly Main Street Institute.

Community Design Activities in Main Street Programs

A typical Main Street program will create a separate standing committee of volunteers for each of the four points. As one might expect, the design committee is most involved in design and creative aspects that affect the program's downtown service area. Areas that design committees address include visual merchandizing, facade grants for buildings, public improvements, the creation of design guidelines, providing local design assistance, creating master plans, and public art. These are areas that the Trust recommends each Main Street program address. Not all programs focus on every item, however, with older programs having a broader array of projects than more recent ones.

Visual Merchandizing

Visual merchandizing focuses on the design of the interiors of stores and what is visible outside the building through windows. Window displays should be updated frequently and represent the "business owner's creativity and understanding of customers" (Steele 2009, 105). The Trust emphasizes issues of lighting, cleanliness, and overall design and organization in these displays in order to increase the visual appeal of shops and thus maximize marketing efforts and increase business. Design committee members learn about consumer shopping psychology and where certain types of goods should be maximally positioned inside stores, the proper colors to use, and how the quality of authentically historic interiors can be "leveraged" to "contribute to the sense of place and the collective experience that certain customers, tourists, and residents seek" (Steele 2009, 109).

Many Main Street programs offer, through their design committee volunteers, assistance to store owners to improve visual merchandizing design, such as the Downtown Sheridan (WY) Association (Sheridan 2014), Victoria (TX) Main

Street Program (Victoria 2014), and the Monett (MO) Main Street Program (Bish-off 2010). Other design committees are more active in their approach, such as with the New London (CT) Main Street Program, which held a series of visual merchandizing workshops that focused on "on store merchandising, design and layout, effective use of window displays, and creation of floor plans that generate the highest sales and attract the most customers" (Woods 2002, 5). Similarly, the Downtown Roseburg (OR) Association sponsored a workshop on storefront design and visual merchandizing from a "nationally recognized retail design consultant" that was vetted by their design committee (Downtown Roseburg 2013).

Facade Grant Programs

While most of the design activities of Main Street programs focus on advocacy, facade grant programs are perhaps one of the most powerful ways that a community can become directly involved in the design of storefronts through volunteers' efforts in a design committee. Typically, state coordinating entities provide funds to Main Street programs or sometimes foundations, corporate entities, or private donors help to fund these programs. In preparation for facade grant applications, a design committee drafts design guidelines against which these applications are

FIGURES 11.1–11.5   Examples of a community-driven design project from a Main Street program (Historic Downtown Kennewick Partnership, Kennewick, Washington) catalyzed by a facade grant program

Source: Jeremy Wells

(Continued)

(Continued)

evaluated. The design committee then reviews applications from business owners wishing to apply for grant funds to repair, restore, or preserve storefronts. If the committee deems that the requested changes are not appropriate, they then work with the applicant to come to a resolution. These negotiations are often facilitated and mediated by a Main Street manager. Example of facade grant programs include Main Street Winter Haven (Florida; Winter Haven 2014), Main Street Hanford (California; Hanford 2014), Cedar Falls Community Main Street (Iowa; Cedar Falls 2014a), and Thibodaux Main Street (Louisiana; Thibodaux 2014).

Public Improvements

As defined by the Main Street program, public improvements "include all streetscape elements, from lampposts and benches to parking and pedestrian amenities" (Lawniczak 2009c, 141). These improvements can also include the redesign, cleaning, or creation of plazas and parks. The way in which a design committee accomplishes these large-scale tasks is by brainstorming ideas and forming a collaborative partnership with their municipality (and sometimes state transportation entities) in order to "be involved from day one in the planning process and remain involved through completion" (Lawniczak 2009c, 142). In some cases, the Main Street program itself may be the recipient of large amounts of streetscape funding, but more frequently, the program writes grants on behalf of a municipality, which, upon funding, become the responsibility of a particular city or town to implement. In other cases, the funding is distributed to the municipality, but the Main Street program manages the overall process. This latter case is particularly prevalent where a Main Street program selects design professionals to prepare plans, drawings, and renderings. The municipality then pays the professionals for their services via the grant funds.

Streetscape improvements typically include installing new lampposts, planters, promotional banners, benches, trash containers, trees, paving materials (e.g., brick, stone), wayfinding signage, information kiosks, and removing elements that "clutter" the environment (Lawniczak 2009c, 141–147). The focus is on creating an environment that is more conducive to the experience of pedestrians and to encourage people to stay downtown, recreate, and shop.

Design Guidelines

Design guidelines describe appropriate and inappropriate treatments for a wide variety of visual characteristics in a downtown area, including the form, massing, and scale of buildings; ornamentation, materials, and color; characteristics of signs; and sometimes landscape elements, such as fences. Many Main Street programs create guidelines out of necessity when implementing a facade grant program or as a prelude to establishing a regulatory design review process, such as an historic district commission. Where they do exist without regulatory requirements, they are tied to funding access or are simply advisory in nature. As the Trust describes, design guidelines "help property owners do the right thing, as well as benefit contractors, carpenters, sign manufacturers, and other tradespeople" (Lawniczak 2009a, 128).

Within Main Street programs, design guidelines are used to help preserve the historical authenticity of the area that is under the purview of a program. For this reason, they often base their general recommendations on the Secretary of the Interior's Standards for Rehabilitation, a document originally created by the National Park Service in 1977 for federal historic preservation tax credits (Weeks and Grimmer 1995) but now widely adopted at the local, state, and federal level for all historic preservation work in the United States.

One typical example, Paso Robles (California) Downtown Main Street Association's guidelines, developed by its design committee, seeks "to revitalize and enhance the appearance, atmosphere, and convenience of downtown Paso Robles [by] provid[ing] preferred design directions for new construction and restoration or remodel projects so that they respect and complement the scale, proportion and tradition of the historic downtown area" (Paso Robles 2014). Along with prescriptive verbiage, drawings make clear what is appropriate and not appropriate in terms of design. Cedar Falls Community Main Street Program's design guidelines similarly foster "desirable aesthetic qualities," maintain a "rich heritage," "provide consistency and avoid arbitrary design" and also rely on prescriptive language and images to convey appropriateness (Cedar Falls 2014b).

Local Design Assistance

While not common, a number of Main Street programs have formed "facade squads," which are volunteer-led efforts to offer design assistance to property owners that are usually associated with design or sometimes promotion committees. As the name would suggest, the primary focus is on improving the fronts of commercial buildings. Committee volunteers work with professionals, such as architects, to create facade renderings and to coordinate contracting services, sometimes in partnership with statewide coordinating programs, such as New Mexico Main Street (New Mexico 2014). Efforts can also be much more basic, such as volunteers helping with demolition work or repainting, as with the Pryor (OK) Main Street program or the Victor (CO) Main Street program, where in the summers of 2012 and 2013, volunteers repainted the facades of fourteen buildings (Hollowell 2014; Pryor 2014).

Master Plans

A master plan is usually associated with municipal planning efforts to create a comprehensive vision for a geographically bounded area that addresses land use and zoning, streetscapes, transportation, parking, historic preservation, and parks and open space. For dense, commercial downtowns with older buildings, there is an emphasis on encouraging pedestrian activity, supporting mixed-use development, converting one-way streets back to two-way, and rehabilitating existing buildings, where feasible. Larger cities with full-time planners frequently create master plans, but smaller municipalities, who often have no planners on staff, often lack this essential guiding document, and downtown development efforts can be chaotic and lack vision.

Main Street programs have successfully stepped into this vacuum and created a master plan in partnership with their municipality. A typical example of this process is Main Street Franklin (North Carolina), which began efforts toward a master plan with a community visioning process, followed by securing a grant to hire a firm to prepare a plan and then hiring a planning firm to complete the plan (Schlott 2011). Municipalities typically welcome the efforts of Main Street programs in developing master plans because it "can help lessen the municipality's workload and financial burden by sharing leadership" (Kalogeresis 2009, 156). Volunteers, representing the community's interests, therefore become directly involved in setting the overall design vision for their own community.

Public Art

Public art projects in Main Street programs range from the visually spectacular, such as murals and sculptures, to less expensive but creative endeavors, such as Orlando (Florida) Main Street's work with local artists to transform twenty engineering utility cabinets into visual art (Orlando 2013). Alberta (Oregon) Main Street program's goal was more ambitious when its design committee invited twenty-five artists to submit proposals for seven permanent public art installations that attached to bus railings. According to the Larry Holmes, the volunteer design committee chair, artists were asked to "propose installations that created a street identity inspired by the texture, character and diversity of the community, provided continuity from end to end, but with diversity of form and concept and satisfied appetites for exciting and provocative sensory experiences" (Alberta 2014). Other Main Street programs have catalyzed the creation of murals, as Historic Downtown Lamar's (Colorado) design committee did when it partnered with the Southeast Colorado Arts Council to create a mural in a downtown park (Lamar 2014).

The Disneyfication of Main Street and Cultural Conflicts

Based on the broad array of potential design activities available to Main Street programs, community volunteers who work in these programs clearly have a significant role in the overall appearance of their downtown. Through volunteer activities, the community's will becomes imprinted in the physical landscape of the downtown. While professionals are often involved in streetscape and facade restorations, it is these volunteers who often make the final decisions as to what is and is not built, especially in the case of facade grants where volunteers have *bona fide* power to control the design of their downtown. In other cases, such as master plans, volunteers' influence is more limited, but still significant.

Critics charge that the resulting design changes these volunteers make to their downtowns look too much like Disneyland's "Main Street USA," which is a scaled-down replica of downtown Fort Collins, Colorado (Francaviglia 1996, 148). Richard Francaviglia (1996, 178, 179) describes:

> The cumulative or overall effect of the Main Street Program has been to either stop change along Main Street or to reverse it, so that the streetscapes are often backdated in appearance. Sometimes through the placing of awnings or the careful selection of signage and paint, these buildings begin to take on a visual uniformity that unites them as a retail marketing package—much in the way Walt Disney marketed in his Main Street.

Street lamps, brick paving, and benches all tend to look similar across the entire country, regardless if the downtown is in Maine or Arizona, which disturbs many historic preservationists and architects who see this homogeneity as injurious to historical authenticity and regionalism. Philip Jackson and Robert Kuhlken (2006, 46) note that Main Street programs "seek to freeze-frame a period of time in hopes of capitalizing on nostalgia." But, as Stephen Williams and Alan Lew (2014, 128) argue, the Main Street program flexibly defines authenticity to recognize that "the postmodern tourist . . . is more interested in the experience, no matter its source, than any objective measure of authenticity."

This rhetoric fails to validate the community's own values used to define what it thinks is important in terms of design. Because Main Street volunteers share similar values in terms of appropriate and inappropriate design interventions that conserve the historical authenticity of their downtown, they form a kind of "revitalization culture" due to their shared beliefs (Wells 2010). This revitalization culture is defined, in part, by its members' rejection of orthodox preservation doctrine, including the reliance on fabric-based definitions of authenticity that is part of what Laurajane Smith (2006) refers to as the "Authorized Heritage Discourse" (AHD) that is created and defined by experts. Because the values expressed by the AHD are in themselves another set of cultural values, rather than objective, scientific "truths" (Waterton, Smith, and Campbell 2006), critiques against the design choices made by adherents to the AHD against Main Street volunteers are not necessarily objective, nor of an intrinsically greater value than the volunteers' own values and beliefs.

Ultimately, the way that volunteers wish to have the historical authenticity of their downtowns expressed usually successfully revives distressed downtowns. Tourists, who have a value system more closely allied to the revitalization culture than the AHD, readily appreciate downtowns under the purview of Main Street programs. Arguably, the penchant that the revitalization culture has for restoration versus preservation (i.e., retention of all layers of changed building fabric from various time periods) results in the loss of informational value. Is it more important to save the downtown by using a more flexible, sociocultural definition of historical authenticity, or should we let it collapse in ruin in order to privilege preservation doctrine and material authenticity? The former solution, which values people and living communities over the physical fabric, is more likely to win advocates than an unsustainable archeological method.

Volunteers, Skepticism, Political Issues, and Advocacy

According to the Trust, "Main Street programs emphasize grassroots support, which is a different philosophical underpinning than most community or economic development strategies" (Adkins and Lynch 2009, 28). As a Main Street manager and later as a faculty member guiding graduate students in planning for Main Street programs, I encountered a common misperception from community members, city staff, and political leaders—that a successful downtown revitalization program requires many paid employees. This staff-heavy model is common with community development corporations (CDCs) or municipalities, which rely on paid employees to drive and implement revitalization programs. If a Main Street program is properly implemented according to the Trust's guidelines, however, volunteers perform nearly all of the program's activities, which makes this volunteer-reliant approach quite different from the way most downtown revitalization entities operate. In the Main Street approach, the members of a community make the decision to create their own program, design it to their needs, and then provide the labor, vision, and know-how to implement it. As the Trust directs, "the Main Street approach relies on creating community-driven, not staff-driven, programs in order to encourage the support and involvement of local stakeholders" (Adkins and Lynch 2009, 25). The purpose of a Main Street manager, who is often the only paid staff person in the organization, is to manage and coordinate the efforts of these volunteers, but not to do their work for them (Adkins and Lynch 2009, 26). Therefore, the more a community "buys-in" to a Main Street program, the more potential volunteers there are to help implement projects, which is why successful Main Street programs not only have a large volunteer base but broad community support.

Volunteers in the organization, economic restructuring, design, and promotion committees, with guidance from the Main Street manager, create work plans that define goals, objectives, specific tasks, and people who are to complete these tasks. The board of directors, also composed of volunteers, then approves these work plans. While it is the responsibility of these committees and the board of directors to create projects, it is also their responsibility to implement them. Ideally, "tasks must be delegated to volunteers, not staff" (Adkins and Lynch 2009, 27).

In what the Trust refers to as the "catalyst phase" (Adkins and Dono 2009, 21), when the program is just beginning, supporters tend to be outnumbered by skeptics in the community. This reaction is understandable, given that Main Street programs begin in distressed, underutilized downtown areas that have long been full of empty storefronts, are dirty and unmaintained, and feel unsafe. In this climate, a few enterprising individuals convince fellow community members to form a visioning group, create a plan for a Main Street program, and then seek the necessary funds from grants and donations to hire a full-time Main Street manager. These early volunteer efforts, if successful, usually attract an increasing number of supporters of the Main Street program, but many communities have persistent naysayers who are, at a minimum, suspect of downtown revitalization approaches, and may be outright hostile, potentially sabotaging efforts (Goforth 2009; Simmons 2013). Sometimes naysayers are members of city councils, which can hurt efforts to create the necessary public-private partnership for a successful Main Street program. Champions of a nascent Main Street program also need to be politically savvy and not alienate potential supporters who could offer funding. This latter aspect can be particularly challenging because, in this early stage before an organization is formed and a Main Street manager hired, all members of a Main Street are community volunteers who have a great deal of behavioral latitude not typically expressed by a paid employee. For this reason, some early Main Street programs earn an activist reputation that may not sit well with conservative, small-town government, especially when trust, stability, and reliability are paramount. On the other hand, volunteers who are too complacent and not willing to question the status quo and exceed expectations will see their early organizational efforts flounder.

This middle ground, most aptly described as "advocacy," requires that volunteers build relationships with elected officials in order to "produce policies that benefit [the] program" and "defend against threats" (Sincavage and VanBellenghem 2009, 60). These efforts include preparing a message on the need for a Main Street program, effectively communicating with elected officials, and developing partnerships with allied organizations in an effort to pool resources. Outreach efforts include the use of websites, social media, e-mail, and plenty of face-to-face meetings. This was a critical component of my work as a Main Street manager, where I had regular meetings with my state and federal representatives and senators, along with local council members, to promote the Main Street approach, my program, and its volunteers and to seek funding opportunities. My volunteer board members met with many of the same people, usually during the day, and sometimes struggled to balance personal and professional commitments with their Main Street work. For this reason, some of my most proactive board members ran their own downtown businesses, which provided the needed flexibility. This relationship with elected officials needs to be carefully cultivated, realizing that the elected officials usually desire a positive public relations opportunity by being associated with a successful Main Street program.

Once a Main Street program is established, a reliable funding stream secured, and a full-time manager hired, the program enters the "growth" phase in which large-scale problems are addressed, such as streetscape design or the development of a master plan. These efforts require a close partnership with a local municipality and the development of a high level of trust between both entities. In my work as a Main Street manager in Quakertown, Pennsylvania, I saw how local government officials and borough council members sometimes resisted the efforts of the Main Street program due to the perception that volunteers were not qualified to make design decisions, that sufficient funding could not be located, and that the interest of the Main Street stakeholders did not match the broader interests of the larger community. The Main Street program in Quakertown persevered and garnered the trust of the borough and downtown stakeholders, although the gains—a couple of community parks—took more than a decade to achieve. The Trust recognizes that these kinds of slow results are fairly typical of most Main Street programs (Adkins and Dono 2009, 21), which mirrors my own experience not only in Quakertown but in other communities as well. For instance, when I volunteered for the Main Street program in Kennewick, Washington, in the first five years of the design committee's existence, its most significant achievement was establishing a facade grant program.

Baby Steps, Funding, Comprehensiveness, and Community Buy-In

Because of the need for patience, the Trust is careful, when describing the development phases of a Main Street program, to stress that the overall process can be distressingly slow. A typical Main Street program may take a decade or more to produce large-scale and dramatic differences for a community (Adkins and Dono 2009, 21). This situation can be frustrating for those involved, especially volunteers who view their donation of time, resources, and money as an investment in their community. During the development and growth of the Main Street program, design projects are more likely to fail than succeed, if for no other reason than a lack of patience. The Trust addresses this issue by advocating the concept of taking baby steps in the work of Main Street programs, which emphasizes quality over quantity. As Vince Martinez from the Colorado Community Revitalization Association advises, these programs recognize the value of patience and that there is no instant solution for a "downtown [that] has gone into neglect over decades" (Darnell 2007).

A perennial issue for most non-profits, including Main Street programs, is securing unrestricted funding sources that can be used to pay the salary of a full-time Main Street manager. Without a manager to coordinate the activities of volunteers, the program is much more likely to fail, based on the early experiences of the Trust in launching the Main Street approach through the first pilot programs in 1976 (Dalibard 1985) and substantiated by four decades of evidence. Most foundations will not allow their grants to pay for employee salaries, which means that the only other reliable sources are direct donations from stakeholders, including membership fees, and government funding sources. A Main Street program should be able to secure an annual source of funding from their municipality, even if it is a small amount, as it shows that the town or city has a vested stake in the success of the program. The lack of this funding source is indicative of a poor relationship between the Main Street program and the municipality, and also indicates a lack of volunteer participation in advocacy and outreach efforts. State economic development departments are also a source of funding for salaries. Until the 2007–9 recession, when the grant program was changed, the Pennsylvania Department of Community and Economic Development held the distinction for the most generous grants for Main Street programs, completely funding most programs' needs for the first five years of their existence, including the Main Street manager's salary.

Even with adequate funding, Main Street programs often fail because they neglect to focus equally on each of the four points (Means 2014, 51). Frequently, there is an overemphasis on promotion, while the other three points are deprecated, especially economic restructuring and, to a lesser degree, design. These "skin deep" programs fail on a number of levels, including the ability to justify their own existence.

But perhaps most importantly, community buy-in is essential for the creation, growth, and maintenance of a Main Street program and appears to be positively correlated with the length of tenure of both volunteers and Main Street managers (Kimmel and Schoening 2011, 4). The relationship between the participation of a community in planning processes and an increase in community-buy is well established (Roberts 2008; Flint 2012; Gallent and Robinson 2012), so it would not be unreasonable to see this same relationship expressed in Main Street programs.

Moreover, this kind of community buy-in translates to empowering a community through ownership of the overall revitalization process. Main Street programs that rely too much on paid staff and/or a small number of volunteers in lieu of a wider community base are much more likely to fail in the long term due to a number of factors, including a lack of constituency support in the eyes of elected leaders.

Conclusion

Main Street programs represent one of the more effective ways that community stakeholders can empower themselves to design significant aspects of their own historic, commercial downtown. A successful program, which is a powerful vehicle to engage a community through volunteer efforts, can be responsible for the design of a wide variety of public amenities, including streetscapes, parks, and public art. Volunteers in Main Street programs can even influence how private owners treat buildings through financial incentives, such as facade grants, and promoting effective visual merchandizing. While sometimes controversial, the design decisions that volunteers make are more reflective of community values than those made by design and preservation professionals.

Volunteers in Main Street programs are afforded this unique opportunity to directly influence the design of their downtown because of the emphasis on the community helping itself. This grassroots approach means that volunteers have to engage in political processes and learn the balance between activism and complacency so that they are seen positively as advocates for their downtowns. Volunteers in these kinds of programs also face the challenge of being seen as unqualified to do their work, yet experience proves that in many cases, volunteers produce superior results compared to hired staff and consultants. The reason for this situation is likely due to the fact that these volunteers feel far more invested in the outcome of their efforts than any outside consultant could ever be. While often thought of as a detriment, Main Street programs' slow process toward revitalization allows volunteers the chance to patiently engage skeptics and change opinions, resulting in a gradual but continual process of community buy-in that is essential to any revitalization program.

My work as a volunteer in Main Street and Elm Street programs helped me better understand my own volunteers' perspectives and challenges when I later became a Main Street manager. At the end of what were very long days, it was easier for me to commiserate with my volunteers' challenges than to complain about the fact that I had to be at meetings several times a week until late at night. In some ways, the work of volunteers is much more difficult than paid staff because you never can truly leave your work behind when you go home. As a Main Street program matures, the community increasingly looks toward their nascent Main Street volunteers as leaders, and with this evolution comes trust, which is essential as the community waits many years for changes to occur.

There are few other programs with the longevity and record of success of the Main Street approach that empower community volunteers to the same extent.

While concrete, empirical data may be lacking to understand causal relationships for success, the fact remains that Main Street programs, when properly implemented according to the Trust's guidelines, are a powerful tool for catalyzing community design.

Notes

1 The National Trust for Historic Preservation is a non-profit organization that United States Congress chartered in 1949 to serve as a nationwide advocate for historic preservation activities. See SavingPlaces.org.
2 Pennsylvania's Elm Street program takes the precepts of the Main Street approach and applies it to a residential area. See http://www.padowntown.org/programs-services/elm-street.
3 See http://www.preservationnation.org/main-street/about-main-street/reinvestment-statistics-1.html.
4 As of 2014, the Trust indicates that there are forty-five statewide and regional coordinating programs that receive direct support from the National Main Street Center. See http://www.preservationnation.org/main-street/about-main-street/the-programs/coordinating-program-types.html.

References

Adkins, Lauren, and Andrea L. Dono. 2009. "Planning Main Streets Work." In *Revitalizing Main Street: A Practitioner's Guide to Comprehensive Commercial District Revitalization*, Andrea L. Dono, and Linda S. Glisson, eds. Washington, DC: National Trust for Historic Preservation, 15–24.
Adkins, Lauren, and Teresa Lynch. 2009. "Running a Community-Driven Program." In *Revitalizing Main Street: A Practitioner's Guide to Comprehensive Commercial District Revitalization*, Andrea L. Dono, and Linda S. Glisson, eds. Washington, DC: National Trust for Historic Preservation, 25–36.
Alberta. 2014. "Woven Chakras." *Alberta Main Street.* http://albertamainst.org/whats-happening/public-art/railing-art. Accessed 27 December 2014.
Banks, Ray. 1988. "The Civic Trust and Amenity Societies." In *Culture, Education and the State*, Michael D. Stephens, ed. London: Routledge, 113–29.
Bishoff, Murray. 24 September 2010. "Monett Main Street Program Begins Downtown Effort." *The Monett Times.*
Bull, Natalie, and Camille Girard-Ruel. 2009. *Main Street: Past and Present.* Ottawa, ON: Heritage Canada Foundation.
Cedar Falls. 2014a. "Facade Grant Program." *Cedar Falls Community Main Street.* http://www.communitymainstreet.org/join/facade-grant-program.aspx. Accessed 2 January 2015.
Cedar Falls. 2014b. "Design Guidelines to Enhance the Downtown Historical District." *Cedar Falls Community Main Street.* http://www.communitymainstreet.org/webres/File/Design%20Guidelines(1).pdf. Accessed 5 January 2015.
Civic Trust. 1967. *Magdalen Street, Norwich: The Story of an Experiment in Civic Design That Became Famous.* London: Civic Trust.
Dalibard, Jacques. 1985. "The Historical Context." In *Reviving Main Street*, Deryck Holdsworth, ed. Toronto: University of Toronto Press, 57–62.
Dane, Suzanne G. 1997. *Main Street Success Stories.* Washington, DC: National Main Street Center, National Trust for Historic Preservation.

Darnell, Marcia. 2007. "What Is a Main Street Program?" *Colorado Central Magazine*, January.

Dono, Andrew L., and Linda S. Glisson, eds. 2009. *Revitalizing Main Street: A Practitioner's Guide to Comprehensive Commercial District Revitalization*. Washington, DC: National Trust for Historic Preservation.

Downtown Roseburg. 1 April 2013. "The 7 Essentials of Eye Catching Storefronts." *The Downtown Beat*, 18: 1.

Flint, R. Warren. 2012. *Practice of Sustainable Community Development: A Participatory Framework for Change*. New York and London: Springer.

Francaviglia, Richard V. 1996. *Main Street Revisited: Time, Space, and Image Building in Small-Town America*. Iowa City: University of Iowa Press.

Gallent, Nick, and Steve Robinson. 2012. *Neighbourhood Planning: Communities, Networks and Governance*. Bristol: Policy Press.

Goforth, Michael. 28 November 2009. "What Main Street Program Had in Mind." *TC Palm*.

Hanford. 2014. "Main Street Hanford Facade Grant Program." *Main Street Hanford*. http://www.mainstreethanford.com/directory/facade.pdf. Accessed 2 January 2015.

Hollowell, Ashleigh. 15 April 2014. "Victor Receives Main Street Designation." *Pikes Peak Courier*.

Jackson, Philip Lloyd, and Robert Kuhlken. 2006. *A Rediscovered Frontier: Land Use and Resource Issues in the New West*. Lanham, MD: Rowman & Littlefield Publishers.

Kalogeresis, Nicholas P. 2009. "Master Planning." In *Revitalizing Main Street: A Practitioner's Guide to Comprehensive Commercial District Revitalization*, Andrea L. Dono, and Linda S. Glisson, eds. Washington, DC: National Trust for Historic Preservation, 149–60.

Kimmel, Chad, and Joel Schoening. 2011. *An Evaluation of Pennsylvania's Main Street Programs*. Harrisburg, PA: The Center for Rural Pennsylvania.

Lamar. 2014. *2013 Annual Report*. Lamar, CO: Historic Downtown Lamar/Lamar Partnership, Inc.

Lawniczak, Joe. 2009a. "Historic Preservation Tools." In *Revitalizing Main Street: A Practitioner's Guide to Comprehensive Commercial District Revitalization*, Andrea L. Dono, and Linda S. Glisson, eds. Washington, DC: National Trust for Historic Preservation, 127–31.

———. 2009b. "Improving Appearances." In *Revitalizing Main Street: A Practitioner's Guide to Comprehensive Commercial District Revitalization*, Andrea L. Dono, and Linda S. Glisson, eds. Washington, DC: National Trust for Historic Preservation, 111–26.

———. 2009c. "Public Improvements." In *Revitalizing Main Street: A Practitioner's Guide to Comprehensive Commercial District Revitalization*, Andrea L. Dono, and Linda S. Glisson, eds. Washington, DC: National Trust for Historic Preservation, 141–8.

Loescher, Doug. 2009a. "Why Main Street Matters." In *Revitalizing Main Street: A Practitioner's Guide to Comprehensive Commercial District Revitalization*, Andrea L. Dono, and Linda S. Glisson, eds. Washington, DC: National Trust for Historic Preservation, 7–10.

———. 2009b. "How the Main Street Approach Works." In *Revitalizing Main Street: A Practitioner's Guide to Comprehensive Commercial District Revitalization*, Andrea L. Dono, and Linda S. Glisson, eds. Washington, DC: National Trust for Historic Preservation, 11–13.

Means, Mary. Fall 2014. "Leadership and Main Street." *Main Street Now*, 48–58.

New Mexico. 2014. "MainStreet Facade Squad." *New Mexico Main Street*. http://nmmainstreet.org/Photo_Gallery/Facade_Squad. Accessed 20 December 2014.

Orlando. 2013. *Orlando Main Street 2012 Annual Report*. Orlando, FL: Orlando Main Street Program.

Paso Robles. 2014. "Design Guidelines." Paso Robles Main Street. http://www.prcity.com/government/departments/commdev/planning/pdf/design-guidelines/DistrictA.pdf. Accessed 14 December 2014.

Pryor. 2014. "Join the Main Street Facade Squad." *Pryor Main Street*. https://www.facebook.com/458908497466381/posts/853039781386582. Accessed 15 December 2014.

Roberts, Nancy Charlotte. 2008. *The Age of Direct Citizen Participation*. Armonk, NY: M.E. Sharpe.

Robertson, Kent A. 2004. "The Main Street Approach to Downtown Development: An Examination of the Four-point Program." *Journal of Architectural and Planning Research*, 21(1): 55–73.

Schlott, Linda F. 2011. *Franklin Main Street Program 2010–2011 Annual Report*. Franklin, NC: Franklin Main Street.

Sheridan. 2014. "Design." *Downtown Sheridan Association*. http://downtownsheridan.org/main-street-committees/design-committee/. Accessed 20 December 2014.

Simmons, Katie. 21 November 2013. "Downtown Newark Partnership Celebrates 15 years." *Newark Post*.

Sincavage, Rhonda, and Stacey VanBellenghem. 2009. "Effective Advocacy for Main Street Programs." In *Revitalizing Main Street: A Practitioner's Guide to Comprehensive Commercial District Revitalization*, Andrea L. Dono, and Linda S. Glisson, eds. Washington, DC: National Trust for Historic Preservation, 59–68.

Smith, Laurajane. 2006. *Uses of Heritage*. London and New York: Routledge.

Steele, Leon. 2009. "Visual Merchandizing." In *Revitalizing Main Street: A Practitioner's Guide to Comprehensive Commercial District Revitalization*, Andrea L. Dono, and Linda S. Glisson, eds. Washington, DC: National Trust for Historic Preservation, 103–10.

Thibodaux. 2014. "Thibodaux Main Street, Inc. Facade Grant Program." *Thibodaux Main Street, Inc.* http://www.downtownthibodaux.org/wp-content/uploads/2012/04/Facade-Grant-Guidelines-2014–15.pdf. Accessed 28 December 2014.

Victoria. 2014. "Benefits of the Main Street Program." *Victoria Main Street Program*. http://www.victoriamainstreet.com/benefits.html. Accessed 21 December 2014.

Waterton, Emma, Laurajane Smith, and Gary Campbell. 2006. "The Utility of Discourse Analysis to Heritage Studies: The Burra Charter and Social Inclusion." *International Journal of Heritage Studies*, 12(4): 339–55.

Weeks, Kay, and Ann Grimmer. 1995. The Secretary of the Interior's Standards for the Treatment of Historic Properties with Guidelines for Preservation, Rehabilitation, Restoration, and Reconstruction of Historic Buildings. Washington, DC: U.S. Dept. of the Interior, National Park Service. http://www.nps.gov/tps/standards/rehabilitation/rehab/stand.htm. Accessed 24 August 2016.

Wells, Jeremy C. 2010. "Our History Is Not False: Perspectives From the Revitalisation Culture." *International Journal of Heritage Studies*, 16(6): 464–85.

Williams, Stephen, and Alan A. Lew. 2014. *Tourism Geography: Critical Understandings of Place, Space and Experience*. New York: Routledge.

Winter Haven. 2014. "Facade Grant Program." *Main Street Winter Haven*. http://www.mainstreetwh.com/art—architecture/facade-grant-program/. Accessed 14 December.

Woods, Kevin M. 2002. "Downtown Merchants Get Tips to Grow Businesses." *New London Main Street*, 4(3): 5.

12

BUILDING STREETS AND BUILDING COMMUNITY

Katherine Melcher

Introduction

Residents of West Oakland, California, build benches outside their homes and businesses. By creating and using these sidewalk living rooms, they become a visible part of the neighborhood, staking claim to the space. Neighbors in Portland, Oregon, turn a street intersection into a painted plaza with community facilities—a bulletin board, a tea stand, and a community library—on the corners. By collectively designing and using the space, they build relationships with each other as well as with the place. In several small towns in Mid-America, residents plan and execute Main Street murals. By expressing their shared past and their future hopes through the murals, they help redefine the community's identity.

Each of these acts claims the public space of a street for community use. Each one challenges the assumption that streets are solely for efficient traffic flow, opening up their potential to become places of connection, meaning, and empowerment.

Although these acts create "self-made urban spaces, reclaimed and appropriated sites" and "have provided new expressions of the collective realms in the city" (Hou 2010, 2), they are not simply ad hoc, spontaneous acts of insurgent urbanism. They are carefully orchestrated hybrids of top-down and bottom-up approaches facilitated by professional practitioners (Steve Rasmussen Cancian, Mark Lakeman of City Repair, and Dave Loewenstein, respectively). These community-built practitioners negotiate the tensions between grassroots efforts and city regulations, individual contributions and communal expression, and inclusive processes and meaningful participation, in order to build place-based communities.

The concept of insurgent urbanism and its relatives (do-it-yourself [DIY] urbanism, everyday urbanism, and tactical urbanism) implies that institutions and professionals create generic places that suppress community expression and ownership, while ordinary people use the tactics of resistance in order to create meaning within those places (Franck and Stevens 2007; Hou 2010; Iveson 2013; Pagano 2013). Community-built practices, such as those listed previously, suggest methods for negotiating this dichotomy, ways to build grassroots community efforts into official streetscapes. This chapter examines three cases in order to better understand how community-built processes can build connection, meaning, and empowerment into community places.

All three of the examples contain community processes that build relationships, meaning, and ownership, but for the sake of simplification, each individual case is explored in terms of a single objective (i.e., relationships, meaning, or ownership). Intersection Repair projects by City Repair in Portland, Oregon, demonstrate how the process of design can create stronger relationships between neighbors. The Mid-America Mural Project facilitated by artist Dave Loewenstein in Oklahoma, Kansas, Arkansas, Missouri, Nebraska, and Texas is used to explore how meaning is negotiated and expressed in downtown mural projects. The Sidewalk Living Room projects started by Steve Rasmussen Cancian along with the West Oakland Greening Project provide insight into the role ownership plays in creating a community space.

Building Relationships: Intersection Repair

> The difference between a thriving neighborhood and an isolated grid city is the communication that happens between neighbors.
>
> *(City Repair 2006, 44)*

It has long been acknowledged that the past century of planning and urban design practices, with their emphasis on efficiency, have been destructive to the social fabric in community and neighborhood life (Jacobs 1961; Appleyard, Gerson, and Lintell 1981). Design approaches such as designing on a human scale, mixing land uses to bring life back to the street, and incorporating elements such as benches to encourage interaction, aim to mend some of the tears in this fabric (Leccese and McCormick 2000; Whyte 2001; Gehl 2010).

In Intersection Repair projects, neighbors use many of the techniques listed previously to collaboratively transform a neighborhood intersection into a community plaza. They convert the street into a pedestrian space by painting a colorful mandala in its centre. They add benches, tea stands, and community bulletin boards on the street corners, giving people a reason to stop and gather.

However, the design elements are not the most important part of Intersection Repair projects: "much of the essence of an Intersection Repair is often unseen. Behind the community kiosks, benches, murals and other structural elements, is a neighborhood that has come together to converse, collaborate and celebrate" (City Repair 2006, 17). It is through the process of designing and building the new space that new relationships are formed and existing ones are strengthened. As Intersection Repair participant Kate Gengo commented, "This is the only way I'm able to meet my neighbors on a personal level" (qtd. in Nelson 2011).

FIGURE 12.1 Intersection Repair at Sunnyside Plaza, Portland, Oregon

Source: Katherine Melcher

Participation in design and planning is not a new concept, but Intersection Repair places it in a central role: "Citizen involvement, participation, and collaboration are the heart of a project, and often even more important than what may be physically built as a result" (City Repair 2006, 44). A review of the City Repair's *Placemaking Guidebook* (2006) and several articles on Intersection Repair projects (Semenza 2003; Semenza 2005; Semenza and March 2009; Nelson 2011) helped

FIGURE 12.2   Share-It Square Intersection Repair, Portland, Oregon

Source: Katherine Melcher

identify five key relationship-building elements that distinguish Intersection Repair from a standard participatory design process.

1. The Effort is Community-Initiated and Community-Led.

Intersection Repair projects are not initiated by the local government; neighbors initiate the project. Rather than neighbors banding together to protest and fight an official decision; they are gathering together to be constructive, literally and figuratively. Although the first Intersection Repair project developed in reaction to a car-bicycle accident and the desire to create a safer street, the neighbors focused on making a concrete change rather than submitting a complaint. In these cases, the neighbors are the agents of change.

2. The Process Emphasizes Having Fun and Socializing in a Relaxed and Comfortable Manner.

Intersection Repair emphasizes taking time to get to know one another before embarking on a project. They recommend that the initial meetings be in a comfortable, accessible setting, and emphasize that projects do not even have to be discussed at this point. Events such as potlucks and block parties can begin the process.

3. Despite the Fun and the Social Atmosphere, Creating Honest Discussion and Meaningful Participation Is Taken Seriously.

Meaningful participation is based on the principle that everyone is invited to participate and that everyone has something of value to give. Outreach is a never-ending process, and the organizers provide multiple ways for people to get involved. For example, consider the Sunnyside Piazza project:

> The homeless participated in all community activities such as the street painting and as a result took pride and ownership in the neighborhood; the homeless helped to clean up litter and waste and have donated materials that were incorporated into the structures.
>
> *(Semenza 2005, 474)*

Part of meaningful participation is that everyone's opinions are acknowledged and respected, which also means that conflicts need to be addressed. Working through conflicts can actually create strong relationships. In one case, an argument over what colors to use resulted in a realization that the relationships between the neighbors were more important than what color ended up being used (City Repair 2006).

4. Working Together to Solve Problems Fosters a Sense of Interdependence.

Because everyone has something to contribute, everyone relies on each other to realize the project. Additionally, the physical act of building something together appears to strengthen those relationships:

> Working together on ecological construction, particularly working with cob (a natural building material), which relies on collective physical labour, stimulates social interactions and increases physical activity. Other activities, such as community organizing and design workshops contribute to expanding social ties as well.
>
> *(Semenza 2005, 465)*

5. The Project Is Seen as a Starting Point, Not an End.

Continued programming in the place, such as movie nights and annual painting parties, keeps the community engaged with the place and with each other. Often, community members move on to create new projects or add new items to the intersection.

To conclude, architects can design spaces that encourage people to interact, but the process of creating those spaces with community residents can develop those interactions into relationships. As Pagano (2013) observed in DIY urbanism efforts, the process of design and construction can be a small-scale experiment in participatory and collaborative democracy.

Building Meaning: The Mid-America Mural Project

> We together, through this process, are reclaiming how the community including its history, current challenges and future aspirations is portrayed and understood.
>
> *(Loewenstein 2013b)*

Even the "best practices" in streetscape design, when reproduced systematically, can result in monotonous, generic places that lack local resonance. On the other hand, when people have multiple perspectives on what their "home" means to them, developing one design that respects this diversity is near impossible. Loewenstein (2010b) observes:

> Working to evoke the history, culture, and people of a place with any sort of objective truth in a public artwork is a daunting task. As you begin to do research, it becomes clear that perceptions of history, culture, and development are rarely static or monolithic. Every place and every community of people

FIGURE 12.3   Community members painting *Storytellers: Sharing the Legacy* mural in East Waco, Texas

Source: Dave Loewenstein

has many overlapping notions about their history and community, many of which are in flux as economic, political, and demographic circumstances change.

The Mid-America Mural Project, sponsored by the Mid-America Arts Alliance, uses murals to express complex stories about a community and its past. Through a process guided by a team of artists, community members develop a mural that contains many different stories and images of their home yet also expresses a unified sentiment.

As in the Intersection Repair process, the mural process emphasizes participation, providing opportunities for many different levels of involvement. The following are elements in the process (as described in the project's blog and local newspaper articles) that help the artists and residents incorporate significant local meaning into the murals.

1. The Artist Team Spends Time to Get to Know the Community: The People They Work With, the Physical Neighborhood, the History, the Stories, and the Cultures.

The artists in the Mid-America Mural Project got to know the community, not just by attending meetings and conducting workshops, but also by walking around, looking at public art, architecture, and other monuments. They checked out the local scene and scenery, combining socializing with work. Along the way, they engaged in informal conversations with residents about the place: "We are visitors here, listening and learning and not as familiar with the history of this place, so we rely on local people to help us understand what is important" (Loewenstein qtd. in Bryan 2012). Through conversations, they learn about what history is important to the residents; sometimes the history would not have been found otherwise: "Right off the bat we heard about a past that's nearly non-existent in Waco's local history books. In all the sources that we could find claiming to tell Waco's story, African-Americans hardly existed" (Loewenstein 2013a).

2. The Artists Ask Community Residents to Move Beyond the Standard Town Symbols to Share Personal Stories of What the Place Means to Them.

What we learned is that although people who live in the same town may share certain cultural and historical symbols, (In Joplin those would include mining, Route 66, and the eagle mascot) their deeper sense of identity is much more personal and is built from first-hand experience. And whether it's kids or grown-ups, this is where the richest material for art is found—in those specific and personal examples of how we know, remember, and envision our home.

(Loewenstein 2011c)

In addition to informal conversations, the artists hold a general meeting where they explain the project, share examples of other murals, and ask for ideas from the audience. They allow everyone to share ideas and write them all down "without criticism or interruption" (Loewenstein 2011a).

> This isn't just to get "buy-in" (a phrase that sounds suspiciously like a bribe to me), it is because the knowledge and experience of residents are what will shape the content of a mural that is authentic and embraced by them.
>
> *(Loewenstein 2012a)*

Sometimes they include exercises for children, with prompts such as "Imagine that all the people, animals, buildings, and bicycles from here dreamed a dream together for [your town]," or "Design a video game that takes players on an adventure through what makes your home town unique" (Loewenstein 2011b).

Interested residents are invited to continue with the design process as a design team. They participate in additional workshops to refine the ideas shared at the first meetings, and they undertake additional historical research.

3. The Artists Acknowledge Upfront That Not Everything Will Be Included in the Mural, and Conflicts Are Addressed Openly.

Because the goal is to create a "a picture story, both meaningful and visually captivating, that conjures the spirit of our conversations, the facts and figures we have gathered, and the input from people in the community that has been shared with us" (Loewenstein 2010a), and "not just a simple enumeration of things" (Loewenstein 2010b), most of the ideas collected end up on the cutting room floor.

To address this concern, Loewenstein lets people know from the beginning that not everything will be included:

> I . . . am quick to admit that it's nearly impossible to include everything that is suggested by participants in the final mural. To do so would make something more like a tourist brochure and less like an artwork. Instead I suggest that we aspire to make a mural that is like a visual poem or folksong, with an emphasis on symbol and metaphor, supported by specific references to place, people and history.
>
> *(Loewenstein 2012a)*

He also acknowledges that conflicts are inherent in the process, but differences can make for a more interesting and more meaningful project:

> The regular discussions, about what scenes and symbols best caught the spirit of Arkadelphia, could become heated at times. Loewenstein said the depth of feelings and the variety of ideas expressed make the creative process of

designing the mural fun. "There were different points of view, but we worked it out together," he said.

(Bryan 2012)

Even if some good ideas get cut from the project, they can be saved for future murals:

> It is an imperfect process, and as I keep reminding everyone who asks whether this or that will be in the final design—this is just the first mural. There are lots of great walls in Tonkawa just aching for a good idea and a little color.
>
> *(Loewenstein 2010a)*

4. To Create an Integrated "Visual Poem" Rather than a Cluster of Ideas, the Artists and Design Team Work Together to Develop Metaphors and Themes That Can Link Several Concepts.

The design team, working in groups of three, does another round of brainstorming around themes and metaphors. The artists share examples of visual metaphors from other murals and introduce ones encountered in local research. For example, in Arkadelphia, Arkansas, bridges, porches, and arches were considered. Design team participants were then asked to draw their own bridge, consider what it is made of, what it connects, what it spans, and what is on it. Another exercise used is creating "word pictures": placing in a rectangle "words and phrases that refer to the imagery to be included in the design, with the size and position of these words and phrases written to correspond to their relative importance" (Loewenstein 2011c).

After each of these sessions, the small groups present their work back to the larger group:

> The conversations that happen around these presentations are always some of the most compelling and fruitful. It seems that holding up an artwork you've made, no matter how modest, stimulates a person's capacity to articulate their intentions by allowing them to speak *through* the imagery they have created.
>
> *(Loewenstein 2011c)*

Through this process of discussion, design, and sharing, an idea that helps bring it all together seems to emerge in an "aha" kind of moment. In Tonkawa, Oklahoma, they used the image of a local pilot delivering local newspapers by dropping them from his plane to deliver the historic news across the mural. In Joplin, Missouri, children's drawings of butterflies came to life, flying across the wall. In Newton, Kansas, the image of a crossroads pulled elements together.

To finalize the mural design, Loewenstein's team of artists takes the word pictures from the design team and the metaphors, synthesizes them into a composition,

FIGURE 12.4   Dance performance and live music at *The Imagineers* mural celebration in Newton, Kansas

Source: Dave Loewenstein

and presents it back to the design team (and other stakeholders) for one more discussion, often adding and changing elements. Finally, the composition is transferred to the wall, and the entire community is invited to help paint the mural in a celebratory event that includes local food, music, and dancing.

The resulting murals become a source of individual and community pride. Even though the goal of the project is to create a mural with personal, shared meanings about the place where the participants live, the project also encourages interaction and development of personal relationships:

> So a big mural like this presents a forum and point of reference for striking up a conversation about the weather, the economy, the government and what it all means. By making it look fun, à la Tom Sawyer, we also get a lot of people to paint and thereby make their mark into their community's unfolding story.
>
> *(Loewenstein 2012b)*

Many parallels between the mural projects and the Intersection Repair process are evident: the project creates an opportunity for people to interact, the process emphasizes fun, and overcoming conflicts can strengthen relationships. Additionally, people made a "mark" on their community's story. They claim the wall and the story as their own, just as in Intersection Repair, residents claim the street as a neighborhood space.

Building Ownership: Sidewalk Living Rooms

> Sitting changes the street from a means of transportation into a place, and specifically, a place defined by who occupies it.
>
> *(Cancian 2005, 34)*

In both Intersection Repair and the Mid-America Mural Project, community residents altered their public environment. Whether officially sanctioned or not, they can both be seen as acts of claiming space. Being able to use the space is a necessary condition for the projects to be built. But, as most public spaces and streets have laws governing who can use the space in what manner, claiming space for local residents requires negotiating a balance between official control and local use. In her review of the legality of DIY practices, Pagano concludes that they exist on a "curiously fluid spectrum of legality" (Pagano 2013, 339).

The Sidewalk Living Room project worked with residents to construct simple benches, stoops, planters, and bulletin boards, and placed them in strategic locations—near areas of potential gentrification and areas with existing activity. The Sidewalk Living Room design process is strikingly similar to both Intersection Repairs and the Mural Projects in the following ways:

- A core group of residents is responsible for the organizing of the project.
- Everyone is invited to participate; outreach is continuous, and there are multiple ways to participate.
- A careful study of the neighborhood precedes the design process.
- Participation is meaningful; conflicts are not glossed over.
- Celebration is an important part of the construction project.

By building benches, residents claimed control of the actual spot for use, and in doing so—in being visible on the street—they also symbolically claimed the neighborhood as their own. Regardless of whether or not the strategy can deter gentrification (the project's original goal), the project did foster a sense of ownership and a symbolic claim to the neighborhood, which is a necessary condition for community-built interventions. Hammett observes, "Sidewalk living rooms are also a positive form of tagging and provide residents with a way to reclaim their right to being active participants in their city" (2013, 4).

FIGURE 12.5 Center Street Living Room, Oakland, California

Source: Steve Rasmussen Cancian

FIGURE 12.6 Living room incorporated into a mural, Temple-Beaudry, Los Angeles, California

Source: Steve Rasmussen Cancian

According to Cancian (2005), organizer of the Sidewalk Living Room project, there are three options for residents who want to build sidewalk living rooms (or claim the street for other uses): obey the laws, ignore the laws, or obey the laws when you can but do not let them stop your project. The West Oakland Sidewalk Living Room used the third approach. They researched local codes and found that placing objects of any kind on the sidewalks was not permitted. Instead of waiting for permits, they installed them anyway. Their rationale was that permission would probably be denied, and waiting for a permit would take too much time and momentum away from the project. "If you let the code hold you back too much, you will forego too many sites, build unsuccessful landscapes and undercut your improvement of the neighborhood and impact on gentrification" (Cancian 2005, 89).

Before installing the project, they made sure that they had support from the businesses and landowners adjacent to the project, and they were respectful in soliciting feedback from the rest of the neighborhood, the theory being, "If your projects are well built, reasonably respectful of the right-of-way and supported by the neighbors, they will more than likely survive attention from City Hall" (Cancian 2005, 90). Additionally, they designed the furniture to be heavy but movable; so if there were complaints, it could be removed.

The city did receive complaints and requested that the furniture be removed. Although removal was the city's official position, after further discussion, city staff agreed to overlook the project as long as it did not cause any problems. Cancian concludes, "Our experiences with the City have made us attentive to any complaints we get from neighbors and aware that we need to cultivate friends in City Hall who will back us up" and "Whichever approach you choose, don't let the regulations stop you. Who knows, your work may end up changing the ordinances as well as the landscape" (2005, 84).

The first Intersection Repair project—Share-It Square—had a similar approach and, in the end, did change the local ordinances. Residents proposed the painting project to the local government, but it was not approved. They decided to go ahead with the project anyway. They carefully documented the impacts of the project (for example, the number of accidents decreased) and shared their evidence with the city. The city not only relented, but also worked with them to create a new ordinance for how Intersection Repairs can be officially approved in other Portland neighborhoods.

Pagano (2013) observes that when DIY interventions are against the law but within the norms of the neighborhood, they are still likely to succeed—and might even change the law. Both the Sidewalk Living Room and Intersection Repair projects support this observation.

A form of place ownership was required for each of these cases to be realized, and in two of them, a form of resistance took place so as to achieve that ownership. But it was not the goal of these projects to change laws in order to reclaim rights to the city. In these cases, disobeying laws only happened when it was necessary in order for the project to move forward. The true goals of the projects were not about realizing rights or ownership but what those rights and ownership could lead to—use and expression in a public space.

Conclusion

Perhaps the key difference between these community-built practices and other public space designs is the emphasis on process over form (but not the total neglect of form). These three cases (and other examples of community-built projects) suggest ways all people—professionals, governments, and residents—can build connection, meaning, and ownership into public space design. Encouraging local control of the process through meaningful and enjoyable participation and developing local control of a site through use are key starting points.

Because theorists tend to see grassroots tactics and top-down governmental strategies in strict opposition, they often conclude that planners and government officials cannot do much to encourage local control of sites (Iveson 2013). For example, Pagano (2013) concludes that government bureaucracies can do little to support community-initiated interventions beyond tolerating "a little disorder" and making "way for experimentation" (388).

For people to build meaning and use into their streets, there has to be a sense of local ownership. But without some form of official intervention, many people might not realize that they have the power or right to change their own environment, especially when typically things are planned and built for them. Many might not want to break the law or social norms. These three cases, organized by planners and designers alongside community residents, suggest that one can encourage people to exercise these rights through participation in something that makes a tangible, visible, and permanent change. These changes might push the boundaries of legality, but hopefully that will lead to laws that better reflect the shared norms of a community.

Much more research needs to be done on how people can develop grass roots—top-down hybrids. One approach to include both official structure and community acts in a public space could be to reconceptualize public space design as an ongoing, evolving process rather than the production of a final product. Borrowing from landscape urbanism, we could shift "attention away from the object qualities of space . . . to the systems" (Corner 2006, 28), not just in terms of ecology but also in terms of human systems. With this approach, a design is not completed upon construction; instead design can provide a structure that supports new life and allows for adaptation.

We have a large amount of knowledge about structures that support human action and interaction on streets and in public spaces. In addition to designing for the human scale and for pedestrian use, research shows that the transition space between the public and private space (or the edge) is an especially fertile ground for these forms of expression and use (Gehl 2010; Thwaites, Mathers, and Simkins 2013). The corners of the intersection are where the tea stand goes. The mural wall is the dividing line between the private building and the public realm. The edge of the right of way, against the building or property fence, is where the living room is set. Creating these edges can be the structure that supports future adaptations.

In ecological design, the structure is not just designed and built; it is seeded to encourage some of these adaptations to take root. Both Intersection Repair and the Mid-America Mural Project offered funds and/or technical assistance to communities through a competitive application process. These competitions support new community projects, and at the same time, by requiring communities to organize and realize the projects, they do not take away local agency. These seeds can grow into community-built projects.

Once the seeds are planted and it becomes apparent that local communities have the right to modify these spaces, other interventions may start taking root, in a sort of reverse broken windows theory. Once established, the interventions express a sense of ownership and empowerment that can lead to greater engagement with the place and open the street up for more interventions and change. This flexibility can support the heterogeneity and inclusivity that is idealized in our admiration of insurgent public spaces. What will a community-built street look like? We don't know, and that is the beauty of it.

Acknowledgments

A version of this chapter was previously published in: *Streets as Public Spaces and Drivers of Urban Prosperity*, Academic Session Papers 2014, Future of Places International Conference on Public Space and Placemaking, Buenos Aires, Argentina. Published by Ax:son Johnson Foundation, Stockholm, 2014.

References

Appleyard, Donald, M. Sue Gerson, and Mark Lintell. 1981. *Livable Streets*. Berkeley, CA: University of California Press.

Bryan, Wayne. 2012. "Painting a City's Portrait: Work Begins on Arkadelphia Mural." *Arkansas Online*. http://www.arkansasonline.com/news/2012/sep/20/painting-citys-portrait-work-begins-arkadelphia-mu/. Accessed 20 September 2012.

Cancian, Steve Rassmussen. 2005. *Sidewalk Living Rooms*. Berkeley, CA: University of California, Berkeley.

City Repair. 2006. *Placemaking Guidebook: Creative Community Building in the Public Right of Way*. 2nd ed. Portland, OR: City Repair.

Corner, James. 2006. "Terra Fluxus." In *The Landscape Urbanism Reader*, Charles Waldheim, ed. New York: Princeton Architectural Press, 21–34.

Franck, Karen A. and Quentin Stevens, eds. 2007. *Loose Space: Possibility and Diversity in Urban Life*. New York: Routledge.

Gehl, Jan. 2010. *Cities for People*. Washington, DC: Island Press.

Hammett, Kingsley. 2013. "Sidewalk Living Rooms." In *The Architecture of Change: Building a Better World*, Jerilou Hammett, and Maggie Wrigley, eds. Albuquerque: University of New Mexico Press, 1–9.

Hou, Jeffrey. 2010. *Insurgent Public Space: Guerrilla Urbanism and the Remaking of Contemporary Cities*. New York: Routledge.

Iveson, Kurt. 2013. "Cities within the City: Do-It-Yourself Urbanism and the Right to the City." *International Journal of Urban and Regional Research*, 37(3): 941–56. doi:10.1111/1468-2427.12053.

Jacobs, Jane. 1961. *The Death and Life of Great American Cities*. Random House: New York.

Leccese, Michael, and Kathleen McCormick, eds. 2000. *Charter of the New Urbanism*. New York: McGraw-Hill.

Loewenstein, Dave. 2010a. "Tonkawa—Research II." *The Mid-America Mural Project*. http://midamericamuralproject.blogspot.com/2012/05/tonkawa-research-ii.html. Accessed 20 April 2010.

———. 2010b. "Newton—Research I." *Dave Loewenstein's Art Bulletin*. http://loewensteinmuraljournal.blogspot.com/2010/07/newton-research-i.html. Accessed 12 August 2010.

———. 2011a. "Joplin—Beginning the Process." *The Mid-America Mural Project*. http:// midamericamuralproject.blogspot.com/2011/07/beginning-process.html. Accessed 19 July 2011.

———. 2011b. "Joplin—Drawing Workshops with Kids." *The Mid-America Mural Project*. http://midamericamuralproject.blogspot.com/2011/07/drawing-workshops-with-kids. html. Accessed 30 July 2011.

———. 2011c. "Joplin—The Design Team." *The Mid-America Mural Project*. http://mida mericamuralproject.blogspot.com/2011/08/design-team.html. Accessed 16 August 2011.

———. 2012a. "Arkadelphia—Community Meetings." *The Mid-America Mural Project*. http://midamericamuralproject.blogspot.com/2012/08/arkadelphia-community-meet- ings.html. Accessed 16 August 2012.

———. 2012b. "Arkadelphia—Painting Begins." *The Mid-America Mural Project*. http:// midamericamuralproject.blogspot.com/2012/09/arkadelphia-painting-begins.html. Accessed 26 September 2012.

———. 2013a. "East Waco Community Meetings." *The Mid-America Mural Project*. http:// midamericamuralproject.blogspot.com/2013/06/east-waco-community-meetings.html. Accessed 4 June 2013.

———. 2013b. "Getting to Know Hastings." *The Mid-America Mural Project*. http:// midamericamuralproject.blogspot.com/2013/09/getting-to-know-hastings.html. Accessed 7 September 2013.

Nelson, Alyse. 2011. "Coloring Inside the Lanes." *Sightline Daily*. http://daily.sightline. org/2011/11/28/coloring-inside-the-lanes/. Accessed 28 November 2011.

Pagano, Celeste. 2013. "DIY Urbanism: Property and Process in Grassroots City Building." *Marquette Law Review*, 97(2): 335–89.

Semenza, Jan C. 2003. "The Intersection of Urban Planning, Art, and Public Health: The Sunnyside Piazza." *American Journal of Public Health*, 93(9): 1439–41.

———. 2005. "Building Healthy Cities: A Focus on Interventions." In *Handbook of Urban Health: Populations, Ethods, and Practice*, Sandro Galea, and David Vlahov, eds. New York: Springer, 459–78. http://www.springer.com/public+health/book/978–0–387–23994–1. Accessed 15 May 2014.

Semenza, Jan C., and Tanya L. March. 2009. "An Urban Community-Based Intervention to Advance Social Interactions." *Environment and Behavior*, 41(1): 22–42. doi:10.1177/ 0013916507311136.

Thwaites, Kevin, Alice Mathers, and Ian Simkins. 2013. *Socially Restorative Urbanism : The Theory, Process and Practice of Experiemics*. New York: Routledge.

Whyte, William Hollingsworth. 2001. *The Social Life of Small Urban Spaces*. New York: Project for Public Spaces.

13

CONCLUSION

Valuing Community-Built

Kristin Faurest, Barry L. Stiefel, and Katherine Melcher

From the creation of community gathering spaces, murals, and gardens, to the development of alternative forms of public space and the reuse of historic buildings and neighborhoods, the examples within this book span a wide variety of projects. Despite this variety, they all fit within the definition of community-built provided in the introduction: they involve local community members in the construction and preservation of community places. They operate within different cultures, such as the African American neighborhood in Hurt Park, Roanoke, Virginia (Clements and Bohannon), and the Jewish-American residents of Charleston, South Carolina (Stiefel). They involve the young (Lasiter; Pratt) and the elderly (Báthory-Nagy). They span different time periods, from the square-log houses built by settlers of the Laurentides in Quebec (Esponda Cascajares) to present day Main Street revitalization efforts (Wells). They also arise out of different political and economic circumstances, as can be seen most vividly in the examples from present-day Hungary (Faurest; Báthory-Nagy; Polyak and Patti).

This diversity demonstrates the complexity within the community-built concept—the many different ways participation can be encouraged and the different manners in which the built environment expresses local culture. In conclusion, we return to the two defining elements of community-built—community involvement and a built-project—in order to describe the concept more fully and to reflect upon what makes community-built projects valuable and meaningful to those involved.

Community Involvement

Community involvement, as Katherine Melcher proposed in Chapter 2, is a central defining element of community-built. Community involvement is key to all cases presented in this book, but these cases also illustrate how participation can take many different forms. In more-established, structured programs (such as the Main Street programs covered by Wells and the professional practices described by Melcher), volunteer participation is organized through committees. Another common form of participation is the integration of the project into existing educational programs, as can be seen in the chapters by Kristin Faurest, Terry L. Clements and C. L. Bohannon, Tiva Lasiter, and Anastasia L. Pratt. Involving youth in community-built projects has additional educational benefits and may even inspire parental involvement, as seen in Faurest's description of the Jam Garden at Eötvös Elementary School, Budapest.

On the other hand, participation can also emerge informally around a project. We observed this in cases where there was no existing organization or structure addressing a particular need. For example, the Jewish communities in Charleston self-organized to create eruvin (Stiefel), and the activist artists and designers in Budapest created their own parallel social services where they felt the government was lacking (Patti and Polyak).

The example that stretches our initial conceptions of community participation the most is Mariana Esponda Cascajares's description of the construction and preservation of square-log homes in Quebec. In her examples, participation spans centuries, tying together people who will never meet in person. Still, as people participate in the construction, relocation, and rehabilitation of these homes, they become connected in a historic community that is grounded in the place.

The diversity of participatory approaches in these examples suggests that there is not a "one-size-fits-all" participatory method; each process responds to the needs, abilities, desires, and fears of the people involved. Standard participatory practices, such as volunteer-run committees, may work in communities who have had positive experiences with volunteer-led work and where trust levels are high. However, in cases where people have not developed the ability to participate on committees, such as the autistic youth and adults in Faurest's chapter or the students in Lasiter's and Pratt's chapters, other processes need to be created. These approaches should be sensitive to people's needs but also involve educational elements to increase their ability to participate and ultimately make decisions for themselves.

In cases where the wounds of the past influence attitudes towards participation, selecting appropriate participatory methods becomes critical. The book contains several powerful examples of this, from Faurest's projects within the new democracy of Hungary, to Clements and Bohannon's work in an African American community who had grown to distrust the "help" of outsiders, to Ildikó Réka Báthory-Nagy's description of a grassroots commemoration of the Holocaust in Hungary at a time when many Hungarians were still fearful of discussing the topic.

These cases grapple with the question: How can we overcome past wounds and lingering distrust to generate projects that are genuinely community-built? Especially in cases where an outsider (as a designer, consultant, artist, and/or community organizer) works with a community group, the commonalities that Melcher noted in Chapter 12 become important criteria for involvement: everyone is invited to participate; the process has multiple means of participation; conflicts are not glossed over; and socializing in a relaxed atmosphere is encouraged.

An inclusive atmosphere where people feel comfortable sharing their thoughts and ideas appeared as an important element in several of the cases (Clements and Bohannon, Báthory-Nagy, Melcher). Báthory-Nagy reflects that one of the key phrases of the yellow-star house commemoration was "'we are all victims of the Holocaust one way or another'…This sentence gave people the right and power to promote their own thoughts and commemoration events" (personal communication with authors, January 2016). In some cases, the simple act of sitting down and listening to the community members can build trust (Clements and Bohannon), while in others, such as the yellow-star house commemoration, social media was employed to reach out to others and build community involvement.

From Involvement to Empowerment

The act of listening can be particularly powerful in marginalized communities. When listening is translated into action, in what Clements and Bohannon call "meaningful community engagement," the ideas are not just listened to but also valued. Through discussions and deliberations (which can involve conflicts of opinion), participants see that not only do their opinions matter, but they can also influence the outcomes of the process, which can lead to a sense of empowerment. Clements and Bohannon reflect, "Without active involvement and advocacy by community members such project work is done *for* the community and does not include developing community social capital or empowerment. Meaningful community engagement has the potential to reshape the way communities build relationships" (personal communication with authors, January 2016).

Ideas are not the only contributions that participants give to community-built projects. As Melcher observed in Chapter 2, projects can incorporate the skills, materials, and other resources found within the community itself. By including and valuing each individual contribution—whether it is an idea, memory, or stockpile of tools—people themselves feel valued. For example, Lasiter, in working with teen youth, developed jobs that gave each student a sense of contributing to the project. Through the sense of pride that comes from contributing to the project, a feeling of empowerment can develop.

Organizing meaningful participatory processes is more complex and time-consuming than the traditional top-down approach led by decision makers or developers. In reflecting on their university-community partnership, Clements and Bohannon said that "the faculty clearly saw that such consensus and collaborative work would and did take longer than most professional consultants normally devote to such work" (personal communication with authors, January 2016). Wells agrees: "a long-term vision, patience, and advocacy, which are critical to a successful Main Street program, contribute to a slow, but inevitable, building of community-buy in and trust" (personal communication with authors, January 2016).

The time is well-spent because community involvement results in projects that reflect people themselves. As Wells reflects,

> Because local community volunteers decide the vision, goals, and objectives of a particular Main Street program, it is innately tailored to serve local needs—in fact, for this reason, it would be impossible for it not to address local needs and issues, including assuring that local identity and culture are consistently represented in all activities.
>
> *(Personal communication with authors, January 2016)*

Through meaningful engagement, community-built projects become about more than simply improving the immediate environment: they are also about improving people's belief in their own power to do so. As participants shape their environment to reflect their needs and identities, they gain new tools, knowledge, and experience. Through projects with high levels of responsibility and accountability, they build collaborative relationships, experience leadership opportunities, develop new skills, create a meaningful place, build self-esteem, and develop a sense of project ownership (Lasiter). In a word, they become empowered.

Additionally, by building trust around a common cause, social capital is increased. The revitalization of a local monument or space is a catalyst that leads to regular festivals, creative events, markets, open-air film showings, or other locally driven happenings. The repeated experience of working together and realizing commonly held ideas continues to motivate and empower community groups for themselves and for the neighborhood. Further, the volunteer physical or intellectual labor that comes with direct participation not only multiplies the value of whatever funding is available for the project but also acts as an investment that encourages people to take care of the place.

Faurest cites recurring events in Teleki Square as an example: "The Friends of Teleki Square are constantly creating programming for it, which contributes to building social capital in the neighborhood by bringing people together for constructive purposes like building holiday displays, planting ornamental annual plantings and putting on theatrical programs." Similarly, Barry L. Stiefel found that even after completion, an eruv can bond people together because of the required continuous maintenance, further reinforcing a social and spatial sense of togetherness.

With a newfound sense of confidence and mutual trust, people involved with community-built projects often conceptualize and realize additional projects. After the yellow-star house commemorative event, Báthory-Nagy's community continued to work on other projects:

> On the bases of the experience gained, [my] residential community . . . started a community-built courtyard garden development project in the following year and successfully built a 46-square meter sized outdoor lounge for community gathering. The repeated experience of working together and realizing

common ideas is still empowering the small community to organize regularly events for themselves and for the neighborhood, such as an outdoor cinema last summer.

(Báthory-Nagy, personal communication with authors, January 2016)

Built Projects in Public Places

The focus on a physical project in a public or semi-public space distinguishes community-built from other types of community development. According to initial descriptions of community-built from the Community Built Association (2014) and Melvin Delgado (2000), community-built projects typically take the form of community gardens, play spaces, public art, and gathering spaces. Within this collection, we have several examples that fit into these categories. The community-built projects covered include community greening projects such as community gardens and fruit gardens (Faurest; Clements and Bohannon), painted and mosaic murals (Lasiter; Pratt; Melcher), and new forms of community space created within public squares, neighborhoods, street edges, waterfronts, and buildings (Faurest; Stiefel; Patti and Polyak; Melcher).

This collection also expands the concept of community-built projects to include architectural preservation and commemorative events (Esponda Cascajares; Báthory-Nagy). Even entire neighborhoods, as in the case of the Main Street programs (Wells), can be considered "community-built" in that local community members had an influence on the appearance and use of the built environment. It is interesting to note that place-based interventions do not have to be highly visible in order to have meaning for people. Community-built interventions as subtle as Charleston's eruvin (Stiefel) or as temporary as in Budapest's yellow-star house commemoration (Báthory-Nagy) can still have significant meaning for those involved.

In all cases in this book, the built-project functions as a gathering point that brings people together. In most cases, designing and building the project becomes the reason for the community to gather; people from within the community come together in order to plant a garden, paint a mural, or build street furniture. As Clements and Bohannon state, "[Communities] are built *around* the making of a thing."

However, in the cases of historic preservation and commemoration where the building exists prior to the community project, we find a slightly different role for the built environment. The buildings—be they the yellow-star houses in Budapest or the square-log cabins in Quebec—become what Báthory-Nagy calls a "physical link" between people. They connect people from the present time to past occupants, and through interactions with the building, people build a community that spans generations. According to Báthory-Nagy (personal communication with the authors, January 2016), the physical link is only the start of such a community; there also must be a social link (understanding the community history) and an emotional link (seeing the parallels between the past and present).

From Built Projects to Local Meaning

In community-built places, the built-project communicates visually; these places tell stories. Community-created and maintained structures can be symbolic representations of intangible expressions of cultural heritage practices. For example, in the eruvin of Charleston, South Carolina, a simple structure composed of poles and wires brought people together in different ways because they had affinity with one another through shared religious identity. Through the selection and application of materials, forms, and symbols, community members express narratives of local culture and identities. As Esponda Cascajares reflects,

> The diverse examples of log cabins are the surviving tangible evidence of the narrative of a society and the transformation of human habitation in the Laurentides. These stories are also about how public perception and community values have been shaped and impacted by a sense of space, identity, and belonging.
>
> *(Personal communication with authors, January 2016)*

As community involvement in creating a place continues, the narrative evolves. Esponda Cascajares continues, "Structures from the past are evidence of the history, but what happens to these buildings depends on the contemporary cultural ideas and values from the current community." Wells has a similar thought about the physical results of the Main Street programs: "Through volunteer activities, the community's will becomes imprinted in the physical landscape of the downtown" (personal communication with authors, January 2016).

This expression in the built environment can arise informally from vernacular construction practices, as in the cases of the square-log houses. Alternatively, the communication of local history can be the explicit goal of an intentional process, as seen in the example of the mosaic project in Clinton County, New York (Pratt). The goal of the mural was not exclusively to bring people together for purposes of built-environment beautification but to commemorate and educate people about local history and culture. Community-built artworks, with their use of images and symbols, appear particularly well-suited for this purpose.

Symbols in the built environment can have powerful effects. The yellow star symbol and the emotions it triggered encouraged Báthory-Nagy to become involved in the yellow-star house commemoration: "Placing yellow star stickers on gates of Budapest's tenement houses in 2014 made the participatory inchoation visible, shocking and definitely a fact to be discussed" (personal communication with authors, January 2016).

For those involved, seeing a project that reflects their culture and values can instill a new sense of pride. This symbolic, visual communication becomes even more powerful when it occurs in the public realm, where it communicates with the rest of the world. Some of the projects in this book took place in neighborhoods adversely affected by neglect and poverty (Faurest; Clements and Bohannon), which come with the attendant prejudices that the people who live there are on public assistance and not contributing to society, or that anyone who has the opportunity to leave the neighborhood will do so. Through community-built projects, residents can assert a certain kind of local identity and produce lasting, visible improvements in their own environments. This not only improves their own quality of life but also provides visual proof to the rest of the city that these negative stereotypes are not true after all.

Community Improvement

Community-built practices often emerge out of a desire to improve a community in a specific manner: for example, the need to slow traffic running through a neighborhood as in the case of City Repair (Melcher), the need to be able to tell one's own version of history as in the case of the yellow-star houses (Báthory-Nagy), or the need to respond to economic disinvestment as experienced by Heti Betevo and VALYO in Budapest (Patti and Polyak) and in the Main Street programs in the United States (Wells).

One common need that many community-built projects serve is to make better use of decaying, demolished, or overlooked spaces such as vacant lots, neglected public spaces, or abandoned buildings. The term placemaking recurs as a theme in the description of several of the cases. As a form of placemaking, community-built takes neglected places and puts them to community use through a creative, artistic process that not only brings new function to a place but also adds beauty and meaning to people's everyday environment.

Community-built can be a means to address immediate community needs when the local government has not been successful at doing so. The gap that community-built projects fill exists for many different reasons. It could be that the government is working on a scale that is too large and it is too far-removed from the community itself. It could be that the government has reduced services due to economic strain or emergency. It could be that the government has different priorities or interpretations, such as in the case of the yellow-star houses. It could be that the problem they are addressing, such as the economic decline of small town main streets, is just too complex for one policy or one entity to fix. However, across all cases, the strength of community-built projects is that the solutions are specifically tailored to the desires and needs of the local residents.

From Community Improvement to Local Control

For local residents to make changes in their own built environment, they need to have the rights or permissions to do so. Historically, local control of the built environment might have been the norm. For example, it may be safe to assume that the early settlers in Quebec did not have building codes that they had to follow. In the instance of eruvin, it is actually an internal requirement of Judaism to obtain permission from the authorities to complete an eruv. But in today's times, gaining the right or permission for local residents to make changes in their neighborhoods can be challenging.

As seen in Part 3, community-built projects can place community members in conflicting relationships with governing organizations. Some community-built practices are overtly political and occur through protest or resistance. Some are built despite the laws, largely ignoring them. Others use a form of advocacy to negotiate a more collaborative relationship with the local government. In community-built projects, there is no one ideal relationship between the local government and community members. Community-built responses are highly contextual: what works for a Pennsylvania Main Street is not what will work in the public spaces of Budapest—two places with very different political and economic histories.

The relationship between the government and the community can also change over time. As seen in the examples from Budapest (Polyak and Patti), projects that started through grassroots efforts may become commercially successful or lead to gentrification, displacing the original residents. Community-built projects could become so successful that the government steps in and takes over the project, removing local control. Conversely, the government could use community-built projects to excuse their own lack of investment in a community. Although community control is a necessary element in community-built projects, governmental support can be equally important to their success.

Despite these differences, in all these community-built projects, local citizens express their right to make changes to their built environment, however small those changes may be, and in a way, claim a right to their city. In Melcher's piece on the sidewalk living rooms built in California cities, she quotes Hammett, "Sidewalk living rooms are also a positive form of tagging and provide residents *with a way to reclaim their right to being active participants in their city*" (emphasis added, 4). Báthory-Nagy's chapter reflects a similar sentiment: "It is up to us to remember, to understand and to comprehend the past: this is our shared moral, civic and human duty. *Our shared history, and thus this city, are ours*" (emphasis added). Finally, Wells, in his piece on Main Street programs, concludes, "Through volunteer activities, the community's will becomes imprinted in the physical landscape of the downtown . . . it is these volunteers who often make the final decisions as to what is, and is not, built, especially in the case of facade grants where *volunteers have bona fide power to control the design of their downtown*" (emphasis added).

The Value of Community-Built Projects

Frequently when we hear or read about projects like the ones discussed in this book, our first response is to perceive them as sweet, cute, or nice—humble homegrown gestures that are signs of humanity in the hard city, something to feel warm and fuzzy about. In doing so, we miss the larger point. Of course, the soft benefits of these projects are obvious and documentable—something looks nicer, plants are growing, students are getting a different experience from what they get in the classroom—but there are much more important, sometimes not always immediately visible, impacts that come from community-built projects.

By involving community members in a meaningful way, community-built processes can help create stronger relationships, feelings of empowerment, and an increased capacity for realizing change. With their emphasis on built projects in public and semi-public spaces, community-built projects can become a forum for new ways of preserving or expressing local culture. Finally, in community-built projects, citizens negotiate their rights to adapt their living environments to better suit their local culture and social needs.

The two defining elements of community-built—community involvement and a built project—appear to be essential to realizing these impacts. In addition to these two elements, local control and a contextual approach recur as important characteristics of both the participatory process and the built project. In the process, local control of decision making is emphasized; while in the place where the project is implemented, local control of what can and cannot be built is a necessary precondition. Successful participatory processes are designed contextually with the local residents' needs, abilities, desires, and fears in mind, while negotiating the use of the place itself requires an awareness of the broader political and economic contexts in which it is situated.

When people are given the opportunity to shape their environment in a way that makes their surroundings more comfortable, more colorful, more personalized, they feel a greater power to make other changes as well. They also have an enhanced sense of stewardship and a closer relationship with the friends and neighbors who helped them realize the project. Within the community-built context, building community consists of, first of all, strengthening relationships between participants and neighbors. Second, building community results from the community group's realization of their own collective capacity for making change. According to Melcher, "By collectively designing and using . . . space, [people] build a relationship with each other as well as with the place." This is an underlying truth to community-built best practices.

The lessons learned from this volume can provide community planners and activists, as well as grassroots facilitators and participants, with a better understanding of what can lead to successful community-built art, construction, preservation, and placemaking. The cases presented illustrate community-built practices in a broad sense, but the examples covered should by no means be considered archetypal. There is more to be explored, as well as made, saved, and restored, and we hope that others will pick up where this volume ends regarding the observation and documentation of success stories and, at times, failures.

The ultimate objective of community-built work is improving the overall quality of peoples' lives and the environment in a social, ecological, and economically responsible manner. The bulk of humanity consists of common people, most with limited resources as individuals. However, as the examples in this volume illustrate, when people come together to pool their resources, time, and social capital, they can achieve great things—forming and strengthening a sense of community—and this intangible aspect of community-built, in and of itself, is the most valuable thing of all.

References

Community Built Association. 2014. "What Is Community Built?" *Community Built Association.* http://communitybuilt.org/about/. Accessed 7 June 2014.

Delgado, Melvin. 2000. *Community Social Work Practice in an Urban Context: The Potential of a Capacity-Enhancement Perspective.* New York: Oxford University Press.

CONTRIBUTORS

Ildikó Réka Báthory-Nagy, PhD, is an associate professor at Szent István University in Hungary where she teaches urban green network and greenway curricula for future landscape architects. As a landscape architect and scientist, she deals with creekside landscapes and also manages a private design practice. She also facilitates community greening and art projects in urban courtyards.

C. L. Bohannon, PhD, ASLA, teaches in the Landscape Architecture Program at Virginia Polytechnic Institute and State University, and received his PhD and MLA from Virginia Polytechnic Institute and State University and BLA from the Fay Jones College of Architecture and Design at the University of Arkansas. His research focuses on community engagement and design pedagogy, community narrative, and landscape literacy.

Terry L. Clements, FASLA, chair of the Landscape Architecture Program at Virginia Polytechnic Institute and State University, received her MLA from the University of California, Berkeley, and BLA from State University of New York College of Environmental Science and Forestry. Her research focuses on design education and pedagogy, cultural landscapes, and women in landscape architecture.

Mariana Esponda Cascajares, PhD, is an associate professor in the Azrieli School of Architecture at Carleton University, Canada. Dr. Esponda has been working on heritage buildings for the last fifteen years to fully understand historical constructions and to allow a new life through contemporary use. Her projects include restoration of modernism historical facades, adaptive reuse, and rehabilitation of existing structures. Her line of investigation is in Sustainable Heritage Conservation, balancing cultural and natural heritage, integrating environmental construction techniques and social and economic practices.

Tiva Lasiter has her BA in Studio Art from the University of Hawaii-Manoa, and her Masters of Science in Community Development from the University of California-Davis. Lasiter leads community-built art projects as a powerful tool to bring communities together and empower youth. She works with community members to involve them in the design and creation of public art.

Daniela Patti is an Italian and British architect and planner. She is a founding member of Eutropian Research and Planning. Specializing in urban regeneration and environmental planning with a particular focus on metropolitan governance and collaborative planning, her recent research and projects focus on the governance of peri-urban landscape, the revitalization of local food markets, and new economic models for urban development. Additionally she has been a guest lecturer at the University of Roma Tre, Tor Vergata, and Universidad de Buenos Aires.

Levente Polyak is an urban planner, researcher, and policy adviser. Polyak is a founding member of Eutropian Research and Planning. His interests are in urban regeneration, cultural development, community participation, local economic development, and social innovation, with a special focus on building development scenarios on existing resources. In the past years, he has been researching new organizational and economic models of community-led urban development projects, including the temporary use of vacant properties and community-run social services.

Anastasia L. Pratt, PhD, is an assistant professor at State University of New York Empire State College and the Clinton County, New York, Historian. She teaches courses in Public History and Heritage Preservation and is actively engaged in connecting the local community with its history. Pratt holds degrees from State University of New York Plattsburgh and the University of Michigan.

Jeremy C. Wells, PhD, is an assistant professor in the Historic Preservation Program at Roger Williams University in Bristol, Rhode Island, and a Fulbright scholar. His research focuses on ethnographic approaches to understanding Main Street programs. He has served as a Main Street manager and volunteer at Quakertown Alive (Pennsylvania), Old Town Cape (Missouri), and the Historic Downtown Kennewick Partnership (Washington).

INDEX

Note: Italicized page numbers indicate a figure on the corresponding page. Page numbers in bold indicate a table on the corresponding page.